LEADERSHIP AND MANAGEMENT IN SOCIAL CARE

TRISH HAFFORD-LETCHFIELD, KATE LEONARD,
NASA BEGUM AND NEIL F. CHICK

SAGE Publications
Los Angeles ▪ London ▪ New Delhi ▪ Singapore

SAGE Publications Ltd
1 Oliver's Yard
55 City Road
London EC1Y 1SP

SAGE Publications Inc.
2455 Teller Road
Thousand Oaks, California 91320

SAGE Publications India Pvt Ltd
B 1/I 1 Mohan Cooperative Industrial Area
Mathura Road, New Delhi 110 044
India

SAGE Publications Asia-Pacific Pte Ltd
33 Pekin Street #02-01
Far East Square
Singapore 048763

Library of Congress Control Number: 2007924721

British Library Cataloguing in Publication data

A catalogue record for this book is available from the British Library

ISBN 978-1-4129-2960-8
ISBN 978-1-4129-2961-5 (pbk)

Typeset by C&M Digitals (P) Ltd., Chennai, India
Printed in Great Britain by The Cromwell Press Ltd, Trowbridge, Wiltshire
Printed on paper from sustainable resources

CONTENTS

ABOUT THE AUTHORS

Nasa Begum

Nasa has worked at the Social Care Institute for Excellence (SCIE) as Principal Advisor for Participation since 2003. She has responsibility for ensuring that service user and carer participation is embedded throughout all of its work. Prior to this, as a qualified social worker, Nasa worked for local authority social services, the King's Fund, MIND (National Association for Mental Health) and the Policy Studies Institute in practitioner and policy/service development roles. She has a background in research and training and has published work on service user participation, race equality, gender, community care and independent living.

Nasa has used social care services throughout her life and has been active in service user and carer participation work both in a professional and personal capacity for over 20 years. Nasa has been on the board of many organizations, ranging from an Asian women's resource centre, a mental health system survivors' organization to a black disabled people's network and the Greater London Association of Disabled People. She was Chair of Waltham Forest Association of Disabled People and the POWERHOUSE, an organization of women with learning difficulties that set up the first ever refuge for women with learning difficulties.

In her 'spare' time Nasa is a board member of the National Centre for Independent Living and part of an 'experts by experience' group focusing on improving social care.

Neil Chick

Neil has a postgraduate certificate in teaching in lifelong learning, a MA in Lifelong Learning and an Advanced Certificate in Coaching and Mentoring qualification achieved through part-time adult learning programmes. Neil has developed and led an inter-agency coach mentoring scheme and believes passionately in widening participation and celebrating and supporting diversity. He is currently Organizational and Learning Manager for a large Housing Association, a learning and development facilitator and consultant, and a coach mentor.

Trish Hafford-Letchfield

Trish teaches at London South Bank University on the MSc in Social Work and on academic development programmes. She is involved with the Leadership and Management Post-qualifying Award. She is also an active mentor to managers and post-qualifying students. Trish has ten years' management experience in adult social care within statutory settings, including supported housing, learning and organizational development. She has published articles and books on management and organizational issues and on diversity in learning. Her main research interest lies in widening participation within higher education and workforce development.

Trish began her career in health as a nurse and gained a wide experience of generic and specialist social work prior to her management career. Trish is currently Chair of her local Age Concern. In her spare time she is a keen amateur musician and is involved in a teaching community orchestra for adult learners.

Kate Leonard

Kate works at London South Bank University where she is Course Director for the Post Qualifying Practice Education Course and teaches on the Postgraduate Certificate in Higher Education and Postgraduate Certificate in Medical Education. Kate is a qualified social worker and has extensive experience of supervising staff and students. Until recently, Kate worked as a Children's Guardian. She is also a freelance mentor, a coach work-based assessor, a trainer and a consultant in health and social care. She has written about the use of direct observation for assessment and the dynamics of interprofessional learning.

ACKNOWLEDGEMENTS

The authors wish to express their special thanks to their families and to people within their support networks. We are especially grateful to those family members who are no longer with us, who we miss terribly and who we know for sure would be really proud of how we have developed our knowledge and experiences in order to share with others.

INTRODUCTION

This book is about *learning* in social work and social care. It is specifically aimed at people who have responsibility for leading and managing learning within organizations that deliver social work and social care services. Government policy, particularly since the modernization of social services (Department of Health, 1999), has placed a strong emphasis in social care on developing choice, independence, participation and control for service users in the process of delivering social care services. These legislative and policy developments give explicit attention to the need for a more skilled, competent and qualified workforce in order to achieve the proposed structural and organizational changes in social care in partnership with other stakeholders (Department of Health, 2004a, 2005a, 2006a). Needless to say, strong professional leadership and effective management hold the key to the successful implementation of these objectives if they are to become meaningful. Therefore people with a role in managing practice or leading service improvements have a joint responsibility with other members of the workforce to promote and facilitate workforce development and particularly continuous professional development (CPD) activities. Managing learning in this sense should enable you to:

- continually develop the competence of staff so that they can do the job to the best of their ability as well as adapt to new ways of working that will bring about the change and cultural shifts required to implement the government's modernization agenda in a way that places service users at the heart of this agenda;
- develop and maintain a style of practice that is self-aware and critically reflective and one which uses evidence-based approaches to improvise and innovate in an extremely challenging social, economic and policy-driven environment;
- take responsibility for the ongoing development of yourself and others in a way that demonstrates an acknowledgement and respect for the diversity, demands and challenges of workforce development based on research and knowledgeable practice.

This book was written principally for leaders and managers of practice as well as other people responsible for staff development in social work and social care organizations. It is *not* a book specifically about management as we acknowledge the existence of other quality texts which focus on the key roles and tasks of social care management. This book, however, is specifically concerned about examining the role and responsibilities that managers hold alongside other professionals for promoting and facilitating learning, a role that is not always emphasized for its contribution to the overall strategic framework for delivering quality care services. This book will also be of interest to any professionals working in a social care setting who have responsibilities for the development, facilitation and assessment of the learning of others. For example, you may be an expert social care practitioner, a member of the human resource team, an aspiring manager or somebody following a post-qualifying award in practice education or leadership and management. This book may also be relevant to a range of professionals from other disciplines who are involved in delivering social care services and/or working and learning alongside other social care professionals. You may want to 'dip into' some chapters or read it as a coherent whole as we have endeavoured to cover a wide range of connected and related issues to workforce development from both a theoretical and practical standpoint.

THE POST-QUALIFYING STANDARDS FOR SOCIAL WORK

This book particularly seeks to provide the underpinning knowledge for candidates following post-qualifying (PQ) frameworks for social work, although not exclusively (GSCC, 2005a). These standards have been developed to describe the different but generic areas which signpost an integrated approach to learning and development within the whole PQ framework, no matter which specialist pathway one is following. The higher specialist level and advanced levels of the PQ framework are associated with complex decision making and high levels of professional responsibility. These programmes are for those who have already demonstrated competence in their specialist practice area to some depth. In order to satisfy approval requirements, higher specialist and advanced programmes will need to show how they will enable qualified social workers to meet the following standards. The advanced level of professional competence incorporates and builds on higher specialist competences, aiming to produce individuals with the ability to lead the further growth and development of the social work profession, drawing on an in-depth knowledge of a specialist area of work and experience of conducting research and applying research to practice. The additional requirements associated with the movement from higher specialist to advanced work are indicated by the use of italics in the criteria listed below. Overall, programmes of higher specialist and advanced social work education and training allow qualified social workers who have demonstrated in-depth competence and who have been assessed as capable of working at both these levels to:

- meet the academic standards for work at level M in the Quality Assurance Agency (QAA) framework.
- use independent critical judgement to *take a leading role* in systematically developing their own practice and that of others in the context of the General Social Care Council (GSCC) codes of practice, national and international codes of professional ethics, the principles of diversity, equality and social inclusion in a wide range of situations, including those associated with inter-agency and interprofessional work.
- demonstrate a substantially enhanced level of competence in a defined area of professional practice, professional management, professional education or applied professional research to the agreed national standards for higher specialist work in this area *and take a leading role in promoting good practice.*
- demonstrate a fully developed capacity to *take responsibility for the use of* reflection and critical analysis to continuously develop and improve own performance and the performance of professional and interprofessional groups, teams and networks in the context of professional practice, professional management, professional education or applied professional research; analysing, evaluating and applying relevant and up-to-date research evidence, including service user research.
- use a critical knowledge and understanding of service user and carer issues to *actively promote,* develop and implement service user and carer rights and participation in line with the goals of choice, independence and empowerment.
- undertake research designed to address issues or problems in the context of professional practice, professional education, applied professional research or professional management.
- work creatively and effectively as a practitioner, researcher, educator or manager *and take a leading role* in a context of risk, uncertainty, conflict and contradiction or where there are complex challenges and a need to make informed and balanced judgements.
- take *a lead* responsibility for managing *key* aspects of complex change processes, including those involving other professions or other agencies, in the context of professional practice, professional management, professional education and training or applied professional research.

- support, mentor, supervise or manage others, exercising practice, research, management or educational leadership to enable them to identify and explore issues and improve their own practice.
- *take a leading role* in the development and implementation of effective ways of working in networks across organizational, sectoral and professional boundaries, taking *a lead* responsibility for identifying, analysing and resolving complex issues, problems and barriers, promoting partnership, collaboration, interprofessional teamwork, multi-agency and multidisciplinary communication and ensuring the delivery of integrated and person-centred services.

Since the launch of the National Training Strategy for the personal social services in 1999, much attention has been given to the concept of learning and development. The research documented that 80% of the one million people working in social care, while working face to face with vulnerable people, had no recognized qualification (TOPSS, 2000). This in turn was linked to a need to develop a workforce beset by recruitment and retention issues. Emerging from this research has been a clear learning and development framework which is constantly evolving in social care. This describes and specifies the standards, knowledge and skills required by a wide range of staff and stakeholders, in a variety of organizations where social care services are delivered. We have just looked at the PQ standards which are tied to an accreditation framework. Other areas of the workforce are also benchmarked by learning and development standards, with nationally recognized qualifications for virtually each and every service area and at every level of employment in the social care workforce, including for users and carers themselves. A key challenge arising from these developments is how to ensure a more robust approach in the workplace where learning and development can be explored and actively facilitated.

However, this approach conceals a number of uncritical assumptions about how individuals learn to practise. It is generally recognized that the learning and development process is integral to overall performance management of an organization (Department of Health, 2000), and should be firmly embedded in workplace culture. As we will see in the debates throughout this book, it is by no means certain that this sort of learning is the best way to acquire the kinds of aptitudes and attitudes that inform sensitive and effective practice (Jordan and Jordan, 2002). In organizations where social care and social work services are delivered, a variety of factors can impact and interact on the successful promotion of learning and development strategies. With these in mind, this book aims to help you unpick and examine the relevant factors and to consider how you might approach some of the challenges in putting these into practice as well as by increasing your confidence in the more straightforward areas.

HOW TO USE THIS BOOK

Starting with an overview of essential practices and processes and the organizational frameworks for examining and thinking about learning and staff development in Chapters 1 and 2, you will be encouraged to develop new ways of thinking about these. Individual topics within this book, for example on diversity (Chapter 5), work-based learning (Chapter 7) and on coaching and mentoring (Chapter 8) will hopefully amalgamate areas of interest in both what we think of as 'formal' and 'informal' learning, at both a strategic and operational level, with reference to models which encourage your active participation in problem solving, critical thinking and reflection in these areas (Chapters 6 and 9). There will be an emphasis on partnership learning and on developing learning partnerships with other agencies and professionals (Chapter 3), service users and carers (Chapter 4), within and across the sector. We aim to help you, the reader, to make the links between the bigger picture and the day-to-day operational functions of an organization; and to facilitate any contribution you might make towards friendly business strategies where the circumstances in which support for learning and development of stakeholders in social care can be strengthened and become part of your daily practice. We will do this by:

- reviewing the established and emerging strategic framework and knowledge base that underpins organizational learning and development strategies.
- clarifying the relevance of these to the role of managers, leaders and practice educators in the field of social care, mediated through the PQ framework and the General Social Care Council's *Codes of Practice* (GSCC, 2002) as well as the legislative and policy framework.
- giving special emphasis to the development of practice knowledge and skills to enable and facilitate others across a diverse range of partnerships, including peers, employees and service users/carers and including the interdisciplinary context that is seen as crucial to effective and joined-up service delivery.
- maintain a strong focus on theories of lifelong learning, reflective learning cultures and learning organizations and the philosophical underpinnings on 'learning to learn'. We will give attention to issues around leading or managing people who have traditionally been disadvantaged in learning.

This book is organized into two main areas. Chapters 1 to 5 introduce readers to the overall framework for learning and development within any organization delivering social care services and to the main themes and issues, as well as providing a reference to the national frameworks within social care that support learning. This will include theories about learning in different contexts. Chapters 6 to 9 aim to help readers to get to grips with the more practical aspects and tasks, following on from the theoretical and ethical considerations covered earlier on, by focusing on models and techniques that can be used to deliver learning and development in practice. The style of this text has enabled us to combine processes, practices and perspectives, drawing on both academic analysis and practicalities of learning and development in the workplace. It draws on relevant research and the evidence base to inform contemporary practice in an accessible way.

CHAPTER SYNOPSES

Chapter 1 briefly examines the historical and policy context and broader debates about the strategies that have been employed to try to transform social work and social care practice through the learning agenda and the dilemmas associated with these. You will develop an understanding of what constitutes 'workforce development', and be asked to think more strategically about the contribution of learning and development activities to the vision, goals and business strategy of organizations delivering social care services. Having established this context, the chapter goes on to explore what is meant by the terms 'leadership' and 'management' by looking at the relevance and usefulness of different models of leadership based on an overview of the management and leadership literature. As this book is essentially about the leadership of *learning*, the process by which learning has become a prominent feature in the current development of the social care workforce is explored. An understanding of this is essential in order to breathe life into workforce development and to narrow it down to a discussion of what your role specifically might be in meeting service standards and delivering quality outcomes for service users.

Chapter 2 examines the more positive aspects of successful organizations and good management of practice in social care, which are often linked to the concept of a 'learning organization'. The complexities, demands and difficulties of working effectively, flexibly, innovatively and proactively in organizations delivering social care in sometimes uncertain, changing and demanding circumstances are analysed and critiqued within this framework. Theoretical models of what constitutes a 'learning culture' are presented, with a focus on the different roles that are played by government agencies, management, staff and users in working towards maximizing success in sometimes adverse situations. The process of organizational development is examined and you will be asked to explore any opportunities for both informal and formal learning in the workplace with reference to the concept of 'life-long learning' (Department for Education and Skills, 2003).

Chapter 3 explicitly explores the dynamics of interprofessional working and learning in social care. As a working definition, the use of terms and language around interprofessionalism is explored as well as the power dynamics between professional, workers, service users/carers and organizations. Interprofessional working and learning is said to be an important aspect of developing best practice across team and organizational boundaries and in giving a prime focus in delivering high-quality services. To explore this in more detail this chapter looks at: the current context of interprofessional learning; the variety of definitions used in the arena of interprofessional learning and working; the evidence base for interprofessional education; the context for leaders and managers facilitating reflective and supervisory practice in an interprofessional context; and what issues leaders and managers should take into account when considering whether learning should/could be interprofessional or uni-professional.

Chapter 4 focuses on the leadership role taken by service users and looks at the specific role of users in staff and service development. Beginning with an overview of the growth and development of user participation movements, it identifies and explores the essential ingredients for promoting successful user participation. This includes the different role taken by users as leaders, managers and partners in service development based on concepts of user involvement and citizenship. The chapter concludes by looking at the specific role of users in facilitating learning through awareness, reflection, partnership working and evaluation, by drawing on the research and the evidence base from service users themselves.

Chapter 5 explores the concept that the effective and progressive social care organizations work with, reflects on and responds to the complex and diverse needs of the community it serves. This chapter refers to the legal and policy framework in relation to diversity and workforce development as well as the evidence base in relation to the changing needs of the population and its workforce. The main theme of the chapter is to explore the challenges for social care organizations and its managers in actively developing creative learning opportunities that appropriately reflect and celebrate the experience and diversity of the workforce.

Chapter 6 develops ideas about the manager's role in helping others to link personal and professional motivations to learn and develop themselves. Focusing on the immediate workplace environment, it looks at policies and procedures that are available to support effective learning, such as supervision, performance appraisal and personal development planning. Opportunities for managers and other staff to improve communication about learning needs and learning styles are considered within a reflective approach. Alternatives to more managerialist prescriptive methods to assisting and facilitating personal and organizational development are emphasized, utilizing theory around motivation and work-based learning. Consideration is given towards the end of the chapter on how to deal with more difficult issues in learning, such as working with people who do not want or are unable to learn, tackling bad practice, and the role of learning and development in managing poor performance.

Chapter 7 examines the context of 'growing your own' within social care organizations and explores the whole area of work-based learning and the concepts underpinning it. It makes reference to the new developments in the PQ framework in social work education, aspiring managers, NVQ candidates and practice learning for social work education. The role of work-based assessors is explored in relation to their role as facilitators of learning and progression. Specific issues are covered, such as methods of collecting and recording different types of evidence, methods, direct observation, involvement of service users and carers, written evidence and the use of feedback. Issues in relation to good enough practice and how to make fair and well evidenced formative and summative assessments are explored. Guidance is also given for those working with learners who are perceived as having difficulties in learning or whose practice causes concern.

Chapter 8 investigates how managers and supervisors can utilize the skills of coach mentoring as a tool for the continuous professional development of the workforce. Within a climate of constant change and demand for innovative services, managers and supervisors must ensure that all employees are positively engaged with the challenges of this agenda, are enabled to identify opportunities and are empowered to respond positively to any threats. This chapter explores how the skills of coaching and mentoring can become a powerful, effective but economic device in the modern developmental manager's toolbox. It identifies the origins of coaching and mentoring and investigates the differences and similarities between these two disciplines. It explores how the skills and practices of coaching and mentoring can be blended and utilized by social care managers and supervisors as a management and developmental tool that can engage the greatest number of social care staff in reflecting on their practice, addressing their own learning needs and developing learning on and off the job.

Chapter 9 aims to help you look at your own self-development and continuous professional development. It begins by examining some of the theories around knowledge management and examines what we mean by the term 'knowledge' in social care. You will be encouraged to think about the role of evaluation and research in learning, and development activities and the types of methodologies available to help us research or to develop our own local knowledge for local services. The chapter then goes on to consider management development and the different approaches to developing managers, topics which have traditionally been much neglected in social care.

At the end of each chapter in this book, there are pointers for further reading and research. Throughout the book, the term 'social care' is generally used to indicate the broad domain in which professional social work operates. We also recognize that other professionals and people involved in delivering social care services may come from different agency and professional backgrounds and our premise is that issues around leadership and management of learning are common to all of these. Enjoy your own learning!

1 THE LEADERSHIP AND MANAGEMENT OF LEARNING

This chapter explores:

- The policy context for workforce development in social care
- The importance of the role of managers in social care in promoting professional and organizational learning
- Theories about leadership and its contribution to developing a culture of learning in social care

INTRODUCTION

In this first chapter, we will be setting the scene for the key topics explored throughout the rest of this book. The management literature has long established the importance of employee development as a managerial responsibility. However, some research indicates that few managers actually regard themselves as a key person responsible for facilitating learning (Ellinger and Bostrom, 2002). This may be because managers either lack skills in this area or perceive staff development to be a distraction from the 'real' work. Managers are often not rewarded or recognized for staff development activities or it is assumed that this is the sole responsibility of staff in their human resource or training departments. Arguably, all workers in health and social care have at least two learning related roles: first, in managing and engaging in their own learning, and secondly, in supporting the learning of others (Eraut, 2006). While managers would appear to have more direct responsibilities for managing the learning of others, we must also recognize that most learning is an important, albeit unrecognized, by-product of work itself and is the essence of professionalism. We know, for example, that only an estimated 20% of all learning achieved and relevant to the jobs that professionals and individuals do in social care occurs in formal educational and training settings. This leaves approximately 80% of learning occurring in more informal ways (Eraut, 2006). These informal learning opportunities are in the majority work-based, largely unmonitored and not fully researched and the role of managers in capitalizing on this is crucial (Bryans and Mavin, 2003).

Any discussion about the leadership and management of learning has to recognize the importance of establishing a positive culture and how the quality of experiences for those working in social care environments is inevitably connected to learning, continuous professional development and effective change management. For example, addressing discrimination and promoting equality and diversity in workforce development is one important area within change management where solutions might not be clear-cut but have to be strongly connected to policy objectives and strategic actions. Attention to the pros and cons of the repertoire of diversity promotion strategies using learning and organizational development techniques is one step to promoting diversity (Butt, 2006). Secondly, current and future social, political and organizational contexts for practice are leading to significant changes in the employment conditions in social work and social care. These conditions are likely to become more fragmented and simultaneous with the demand to deliver more coherent, consistent and systematic approaches to high-quality services against clearly defined national service outcomes (Fook, 2004; Association of Directors of Social Services, 2005). Taking into account contemporary changes in both children and adult services at the time of writing (Department of Health, 2004a, 2005a) and other areas of the social inclusion agenda, it appears no longer possible to derive a long-term sense of professional identity from working within one particular organizational setting. The structure, and hence the culture, of organizations delivering social care services will inevitably change and evolve on a continuous basis. This raises questions about how we might learn to develop and reframe the essential skills, knowledge and values of social care to meet the demands of an also increasingly regulated and constantly changing environment. This must also be done in a way that suits or can be adaptable to other contexts when necessary. For example within interprofessional relationships and service delivery.

Throughout this text we will be constantly referring to the importance of evidence-based practice and practice wisdom and particularly how these and other forms of knowledge can be managed and utilized in social care. Partnership working is a constantly reiterated theme in public services and any strategy to promote partnerships at the strategic and local level has to recognize active support for learning alongside this.

The study of leadership and leadership development is based, as we will see in the latter part of this chapter, on the idea that public service leaders help to create and realize possibilities for the twenty-first century and that organizational learning and adaptation are part and parcel of any management development strategy (Skills for Care, 2005b). We are not suggesting here that attention to the leadership of learning can be made solely responsible for controlling or monitoring all the details of practice in an organization. If you are an educator, then you will recognize this common expectation from people towards your role in the organization, which carries with it an unspoken assumption that training can offer solutions to many dilemmas in practice. On the contrary, it will be asserted throughout this book that managers and leaders of learning themselves have a specific and integral role in enabling professionals and practitioners to think and act creatively and flexibly so that they can adapt their own abilities and take direct responsibility for developing and improving practice. It is also almost inconceivable to imagine that leadership development can evolve without the active participation of users in leadership and improving the lives of people who use social care services. The promotion of user participation and the role of users in facilitating learning through awareness, reflection drawing upon evidence, partnership working and evaluation is essential. In summary, while this text is aimed at managers and people with specific roles for learning and organizational development, this is a facilitative and partnership process. Predicting change in order to position your organization and the individuals within it to meet potential demands requires *everyone* to understand and engage in the process of individual as well as institutional learning. We will be drawing attention to the creation of learning opportunities and the use of supervision, appraisal and team work within 'communities of practice', while at the same time we will be looking at the more practical aspects of assessing work-based learning and the use of coaching and mentoring techniques.

In conclusion, learning within the organizational context implies approaches that include collaboration, interdependence and independence between those involved inspired by leadership. Before turning to look at how leadership theories can help us in this endeavour, we will first examine the policy context for workforce development in social care and the key principles underpinning these.

WORKFORCE DEVELOPMENT IN SOCIAL CARE

Social work and social care are a major enterprise in the UK with around £12 billion expenditure and a workforce of over one million

(Skills for Care, 2005a). Marsh et al. (2005) go further to state that it also plays a key role in fostering social coherence and represents a major commitment to a socially just society. Yet it is only since the turn of the twenty-first century that any real active scrutiny of who was working in the workforce as a whole, their backgrounds, skills, knowledge and training took place (TOPSS, 2000), resulting in the development of organizations such as Skills for Care (SfC) and the Children's Workforce Development Council (CWDC) to manage and oversee these strategic developments on behalf of the government. Across health and social care, the government and its employers have been working towards the development of an approach to a workforce strategy that promotes the well-being of users and ensures the best outcomes in their care and support. Irrespective of their employing organization or professional position, staff will need to share a set of competencies so that workforce planning across all services is linked to improving services and allows for progression and transfer of staff as these develop. Finally, a coherent workforce development strategy is needed that it is supportive of the implementation of improved services (Skills for Care, 2005a).

The Modernizing Social Services agenda (Department of Health, 1998) sought to raise the quality of service outcomes through increased regulation and integration of social care services. All service areas have since felt the impact of the government's agenda and target setting to improve standards in the workforce through increased quality, inspection and regulation. Because attaining higher-quality outcomes for users is related to the better training of those delivering services, a parallel agenda has sought to raise the quality of education and training through more rigorous regulation of the workforce. There have been a number of policy drivers and initiatives since the first National Training Strategy was developed by the Training Organization in Personal Social Services (TOPSS, 2000) to achieve this. Research has documented that 80% of the one million people working in social care, while working face to face with vulnerable people, had no recognized qualifications. The National Training Strategy (Department of Health, 2000) aimed to give a new status to those working in social care which fits the work that they do. As illustrated in Figure 1.1, a network and infrastructure of national stakeholders in workforce development have since combined to support workforce development across the sector and have developed different roles in setting quality standards, for example, through legislation, national service frameworks, a coherent qualifications framework, and the process of regulation, inspection and quality assurance in social care.

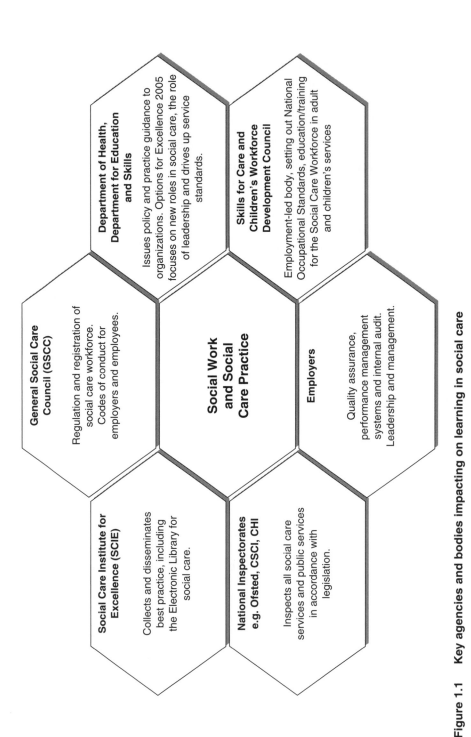

Figure 1.1   Key agencies and bodies impacting on learning in social care

Source: Hafford-Letchfield (2006: 44) Reproduced with kind permission from Learning Matters

The figure contains the following labelled hexagons:

Department of Health, Department for Education and Skills

Issues policy and practice guidance to organizations. Options for Excellence 2005 focuses on new roles in social care, the role of leadership and drives up service standards.

Skills for Care and Children's Workforce Development Council

Employment-led body, setting out National Occupational Standards, education/training for the Social Care Workforce in adult and children's services

General Social Care Council (GSCC)

Regulation and registration of social care workforce. Codes of conduct for employers and employees.

Social Work and Social Care Practice

Employers

Quality assurance, performance management systems and internal audit. Leadership and management.

Social Care Institute for Excellence (SCIE)

Collects and disseminates best practice, including the Electronic Library for social care.

National Inspectorates e.g. Ofsted, CSCI, CHI

Inspects all social care services and public services in accordance with legislation.

As established earlier, learning is very much linked to change management and therefore people who understand how to facilitate learning can make an important contribution to the change process. Actively managing learning is also a way of ensuring a balance as well as a match between the needs of professionals with the goals of the employing organization. To achieve this, it is absolutely imperative that there is a close relationship between managers and those involved in learning which is mirrored throughout the organization. To achieve the dramatic step changes as well as the small day-to-day changes to meet the needs for new approaches to services, learning should be understood as more than just as a series of technical processes and issues. It must be supported by a range of other activities, such as supervision, appraisal systems, external and internal training programmes, and the use of reflective learning models, reflective practice and experiential learning are equally important. We will be exploring these more tangible aspects of learning in later chapters of this book.

Paragraph 3 of the GSCC code for employers states:

As a social care employer, you must provide training and development opportunities to enable social care workers to strengthen and develop their skills and knowledge. This includes providing induction, training and development opportunities to help social care workers do their jobs effectively and prepare for new and changing roles and responsibilities. (www.gscc.or.uk/codes_practice.htm)

This responsibility is linked to workforce development planning that is essential for effective organizational learning. The key components of such a plan include:

- A vision for the organization
- How the organization proposes to meet national targets and its own aspirations
- A clarity about access to opportunities which addresses equalities issues
- Definition of training partnership opportunities
- Clarity about the organization's training priorities in the context of service requirements
- Expectations about the individual learner's contribution and responsibilities;
- Cost analysis inclusive of indirect or hidden costs
- Support structure for learners
- Underpinning accurate data, both local and national
- How movement towards development through knowledge management, practice/evidence-based training, mentoring and coaching is going to be achieved

- Strategy for investing in training social workers
- Plan for quantifying and meeting practice learning requirements.
  (Association of Directors of Social Services, nd: 21)

At the time of writing, some of the most significant achievements in workforce development have been the establishment of induction systems for all new staff and the setting of targets for learning, for example vocational and professional standards, including making social work education based on a degree with a new structure for post-qualifying awards for social work. A number of strategic bodies have been established nationally and regionally which are employer-led in the form of regional planning committees and learning resource centres to take these strategies forward. These aim to facilitate networks between employers, government bodies, commissioners and educa-tion and learning providers, and set targets for performance and monitor progress. Improved workforce intelligence and collection of minimum data sets for agencies where social care is provided has meant that there is an acceptance by the sector that it needs to estab-lish and maintain a competent workforce which requires excellence in leadership and management linked to how services should be delivered.

However, the recruitment, retention and ongoing development of the social care workforce continues to be an enormous challenge fraught with difficulties and constrained by inadequate resources to realize this. Improving recruitment into social work, for example, needs a genuine commitment to enhancing the status of the profes-sion, which in turn requires that government policies and public atti-tudes also reflect an ethical and positive approach to the sections of society with whom social workers engage. McLenachan (2006) points out that this does not always occur in the context of campaigns and policies that marginalize and criminalize those in need of guidance, support and the resources to enable them to lead worthwhile, valued and independent lives. McLenachan cites the changing nature of the workforce as another key factor where discrepancies in pay and status have been highlighted by social workers within interprofes-sional teams, who feel that 'the professional status of the social work role is less valued and respected' (2006: unpaged). Strategies to enhance social work recruitment and retention therefore need to reflect the nature of the settings in which social workers now func-tion and ensure that there is parity between professionals, in terms of pay, status and recognition.

In July 2005, the government announced a review of the social care workforce in England to be led jointly by the Department for Education and Skills (DfES) and the Department of Health (DH) to draw together different strands of work in workforce development. The resulting *Options for Excellence* review (Department of Health and Department for Education and Skills, 2006) made recommendations to increase the supply of all workers within the sector, such as domiciliary care workers, residential care workers, social workers and occupational therapists. It also looked at measures to tackle recruitment and retention issues, improve the quality of social care practice, define the role of social workers (including training and skill requirements), and to develop a vision for the social care workforce in 2020 and a socio-economic case for improvements and investment in the workforce. Evidence gathered for this report suggested that a continuing high vacancy rate in social care included poor perception of those working in social care and a lack of quality career advice. The highest vacancy rate in social care was found in children's homes (15.1%) and in care staff in homes for adults with physical disabilities, mental health and learning difficulties (13.2%). Vacancy rates in social care doubles that of all types of industrial, commercial and public services employment, including teaching and nursing, yet demographic trends suggest that demands for social care staff will increase by 25% to meet projections for 2020.

To address these challenges, the government has identified a number of key priorities which will subsequently be addressed in the topics within this text:

• Appropriate support not only for new workers, but also for leaders and managers, in a way which values and shows commitment to their roles.
• Support for continuous professional development to enhance career progression. This support should be focused on practice-based learning and should not just be provided for professionals who require ongoing training to renew their registration.
• Career development and progression opportunities in addition to management ones with supported training programmes and induction.
• Effective supervision and systems for workload management as the norm. This is felt to be important in reducing absence brought about by stress and sickness and for improving staff retention.
• Leadership and management development strategies, including for those working in smaller organizations.
• The improvement of human resource management, for example through developing 'growing your own' initiatives.
• Following on from the Laming Report (2003) into the death of Victoria Climbie, the importance of drawing up clear lines of accountability and management to define roles and to avoid negative outcomes.

- Extending registration to increase the accountability and professionalism of the social care workforce.
- Using commissioning as a tool to raise quality in the social care workforce. This should include ways of improving the skills of commissioners themselves so they can focus on outcomes of commissioning and workforce quality as part of the commissioning process. Department of Health and Department for Education and Skills, 2006: 18)

How far these recommendations filter down to your direct workplace and impact on your own roles within the teams and services you work in will be discussed in more detail later on. In the meantime, we will now look at the role of formal learning as one of the many initiatives with human resource management strategies, starting with an overview of the National Occupational Standards and the national qualifications framework.

NATIONAL OCCUPATIONAL STANDARDS AND THE QUALIFICATIONS FRAMEWORK

National Occupational Standards (NOS) were designed to describe best practice in social care by bringing together the minimum skills, knowledge and values for each service area and level of employment within the social care workforce. NOS are used as benchmarks for learning within National Vocational Qualifications, (NVQs), the social work degree, and post-qualifying (PQ) awards as well in defining work roles and benchmarks for staff recruitment, supervision and appraisal. This process has enabled the development of a national qualifications framework, which is understood by and relevant to all staff and employers in social care. This framework ensures that employees are trained and developed as 'fit for purpose', and that they hold a portable, transferable and nationally recognizable qualification. This should prove effective in promoting career progression for moving into more advanced practice and across related occupations or working with specific service user groups.

Likewise, national leadership and management standards and social work post-qualifying awards at higher specialist and advanced levels have been instrumental in mapping the required competences for managers across all social care services linked to best or desirable practice (Skills for Care, 2004) (see Box 1.1). This qualification strategy is designed to support the expansion and coordination of integrated service delivery and you should make sure that you are familiar with the NOS that is relevant to your own service and the skills and competences that your staff need to develop to meet them.

BOX 1.1   THE PQ FRAMEWORK (GSCC, 2005A)

Degree in Social Work

(or CQSW, CSS, DipSW, or international qualification)
GSCC registration as 'Social Worker'
Generic qualification

Post-qualifying Award in Specialist Social Work

(Minimum honours degree level) Pathways

Child care	Adults	Mental health (MH)	Leadership and management*

- *Consolidating and extending* initial competence
- Developing *competence in depth* in a specific area of practice
- Mentoring and *practice education*

(*for Residential Care Managers only)

Post-qualifying Award in Higher Specialist Social Work

(Postgraduate diploma level) Pathways

Professional practice (Child care/Adults/MH)	Leadership and management	Professional practice education

for *complex decision making* and *high levels of responsibility*

Post-qualifying Award in Advanced Social Work

(MA degree level) Pathways

Professional practice (Child care/Adults/MH)	Leadership and management	Professional practice education

and take a *leading* role in promoting good practice and *applied professional research*

Reproduced by kind permission of Jane Lindsay © School of Social Work, Kingston University 2006

This approach to developing staff focuses on the specific tasks done by staff and equips them with the technical competencies they need to perform to the required national minimum standards. One criticism of this approach is that it is highly instrumental, mechanistic and managerial (Jordan and Jordan, 2002). In relation to social work, for example, Jordan and Jordan (2002) suggest that state intervention via regulation and enforced mandates for education and training has the potential to reduce the scope for professional judgement or experienced creativity. A number of uncritical assumptions are thus concealed about how individuals learn and the resources available within an area with such specific competencies for training and assessment specific to each level. This can result in a hierarchy of roles and tasks connected with care and its management. A taken-for-granted approach in which awarding bodies and curriculum development authorities identify appropriate occupational skills and standards and train people in competencies appropriate to their work can amount to a general philosophy of how social care should be regulated. Jordan and Jordan (2002: 129) states that where this is seldom questioned, it forms an inappropriate basis for learning and does not address the need for more adaptable and effective practice.

The emphasis on developing specific occupational standards for specific roles has also diverted attention from the issue of the transferability of knowledge and skills which is an essential and valuable tool for employability in new roles as future practice develops. For example, in 2005, the Children's Workforce Development Council (CWDC) and Skills for Care launched a 'Sector Qualifications Strategy' which specifies the current and future qualifications (Department for Education and Skills, 2005b) and broader achievements needed by the sector to respond to the whole systems approach to meeting children's needs within *Every Child Matters* (Department fo Health, 2003). While this is progressive, it will require much information, analysis and activity by the organizations involved to examine what it means to be 'occupationally qualified' and to be effective in meeting the five outcomes for all children's services. Equally problematic is how people following vocational qualifications will acquire the necessary knowledge base to develop their practice, since vocational qualifications have tended to be seen as performance assessment systems, rather than learning and teaching systems (Higham et al., 2001) and highlights the need for a model of learning which promotes partnership between academic and vocational awards within a skills escalator approach (Department of Health, 2002b).

BOX 1.2   REFLECTION BREAK

How far do you agree with the above critique and how successful do you think that learning using competences and the above type of task-specific model has been in improving standards or generating more reliable or flexible forms of care and support services?

As we have seen, broad changes in the economic, social and political context of social care inevitably requires specific changes in both the labour market and notions of occupations, professional expertise and education and training for the parallel transformation of social care. It is therefore crucial that, if professions are to survive and change in the current climate, those affected and those responsible for leading learning understand the nature of the changes that are occurring. We have seen above that as services become more fragmented, intensified and specialist, professional practice may become more programme-based. This may result in skills and knowledge becoming conceptualized in relation to specific services, rather than in terms of generic professional orientations (Fook et al., 2000). Primary responsibility for educating and training its workforce lies with employers who work closely with its partner agencies, sectors and organizations. Within the organizational context, employer and employee responsibility for training and development lies at all levels within social care organizations: for example at a strategic level, to devise an appropriate staff development strategy; at an operational level, where line managers have a responsibility for identifying staff development needs, plan how they should be met and take responsibility for implementing and evaluating the action arising from the plan; and finally at an individual level, staff must also play an active part in their own training and development.

According to Gould (2000), at the heart of organizational theory is the problematic concept of learning: what it means, how it relates to organizational structure and behaviour, and whether there are any real differences between the concept of 'organizational learning', defined as the processes through which learning takes place, and 'the learning organization', defined as the characteristic of an organization that learns. Gould identified the two fundamental premises underpinning these concepts. First, that individual learning is a necessary but not sufficient condition for organizational learning. Secondly, that the learning experience is more pervasive and takes place across multiple levels within the organization. We will be exploring these ideas further in Chapter 2.

THE ROLE OF MANAGER IN DEVELOPING THE SOCIAL CARE WORKFORCE

We referred earlier to the many issues affecting recruitment and retention of staff in social care organizations (Skills for Care, 2005a). We also saw from some of the recommendations coming out of the *Options for Excellence* report (Department of Health, and Department for Education and Skills, 2006) a clear indication for the role of managers in providing quality support to staff and users as key to taking this forward. According to one study done by the Audit Commission (2002a), quality support should incorporate five core characteristics: consistency and fairness; acceptance and respect; integrity and honesty; reliability and trustworthiness; empathy and understanding. Managers at all levels need to continue to develop greater levels of skills, including new ones, supported by a management development strategy, to respond to the changing policy environment within which social care is delivered. Likewise, practitioners need to be able to confront and engage in day-to-day dilemmas to avoid demoralization caused by constant organizational upheaval and to manage conflict effectively (Lymbery, 2004). The government's vision for social care requires major culture and mind-set shifts from the social care workforce so that empowering and partnership approaches can be developed. As stated earlier, these shifts will lead to the relocation of many social work functions and joining together of social care with other agencies, namely education, health, housing, criminal justice and the independent sector, and are powerful factors currently impacting on learning cultures. The development of evidence-based practice in social work and social care has also been seen as a means of shaping interventions and the modernization of social care (Marsh et al., 2005).

Underlying this development is the assumption that the best quality evidence for practice is easily available and applicable to different settings. However, this concept needs to be carefully examined given the highly mechanistic and bureaucratic procedures that exist within some organizations delivering social care (Dominelli, 2002). There is a plethora of different organizations and stakeholders involved in its planning, delivery and regulation as well as in the support of social care education. As a result, learning and development can be confusing and piecemeal. Secondly, in order to be of maximum value, learning has to be managed and properly resourced. Eraut's (2004: 111) exploration of whether 'we are learning to change or changing to learn' highlights how the change process often tends to be regarded as a political and administrative process rather than as a learning process in itself. Less attention is therefore given by managers in learning how to facilitate change through the many different clusters of activities for which they are responsible. Employee development is but just one of the activities and is not always at the top of a manager's agenda or a priority in change management. In conclusion, strong managerial, professional and political leadership is needed to reassert the central importance of learning in social work and social care practice and is often cited as a key determinant of high-performing organizations (Skills for Care, 2004). At both a national and local level this will also be based on power sharing with users and carers (SCIE, 2005).

The leadership of learning is a complex activity which involves those responsible being able to navigate through overwhelming demands for learning as well as unlearning knowledge and skills because of new developments or changes in the organization or wider social policy environment. These learning curves or 'rollercoaster' experiences are an inevitable part of professional life for which managers and staff are not always adequately prepared. It has been shown, however, that managers who use a wide range of leader behaviours are viewed as more effective than those who use a more limited range (Ahearn et al., 2004). To illustrate this, we will now turn to look at theories of management and leadership in order to familiarize ourselves with what is meant by these terms and what leadership as a concept can offer to learning in social care.

WHAT DO WE MEAN BY MANAGEMENT AND LEADERSHIP IN SOCIAL CARE?

If leadership is a key to improving organizational performance, then by implication, leadership development within organizations responsible for delivering social care services is equally critical. An overview of the generic literature on leadership shows that while leadership and management are often linked together, there has been a growing interest in *leadership* as opposed to *management* (Ribbins, 2004) and there are literally thousands of studies presenting various viewpoints and definitions of leadership (Clegg et al., 2005). Considering the relevance of classic leadership theories and their transferability to the context of social care can be useful to help us understand how leaders think and act. At face value, leadership appears to be a simple sphere of interest, but we will see when we review the different leadership theories that confusion and contradictions arise from differences of opinion about what leadership is and how useful it is as a concept. Nor is the implicit assumption that leadership is an important component of organizational performance necessarily substantiated by empirical evidence (Lumby et al., 2005: 12). Leadership has been studied from a variety of perspectives, including the different traits, behaviours and situations that inform leadership theories and the development of concepts such as *transformational* and *charismatic* leadership. So let's start by having a look at how useful these theories and concepts are to us in the social care context.

THEORIES ABOUT LEADERSHIP

TRAIT THEORIES

Ideas about leadership put forward by trait theorists originated from a series of psychological studies which identified certain characteristics, qualities and attributes in people based on physical, psychological and demographic variables such as gender, ethnicity, intelligence or personality. Critiques of this approach contest the idea that some people are superior or possess inherent leadership traits. Instead, they argue that emergent leaders are the product of other influences, such as the norms and culture of an organization. Further, the failure to recognize these other influences can lead to discriminatory practices in leadership development and through the impact of leadership itself. In social care there are many studies highlighting the institutional effects of certain types of leadership, particularly higher up in the organization hierarchy (Liff and Dale, 1994; Davidson, 1997; IDeA, 2004). Barker (1997) suggests that leadership development should be based on the relationships that occur within the leadership situation in response to particular issues or challenges, implying a form of leadership which is more context-specific and situational. For example, a leadership role might be taken by a person progressing an improvement or change in response to legislation or feedback from users and carers and builds on the recognition of their expertise, experience or interests as well as the need to drive or implement significant change. Therefore the characteristics of a leader might emerge as a result of an individual's opportunities, experiences and behaviour rather than from an inherent ability or natural flair, as the case study in Box 1.3 illustrates.

BOX 1.3   LEADERSHIP AND DIVERSITY – A CASE STUDY

The Improvement and Development Agency (IDeA) commissioned a study to examine the career prospects of different groups of people working in local government. It sought to find out why some groups were under-represented at senior levels of management and the nature of any discrimination experienced. A survey of more than 10,000 white, black and minority ethnic male, female, disabled and non-disabled managers asked

(Continued)

them about their level of education, career satisfaction, level of supervisory support, access to training and development, the quality of feedback offered to them, their interaction with colleagues and whether they felt included at work, and their desire for career progression, among other aspects of their jobs.

Findings found that white males were significantly more likely to have a professional qualification or undergraduate degree. Black and minority ethnic managers were found to be generally better educated academically. As with female managers, they were more likely to have obtained a master's degree. However, they received less supervisory support, training and development opportunities and high-quality feedback than white managers. They also believed that despite their abilities, they would not be given leadership responsibility without appealing to those in positions of power. Female managers were found to be at a lower level of management overall than male managers, despite the fact that they were significantly more likely to engage in a variety of career strategy behaviours. Disabled managers did not exhibit any greater or lesser interest in progressing within their organization compared to non-disabled managers, yet they were also at a lower level of management overall.

The findings conclude that diverse groups of managers will continue to face barriers to their career progression until organizations effectively commit to managing diversity fairly and consistently.

Source: iDeA (2004)

BEHAVIOURIST THEORIES

The behaviourist school have studied behaviours exhibited by leaders and suggested that styles of leadership can be adopted based on two key underlying behaviours: first, an orientation or concern towards people which builds on developing good communication, interaction and relationships with others; and secondly, an emphasis on the task at hand, or to the more 'technical' side of work. Blake and Mouton (1985) note how leaders' behaviours are ranked according to these two dimensions. Depending on whether one is more focused on concern for *people* or *production*, this then determines whether one is an *employee* or *job-centred* leader. These two styles can be adjusted depending on the requirements of the situation and can contain extreme, middle-of-the-road or maintenance positions. The origins of debate about managerialism in social care, which emerged through the 1980 and 1990s, illustrate these tensions.

Managerialism is led by the belief that efficiency, value for money and getting more from less could also be delivered by stressing the customer or consumerist approaches to social care within a strong hierarchy and performance management culture (Dominelli, 2002; Harlow, 2004). Managerialist approaches value the knowledge and expertise of management itself, which dominates and supersedes professional expertise or specialist knowledge and practice. Likewise, professional staff are expected to take on more managerial-like tasks within the organization. Management in the personal social services has always been unique through its emphasis on human relationship issues and its tradition of supervision, care for staff and more cooperative or humanistic approaches. According to Walton (2005: 598), managerialist approaches are more preoccupied with tasks such as 'drafting specifications and contracts for commissioned services, overseeing and monitoring contracts, providing a wide range of additional information for audit, inspection and central government, drafting proposals for targeted allocations from central government for diverse projects and services and managing budgets'. These approaches can significantly divert staff away from a more unique approach necessary for effective social care. Within this context it is not surprising that managers have little time for learning and staff development.

Behaviourist theorists on leadership also draw on theories of motivation and stress the importance of recognizing motivational factors which underline the way in which employees relate to the vision, values and goals of the organizations in which they work. McGregor's theory of X and Y management contrasted two assumptions about what motivates people at work (McGregor, 1960). Theory X assumes that people inherently dislike working requiring leaders (who are usually remote) to take decisions, be directive and control those involved. Managers subscribing to Theory Y, however, assume that people enjoy being given responsibility, are self-directive and that the role of leaders is to facilitate and collaborate with them. These contrasting approaches can be observed in the tensions experienced between central control and local decision making in social care organizations today and represent one of the features of how we might experience opposing styles in leadership and the different organizational cultural contexts for learning.

SITUATIONAL AND CONTINGENCY THEORIES

When discussing the notion of effective or ineffective leadership in social care, we often refer to the influence of social, political and economic contexts in which leadership develops, and this is where situational and contingency theories can help. Situational theorists believe that leadership emerges in certain situations, such as a crisis or event where leadership is required. Underlying contingency theory is the notion that leadership is all about being able to adapt and be flexible to ever-changing situations and contexts, and this focuses more on the interactions between those that lead and those that follow. Adair (1983) believed that a leader also has to balance three different needs in approaching a task: the needs of the task itself, the needs of the group or team working on the task and the needs of the individuals within the group. Attention to detail within all three aspects should help leaders structure their approach to a new situation and do a thorough job.

Contingency leadership theories have made an important contribution to the evolution of leadership theory and can easily transfer to the social care arena. Contingency theory takes into account the *context* of leading and the nature of the work being led. It considers the internal working environment and the external economic and social environment (House, 1995). A perspective shared by many organizational theorists is that work environments are inherently political. The acquisition of 'political skills' will help managers become more adept at using their interpersonal and information management skills to more positive effect (Ahearn et al., 2004). Mintzberg (1985) defines political skills as the ability to effectively understand others at work, and to use such knowledge to influence others to act in ways that enhance one's personal and/or organizational objectives. By working with and through others, managers can become more effective at networking, coalition building, and creating social capital. Leaders who network are therefore in a better position to secure more resources for their units and are more valued by their teams. Their accumulation of friendships, connections and alliances allow them to leverage this social capital to then facilitate change within a climate that encourages learning for service improvement (House, 1995).

MODERNIST AND POSTMODERNIST LEADERSHIP THEORIES

More recently, the whole notion of leadership has been critically questioned and challenged by arguing that there is no such thing as leadership *per se*. Leadership is perceived as a socially constructed concept which only exists in accordance with what people within an organization perceive it to be (Boje and Dennehey, 1999). In social care, substitutes for leadership can be found in one's professional experience. Professionals who possess a high level of expertise are one of several members of a team who may be involved in decision making, goal setting, performance measurement and evaluation, and will hold responsibilities for determining the way in which issues are dealt with in an organization. Therefore, leadership is less likely to be prominent in situations where there are high levels of trust, shared responsibility, interdependence and support, and likewise in jobs with highly formalized and routinized procedures where people work with less supervision and support.

Some of these ideas are strongly related to the notion of empowerment in social care and originate from social democratic practice and anti-discriminatory and anti-oppressive practice which aim at enabling people to overcome barriers in achieving life objectives and to gain access to the support they need (Payne, 2005: 295). These ideas are also in tune with the principles of lifelong learning. As a real substitute for leadership, the process of empowerment enables steps to be taken to address the power inequality inherent in subordination. For example, many practitioners develop strong professional relationships of mutual trust with some of their colleagues. These relationships contribute to their professional identities, provide important emotional support and lead to considerable informal mutual learning (Eraut, 2006).

Empowering managers will be concerned with motivating individuals and teams to achieve more towards organizational objectives by granting them greater independence from managerial control. This is not an easy concept to promote within the public sector, where legislative and regulatory responsibilities can take precedence. A true learning climate is one where managers' primary task is to facilitate experimentation from experience. Mistakes are allowed and there is no such thing as a failure. However, in health and social care we have many examples from extensive public inquiries and media criticism where a blame culture emerges. This inhibits openness, risk taking and the ongoing reflection necessary for learning and communicating this vision to others. Allowing people or professionals to participate in planning, through representative consultations and mutual self-help using empowerment, will inevitably lower their reliance on or need for leadership. In this scenario, boundaries between leaders and followers become blurred and leadership skills and responsibilities are dispersed or shared throughout an organization. Emphasis is instead placed upon the *process* of leadership as an alternative to the attributes or style of one particular person or persons. These are concepts that we will build on throughout this text, particularly in relation to service users as leaders and the leadership of staff in developing others within the workplace environment.

DISPERSED OR DISTRIBUTED LEADERSHIP

This leads us to consider the theory of dispersed or distributed leadership, where leadership is described as an entity shared through the organization and is an idea that continues to gain interest and validity in postmodernist thought (Boje and Dennehey, 1999). In theoretical terms, distributed leadership means that multiple sources of guidance and direction, related to the expertise in an organization, are made coherent through a common culture. This type of léadership may lend itself or be an aspiration in some social care organizations, where tasks and goals are shared and based on a common framework of values and where the members of the organization work together to pool their expertise. Essentially, it is defined as leadership which 'concentrates on engaging expertise wherever it exists within the organization rather than seeking this only through formal position or role' (Harris, 2003: 13).

Distributed leadership is therefore largely equated with team working and collaboration. It can contribute towards an ideal culture for learning and is strongly influenced by the professional cultures and subcultures which have helped to shape each practitioner's identity and the organizational or departmental cultures in which the team is situated (Eraut, 2006). It is often enacted as a distribution of responsibilities to meet operational needs rather than as an aspiration to the distribution of power in itself. Size and complexity of an organization may be one factor which affects its ability to distribute leadership effectively. If you are not familiar with the concept of organizational culture, this can be defined as the deep, basic assumptions and beliefs that are shared by members of an organization which are often hidden and unconscious and represent the way in which an organization perceives itself and its environment (Schein, 1997). Put simply, culture is learned, shared and transmitted based on a combination of assumptions, values, symbols, language and behaviours that manifest the organization's norms and values.

Although many features and practices in social care are framed by national, organizational or professional regulations, pathways or guidelines, their usage, meanings and practical detail are usually subject to interpretation within the culture in which they are implemented. While work cultures provide a major source of practice expertise from which most participants can benefit and leadership can emerge, they can also sustain outmoded practices, ineffective ways of working, and negative attitudes towards learning (Eraut, 2006). This relates to the final form of leadership described within this section, the notion of *abdicated* leadership. Abdicated leadership refers to a situation where the absence of leadership leaves people with a lack of direction and decision making, resulting in a poorly motivated work culture where conflict or indifference thrives (Martin, 2003).

BOX 1.4   REFLECTION BREAK

Choose two perspectives or theories of leadership from the above explanations which you found most accorded with your own thoughts, beliefs and values. What are their strengths and weaknesses? Make notes on how and why you think you agreed or disagreed with them or how these might be applied to your own practice setting.

LEADERSHIP AND LEARNING

Researchers have long attempted to understand the determinants of effective leadership and, following the above exercise, hopefully you were able from your own experiences to identify with some of the aspects of both classic and modern theories of leadership. One theme among much of the research is the idea that leadership behaviours and actions are important determinants of organizational effectiveness and it seems reasonable to conclude that to be successful, leaders must be concerned with both task- and people-related issues in the workplace (Mastrangelo, 2004). The task of leadership is often expressed as being able to motivate people to achieve outcomes that benefit the individual, the team and the organization. Hopefully you will recognize that we need to have a balance between all of these. Attention to a range of issues was illustrated in a study undertaken by the Audit Commission in 2002 of why staff leave social care. It identified six key influential factors:

- The sense of being overwhelmed by bureaucracy, paperwork and targets.
- Insufficient resources leading to unmanageable workloads.
- a lack of autonomy.
- Feeling undervalued by the government, their managers and the public.
- An unfair pay structure.
- A change agenda that feels imposed and irrelevant. (Audit Commission, 2002a: section 3)

Within social care, leadership also makes a significant contribution towards collaboration and collectivist approaches by promoting the principles of social justice within communities and society. Boundaries between leadership and followership can also become blurred and make way for the leadership roles taken by users and other professionals during the learning and development processes. Whether you are a leader or a follower, or both, these principles should underpin the commitment of people working in social care and their personal and professional commitment to update their knowledge, advocate on behalf of users and to critically examine their practice. Signing up to this is embedded in the General Social Care Council's *Codes of Practice* (GSCC, 2002):

Code 6

Be accountable for the quality of your work and take responsibility for maintaining and improving your knowledge and skills. (www.gscc.org.uk).

A significant feature of leadership is a willingness to challenge rigidity or narrow thinking to develop new perspectives and this means that anyone within the organization can take on this role as long as it is recognized, encouraged, facilitated and supported.

TRANSFORMATIONAL LEADERSHIP

As we have already established, leadership theories are very much associated with change and organizational development and are an essential ingredient in being able to achieve transformation. Mezirow (1991) was a key observer on how learning transforms the way we think. He differentiates between *transformational* and *informational* learning. Informational learning occurs when we change the amount we know about something based on our acquisition of knowledge alone. However, learning that involves us in changing the way we think about things will also challenge our frame of reference, and if we are successful in this, can lead to our thinking and feelings being transformed. This is what is known as transformational learning. Transformational learning in the literature is associated with leadership because it is essentially about taking control of your own life as a key to making transformations (Senge, 1996). Our capacity to make transformations or develop our ways of knowing have affective, interpersonal and moral dimensions. Individuals who learn through critical reflection and who are able to make personal transformations are well equipped to translate this into achieving action and results in a wider context through a leadership role. Transformational leadership is one of a number of different approaches to leadership styles described in the literature and Table 1.1 summarizes three most common key leadership styles.

Table 1.1   Characteristics of leadership approaches: transactional, charismatic and transformational

Approach	Description
Transactional	Transactional leaders build on trait, behaviourist and contingency theories and pay attention to all the necessary and critical management functions, such as clarifying the roles and tasks and allocating work through the exchange of rewards and sanctions. They adhere to organizational policies, values and vision and, are strong on planning, resource management and meeting schedules, but do not cope well with major change or managing the change process.
Charismatic	Charismatic leaders create the impetus for change and have a motivating effect upon others. They are able to create a grand and idealized vision. They unify people towards that vision and foster conditions of high trust.
Transformational	Transformational leaders inspire change and innovation and are the opposite of transactional leaders because they deal mainly with bstract and intangible concepts like vision and change. Key factors in successful transformational leadership have been identified as concern for others, approachability, integrity, charisma, intellectual ability and an ability to communicate, set direction and manage change.

Source: Clegg et al. (2005) Reprinted with permission from SAGE.

FOLLOWERSHIP, POWER AND INFLUENCE

In social work and social care there is an increasing impetus to use reflective practice as a method of learning for continuing professional development. In the previous section we identified that reflective practice has the potential to be transformative, resulting in changes in professional practice and society. This only occurs when underlying power relationships are identified, challenged and redirected (Sandars, 2006).

It may also have occurred to you while reading this chapter that throughout history there have been leaders whose influence has not always been positive or desirable. An understanding of the appropriate use of power and authority in social care is influential in the way in which those being managed or led will respond. One much discussed aspect of leadership, which is said to differ from management, is the ability of some people to get others to do things above and beyond rewarded effort, which is not purely dependent on sanctions or the use of power and authority. This is attributed to the followers' expression of beliefs and emotions towards certain ideas or people who possess a greater influence over them. It is this influence that is often described as the *essence* of leadership and, according to Popper (2003), is essentially an *emotional* influence or a process which moves a group or groups of people in some direction through non-coercive means (Kotter, 1988). This emotional influence, or 'emotional intelligence' as it is more commonly called, is thought to carry great significance in accounting for excellence in work performance. As stated earlier, while these characteristics can also be used negatively, 'socialized leaders' (Howell and Frost, 1989) are motivated by a sense of responsibility or through the influence of social structures which form the basis of empathy, giving, and the need to relate to the emotions of others. Working in social care can trigger stress and anxiety because we are often working with very difficult and challenging situations. Goleman (1996) identified the ability to understand oneself and others, including competence in self-awareness, self-control, empathy, listening, conflict resolution and cooperation, as characteristics of someone who is emotionally intelligent. Emotional intelligence helps us to cooperate and work together within highly emotional interpersonal relationships to achieve better conditions for change.

These characteristics are very much in tune with the ethos of social care and embodied in its national leadership and management standards (Skills for Care, 2006b) and GSCC *Codes of Practice* (www.gscc. org.uk). Good social care managers are said to possess distinctive qualities. They:

- inspire staff;
- promote and meet service aims, objectives and goals;
- develop joint working/partnerships that are purposeful;
- ensure equality for staff and service users driven from the top down;
- challenge discrimination and harassment in employment practice and service delivery;
- empower staff and service users to develop services people want;
- value people, recognize and actively develop potential;
- develop and maintain awareness and keep in touch with service users and staff;
- provide an environment and time in which to develop reflective practice, professional skills and the ability to make judgements in complex situations;
- take responsibility for the continuing professional development of self and others;
- demonstrate an ability to plan organizational strategies for work-force development. (Skills for Care, 2004)

These principles explicitly have a 'people' emphasis. Ideas about transformational leadership are useful in critical periods when an organization needs more intensive development. Transformational leaders are those who: 'broaden and elevate the interests of their employees when they generate awareness and acceptance of the purposes and mission of the group, and when they stir their employees to look beyond their own self-interest for the good of the group' (Bass, 1990: 20). Management researchers have begun to pay particular attention to the concept of self-awareness and its effect on individual and organizational outcomes and have found that individuals who are self-observant and more self-aware are also likely to have a positive impact on an organization's culture (Atwater and Yammarino, 1992).

DIFFERENCES BETWEEN MANAGERS AND LEADERS

By now you will have realized that managers and leaders are quite distinct in their role and functions (Kotter, 1988). Management is mainly to do with planning and organizing whereas leadership is associated with creating, coping and helping to adapt to change. Management is about implementation, order, efficiency and effectiveness, whereas leadership is concerned with future direction in uncertain conditions (Boydell and Leary, 1994). In conditions of relative stability, management suffices, but in conditions of complexity, unpredictability and rapid change, leadership qualities are required. There is no doubt, however, that while these two functions are distinct, there is an overlap between them and the development of managers and leaders needs to be an integrated process, set in its organizational context and shaped by the particular challenges facing an organization at any one time. Within this process, managing learning is a central task and, according to Salaman (1995), cannot be achieved as a separate and discrete activity from either management or leadership. Integrating the management of learning as a core task in organizations may well help to place learning on the mainstream organizational agenda. Users own feedback has highlighted the importance of leaders and managers knowing how to 'show the way, keep people on board and together, listen to customers, make change happen and get results through the best use of people, money and other resources' (Skills for Care, 2004: 1). Whatever the focus, effective leadership and management are essential to manage the increasing complexity of social care arrangements, which often entail managing staff from different professions and disciplines across integrated and multi-agency settings within a range of partnerships. From this we may conclude that staff support and development are integral to achieving good services and implementing social care objectives.

LESSONS FROM THE LEADERSHIP LITERATURE

In the section above we have looked at the main theories about leadership and management in social care and identified factors which provide the appropriate conditions for leadership development in order for learning and subsequently change to be supported. Leading others often means being out front and providing direction, particularly in defining a common purpose or, as it is mostly described, a 'mission', 'vision' and 'philosophy'. Providing, implementing and managing a systematic process of learning is also critical to the success of leader direction. Ensuring this process is effective requires the confidence of each member in the organization. Staff need to know how their job contributes to the overall effort as well as towards continuous service improvement. These assumptions are what lie behind the government's drive towards 'workforce development' in social care (Department of Health, 2000). Organizations need to develop cultures and structures that will encourage leadership and management capability as well as being proactive in working with the diversity of staff, users and carers in promoting social inclusion (Skills for Care, 2004).

Hopefully so far, this chapter will have provoked you into considering how this fits with your own current role? Whether you are a manager, practitioner or in another significant role, our politicians, policy makers and the public have rightly called for better knowledge, skills and evidence in the workforce to underpin the modernization of welfare. Resources cannot be targeted or used wisely without those involved in delivering them having a better knowledge of which ones are effective in meeting the requirements of people in need (Marsh et al., 2005). Nor can the different stakeholders work effectively together unless they share a commitment to developing the workforce and, through evidence-informed practice, developing a shared understanding of how to achieve better outcomes for people through those working for and with them. Awareness and understanding of strategic influences can help those of you who are contributing towards developing learning and development and your understanding of how this activity is linked to achieving improvement and better outcomes in service delivery in a way that builds on the job satisfaction and cooperation of those engaged in the process.

CHAPTER SUMMARY

Developing the capacity of the workforce has to consider the range of qualifications required and which award schemes are appropriate to the social work and social care workforce which link with professional qualifying training and continuous professional development. The capacity to produce knowledge and evidence to inform practice developments are a further strand of workforce capacity development. Research literacy is an integral part of professional education and learning. Fook et al. (2000: 242) highlight a number of challenges for learning and organizational development in the current climate, where it is suggested that professional skill and knowledge is devalued, disaggregated and decontextualized so that it can be measured and evaluated. The representation of professional knowledge in terms of managerial, rather than professional, discourse can lessen professional autonomy and control and distances professionals from sources of policy and decision making. Fook et al. also remind us that competition between different professional groups potentially increases and dominates boundaries between them, resulting in a shift to the aggregation of skills for specific programmes rather than orientations of value bases and approaches.

These challenges force us to look at the knowledge hierarchy differently. We have to make a commitment to all stakeholders within social care by researching and developing knowledge from the perspective of the practitioner and the user/carer and by having the courage to conceptualize our practice in professional rather than in managerial terms. As we have seen, the ever increasing external scrutiny, regulation and performance management in social care do not always sit comfortably with its core values and the learning process. The use of leadership to reassert the importance of learning in social care and social work practice can help staff and stakeholders to be more critically reflective and seriously pursue the aspirations laid down by national standards and the GSCC *Codes of Practice* (GSCC, 2002). Social workers will have to develop their practice in the face of political, professional and organizational environments that can enable as well as disable progress (Lymbery, 2004). The dilemma is deceptively simple: how can a more progressive form of practice be developed within the drivers for workforce development in a way that makes much of its rhetoric a reality? This responsibility sits with the individuals in an organization and their commitment to develop knowledge, skills and practice along with users, carers and other significant people who, with the appropriate support and encouragement, can take a lead role in the development of social care workforce.

According to Uttley (1994: 191), professions have a kind of pact with the state in that many depend on state patronage to maintain elite positions. They are socialized to comply with employing organizations. Some of these issues came up when we looked at the different theories about leadership and leadership styles. You may have concluded that the more repressive the environment, the more attention is needed to be able to adapt current conceptualizations of the skill and knowledge required to be effective in new situations. The domination of a managerialist culture, curiously, can in fact encourage practitioners to be more critically reflective, whereby locating the source of this domination creates a local dialogue about how to achieve change. If you are a leader or manager of learning, you will appreciate that managers' and professionals' objectives are not necessarily dissimilar in their mutual need to record and develop practice. Shifting the debate and defining professional identity in terms of meaningful systems that transcend the day-to-day workplace will enable all those involved to frame their knowledge and skills and acknowledge commonalities of professional practice. This means striving to become an expert practitioner, no matter what level in the organization you are operating in, and consciously reflecting upon practice in its widest sense.

Recommended further reading

Vivien Martin (2003) *Leading Change in Health and Social Care* (London: Routledge) provides a practical guide to change management drawing on leadership, management and change management theories, tools and techniques.

Web-based resources

Skills for care (www.skillsforcare.org.uk) – an organization responsible for raising standards for adult social care in England by ensuring qualifications and standards for training are constantly developed and adapted. Through its regional committee structure, Skills for Care coordinates a network of statutory and independent sector employers in all aspects of social care alongside representatives of service users, informal carers, staff associations and education and training providers.

    Children's Workforce Strategy (www.everychildmatters. gov.uk) – the Children's Workforce Development Council (CWDC) aims to improve the lives of children and young people by ensuring that people working with them have the best possible training, qualifications, support and advice. The strategy developed in 2005 aims to develop an integrated qualifications framework for the Children's Workforce in partnership with all stakeholders concerned.

2 DEVELOPING A CULTURE OF LEARNING IN SOCIAL CARE – A WORK IN PROGRESS?

This chapter explores:

- Organizational processes that encourage and support learning in social care
- The relationships between individual and organizational learning

INTRODUCTION

In the previous chapter we looked at the drivers for workforce development. This raised questions and dilemmas about how the rhetoric on organizational processes to facilitate learning might become a reality and who might take a lead in these developments. As we saw earlier, a number of government policy initiatives in health, social care and education have indicated that delivering a vision of lifelong learning requires organizations to develop and foster a learning culture in which leaders and managers take responsibility for having systematic learning and development strategies in place for implementing them. Effective learning cultures are ones that are inclusive and shared with staff, and follow a process which not only enables staff to develop and fulfil their potential, but also enables the organization itself to learn, develop and evolve. The critical characteristics of organizations that describe its capacity to learn from experience and adapt continuously to changing external conditions are often referred to as those of a 'learning organization' (Gould, 2000).

The term 'learning organization' has become a new buzzword within the field of management and organizational research. Striving to become such an organization is often cited as the solution to how organizations can increase their chances for survival and strengthen their market position (Schein, 1993; Senge, 1996). For that purpose, becoming a learning organization is said to offer flexibility and adaptability (Thomsen and Hoest, 2001). The concept of a learning organization is relatively unexplored within social care research and much of the literature in this field comes across as very normative and prescriptive by describing useful instruments or frameworks for working with learning, thus implying its applicability to practice. This chapter will explore some of these discourses in relation to learning organizations in an attempt to grasp how both employers and employees can develop a meaningful but accessible learning culture that has the potential to engage and empower the greatest number of employees and celebrate work based learning.

On the whole, social care knowledge and research still depends heavily on its source from education and academia. The evolution of knowledge and learning, however, needs to be examined alongside developments and trends in services and continuing interest in qualitative research and practice evaluation – including reflective practice. Supervision, coaching and mentoring, interdisciplinary working and team working provide alternative mechanisms capable of fostering this ideal. We will be looking at some of these ideas in later chapters of this book.

Walton's (2005) analysis of learning organizations in their wider context proposes that a learning organization is one which enables the liberation of learning from the political and administrative preoccupations of central government but is also able to recognize and accommodate the development of government and audit targets against which social care employees and their agencies are evaluated. It facilitates the connection between extending and disseminating knowledge to maintain and improve the standards of practice. It also consciously delivers opportunities to forge partnerships which provide support for the expansion of staff development and opportunities for practitioner involvement in organizational learning and the provision of high-quality services.

We will begin by defining the characteristics of a learning organization in social care, with reference to any theoretical frameworks offered from management and organizational research. In Chapter 1 we alluded to the importance of a value-based approach to leadership development as one where individuals are encouraged to take ownership of learning within their own context. We referred to this as 'dispersed leadership'. Managers could, for example, look for ways of engaging the community in finding a common ground for developing services and the learning needed to support this. We will be talking in more detail about this challenge when we look at the leadership of service users in learning in Chapter 4. Service user participation is a significant factor in ensuring that any staff developmental activity has an impact on service delivery.

Leaders and managers of learning also need to have a working knowledge of major theories of learning, particularly those which either explicitly or implicitly place experience at the centre of an organization's learning culture. We will give a brief overview of learning theories to help us to consider how organizational learning can be understood and operationalized and how the learning process can be more holistically managed in organizations. In summary, this chapter is concerned with a wider interest in how the management of the learning process can be related to individual learning and how individual learning can be related to organizational learning and the balance that can be achieved between these.

DEFINING A LEARNING ORGANIZATION?

As we discussed in the previous chapter, if organizations, and importantly the people they employ, are successfully to continue to adapt, survive and develop in a complex culture, where change is the norm and resources are often limited, there has to be a work-based learning revolution. This inevitably involves a shift away from the reliance on directed learning and 'command and control' management styles towards a culture of facilitation, creative learning and development strategies. These will recognize and support widening participation, empowerment, personal responsibility and collaborative working. These ideas are related to the concept of what we mean when we refer to a 'learning organization'. We will try to define what a learning organization is in order to see what relevance it has to social care.

LEARNING ORGANIZATION THEORY

The 'learning organization' and 'organizational learning' are two sides of the same coin. In any organization, the positioning of employees is linked to the specific tasks and roles that they are expected to carry out within overall organizational work practice. Employees, their position and the organizational work practice are, in turn, aspects of the organization that make up the workplace. This unity – employees, work practice and organizing – provides a context for organizational learning. Thus there is an element of 'community' and collective work practice in an organization which employees are part of and which is the frame of reference (Elkjaer, 2003). There is also an assumption that learning is possible to measure as, according to Garvin (1993: 89), 'if you can't measure it, you can't manage it'.

Proponents of learning organization theory write from within a commitment to humanist radicalism (Dovey, 1997) and reflective practice (Jarvis, 1999, cited in Gould, 2000: 585), where learning is not limited to training events or courses, but describes a set of processes located within the organization where learning purposively engages with practice, is experiential and is achieved through shared problem solving and quality improvements. Revans (1980), an advocate of action-learning approaches, proposed that for an organization to survive, its rate of learning must be equal to or greater than the rate of change in its external environment. Associated with this idea is an implicit change of metaphor for conceptualizing organizational life, from the dominant Taylorist image of the organization as a *machine* towards a metaphor of the organization as a *system*, one which has to adapt through learning to the changing demands created by its environment (Gould, 2000).

Therefore organizations with transparent boundaries, exposing more employees to the external environment, flatter hierarchies, more widely distributed managerial responsibilities and high involvement of employees in product and process development, are more conducive to learning. This, in turn, facilitates the development of horizontal learning networks which include more experimental techniques and acceptance of mistakes. Ultimately, as the theory goes, access to learning resources within such an environment enables people to cope with the day-to-day pressures of work. The provision of vocational advice and guidance and human resource policies to reward achievements are therefore very important.

The relevance of all this to social care is that learning and development have been identified as key to delivering the government's vision of service user-centred care in service provision. This means making sure that staff, the teams and the organizations they relate to and work in, can acquire new knowledge and skills, both to realize their potential and to help shape and change things for the better (Department of Health, 2002c). What is important for leaders and managers is the ability to identify and utilize concrete tools for promoting learning as well as fostering the culture and environment within which learning thrives.

The Social Care Institute for Excellence (SCIE, 2004) puts culture and environment at the forefront in their identification of the key characteristics of a learning organization specific to social care. Both structure and culture are important vehicles for learning in order to facilitate users' and carers' feedback in a way which is properly valued, resourced and utilized so that it can rightfully influence and inform practice itself. Any structure or culture should also promote cross-organizational and collaborative working in a way that makes the best of use of staff skills and potential. As we will see in the next chapter, a system of shared beliefs, goals and objectives with our partner organizations will, in turn, provide an open learning environment that not only leads to opportunities to try to test out innovative practices but will also allow learning from mistakes. As a manager, you will have an impact on both developing and implementing human resource practices and these must include a clear supervision and appraisal system as a basis for continuous professional development. While any information system in an organization needs to be effective and include a range of policies and procedures to standardize and regulate practice, the effectiveness of these, and the way in which these are communicated, can help to make them more meaningful, especially if underpinned by a human rights and social justice approach (SCIE, 2004).

As a manager or leader of learning, you will recognize that achieving learning organizational status therefore involves a range of complex tasks. Breaking these down into their various constituent elements will enable you to consider which areas you may have some direct control or influence over, and therefore to determine what contribution you can make towards developing a more positive learning culture. We will be looking at some of the practical implications of this in more detail in later chapters of this book. Of course, organizations are not monolithic in terms of their culture, and influencing culture is a slow and difficult process which requires a series of shifts over time and action on many fronts over an extended period (Fryer, 1997). It requires 'winning people to new ways of working, new priorities and a new sense of what is seen as normal and largely unremarkable' (Fryer, 1997: 8), and leadership is important to achieve this. Professional values also underpin the characteristics of a learning organization, where stakeholders are empowered to make relevant decisions and where organizational structures themselves support team work and strong lateral relations instead of just vertical ones. Networking for managers, teams and services should be enabled across organizational and hierarchical boundaries both internally and externally (SCIE, 2004). How these exist within your own organization and the different levels at which support is available will determine how active and effective you can be in your own particular role or sphere of influence. You need a range of practical and theoretical tools when working with your immediate teams and workgroups in order to promote and develop any of the above characteristics of a learning organization.

At the time of writing, the issues being examined by the government's review of its workforce development strategy are clearly complex (Department of Health and Department for Education and Skills, 2006). These issues are not only centred on themes of learning and development. Equal attention has been given to the reform of recruitment and retention practices within the sector to ensure that all parts of the social care system, not least the private, independent and voluntary sectors, facilitate appropriate opportunities for training and development in a consistent way. The *Options for Excellence* review (Department of Health and Department for Education and Skills 2006) looks at how best practice can be disseminated and replicated across the sector, for example, by looking at and extending the use of new technologies, both to free up staff time and to act as a tool for professional development. This approach embodies the view that managing the organizational culture must happen in tandem with improved learning (albeit overseen by close external monitoring) in order to deliver substantial gains in performance. In summary, although learning is something that is often undertaken and developed by individuals, it is important to recognize that the organizational arrangements or culture can foster or inhibit the process by which individuals subsequently engage with any learning. It is very difficult indeed to substantiate and prove how an organization can harness the learning achieved by its individual members. The example of continuing professional development, which has long been a part of social work and social care, is undertaken by individuals who may come and go, yet the organization as a whole has to endure and survive. The question remains, therefore, as to how organizations can still accumulate competence and capacity within its workforce despite the turnover of staff. Demands made on human or workforce development can often make it difficult to reconcile the needs of the business with the needs of the individual. This might present a useful opportunity to visit the concept of single-, double- and triple-looped learning, which is linked to how organizations learn and may take us one further step towards understanding the above dilemmas.

ORGANIZATIONAL LOOPS OF LEARNING

In their seminal work on organizational learning, Argyris and Schön (1990) describe three different levels of learning. At the most basic level is the detection and correction of error, which they label as 'single-loop learning' as it is analogous to maintaining a steady course through the use of a direct feedback loop. Single-loop learning tends to leave organizational objectives and processes largely unchanged. Some performance management targets, for instance where existing practice is compared with explicit standards, are typical of this type of learning. However, going beyond basic error correction to more sophisticated learning in order to change fundamental assumptions about the organization is possible.

The desire to further redefine the organization's goals, norms, policies, procedures, or even structures, is what Argyris and Schön term 'double-loop learning'. It calls into question the very nature of the course plotted and the feedback loops used to maintain that course.

Development of new and innovative models of service and redesign of service from the ground up represent attempts at this more radical form of learning. Unfortunately, many of the pressures on 'care' systems as we know them impede such a rethink. Radical change often fails to materialize unless it is precipitated by a crisis or critical event.

'Triple-loop learning', on the other hand, is one which pays attention to the system of power in an organization in order to influence *all* actions. Adopting the right approach to a problem and transparent discussion of the underlying purposes and intentions of any actions will inevitably involve some conflict. Allowing conflict and debates to emerge and different viewpoints to be challenged alongside a consideration of new approaches can lead to truly transformative learning in an organization. The approach to triple-loop learning, therefore, is one which acknowledges the importance of power relationships in society and capitalizes on transformation leadership styles (Sandars, 2006). As Sandars (2006: 8) tentatively puts it, relationships that acknowledge power are able to avoid the reproduction of a system in society that is 'inherently exploitive, racist, sexist and divided by social class. ... These underlying values and assumptions need constant questioning to achieve a more "rightful society"' In summary, the main questions for each learning loop are:

- Single-loop learning: are we doing things right?
- Double-loop learning: are we doing the right things?
- Triple-loop learning: why should we be doing it that way? (Flood and Romm, 1996)

Another, usually underdeveloped, aspect of exploiting learning capacity within organizations is the organization's ability to learn about the contexts of its learning. This means being able to identify when and how organizations learn and when and how they do not, and then adapt accordingly. Thus, successful learning organizations build on their experiences of learning to develop and test new learning strategies. This can be thought of as 'learning about learning' or *meta-learning*. It should be emphasized here that learning is not always about acquisition. Much of social care is actually based on custom and practice or on following government strategies and guidance, rather than on evidence itself.

This is a controversial topic which we will look at later in the book. Learning strategies should equally focus on 'unlearning' previously established ways of doing things. This is not just about practitioners changing their practice. More importantly, as demonstrated in the looped learning theory outlined above, it involves the organization in developing its ability to identify, evaluate and change whole routines that were previously embedded in organizational custom. For example, as we will see in Chapter 3, moving social care services into multidisciplinary teams and working with other professionals as equals may be especially difficult because of the personal investments that people inevitably have in their current ways of working.

Within a national context, the Performance Assessment Framework tends to facilitate single-loop learning by providing clear measures of performance and benchmarks against which these can then be judged. This can inhibit the questioning of underlying assumptions and objectives required for double-loop learning. Likewise, continuing professional development programmes, which meet both the learning needs of social work and social care professionals, must also meet wider service development needs. Building learning organizations is, in effect, an attempt to manage the culture of that organization and requires attention to some key cultural values if it is to be successful. Despite these insights, research continues to show a significant gap between strategy and its delivery across learning and development. To tackle this gap, learning and development professionals can be encouraged to work with line managers to build and support learning cultures that will make learning and development plans come to life in the workplace. This is easier said than done, and in a way is one of the underpinning values of this very text. Frontline managers in particular need help in supporting their learning and development responsibilities as they come under other pressures in organizations that are regularly restructuring (Harrison, 2005).

BOX 2.1 REFLECTION BREAK

What values do you think underpin the processes of a holistic modern human resource development strategy that enable the development of effective practice within social care organizations?

Some of the key values that you identified may have been at different levels and those at the organizational level may echo those identified by the Association of Directors of Social Services (ADSS). For example:

- Recognition of people's motivation and desire to make a difference.
- The creation of cultures that value and respect everyone.
- The promotion of lifelong learning.
- Fair, effective and safe employment policies.
- Open and ongoing consultation.

- Commitment to implementing national initiatives.
- Cooperative development with partner organizations.
- Measurable results.
- Positive, integrated service development. (Association of Directors of Social Services, nd: 2–3)

These values also emphasize how leaders in organizations allocate their time, support, personal attention, and other intangible as well as tangible resources, such as financial resources, to manage learning in organizations. We are often concerned with the process of how learning is constrained by or facilitated by resources, for example time, money, power and support. For instance, in learning organizations the resources that are made available in the staff role negotiation process, among other factors, and engagement in learning roles create favourable or unfavourable conditions for the individual to learn either in a routine or in an innovative way. This means influencing the types of action taken by the individual, resulting in different experiences from which something is learned (Kolb, 1984). As many tasks in social care are now accomplished through the division of labour and specialization, at the organizational level they require both specialization and integration of efforts.

Integration at the organizational level by individuals involves them transferring their individual learning into systems and structures, or forming communities of practice in which knowledge is shared through social constructions of reality and meaning (Lave and Wenger, 2002). The design of job roles and the movement of employees through the organization also enable the gathering of knowledge, in breadth and in depth, about the organization and its systems as well as creating different levels of learning and skill formation.

THE CONCEPT OF INDIVIDUAL LEARNING AND LEARNING TRANSFER

So far, throughout this book, we have been using the term 'learning' without necessarily defining or saying what we mean by this. Learning has been described as a lifelong process; something that continually takes place throughout the life-cycle consciously and unconsciously. Each person's awareness of, and commitment to, personal and professional learning will depend on their differing ability to learn and develop based on a variety of reasons, including intellect, interest, preferred learning styles, patience, etc. Major theories on learning and development either explicitly or implicitly place experience at the centre of the learning process. For example, learning theory, associated with Skinner (1989), is based on the law of effect, where behaviour is guided by reward and effort. Likewise, vicarious learning, which is based on the observation of others' behaviour or through observation, is understood to be strengthened by the receiving of positive reinforcement (Bandura, 1977). The possibility of learning by observation is important because it expands the opportunities for learning a broad range of behaviours occurring in situations that are too complex to be created artificially for learning purposes. The importance of managers in acting as role models in this paradigm cannot be emphasized enough, and highlights the relevance of leadership.

Transformational learning is another theoretical approach which we visited briefly when discussing organizational triple-loop learning in the previous section. This refers to critical periods when experiences and learning leave their stamp and is more clearly linked to leadership styles and influences. Developmental psychologists, such as Erikson (1959), have looked at the entire lifespan where each period is prone to internalizing a different aspect of learning. In conclusion, despite the various theoretical offshoots in developmental psychology, the following principles appear in most of the leading developmental theories:

- the central importance of direct experience of role models in emotional and social development; and
- the existence of periods of more intensive development in various aspects.

The learning process can not only be conceptualized as an individual, cognitive process that takes place strictly in the mind of an individual person, but is frequently defined as a socio-cultural process which takes place through interaction with others and is fundamentally the product of and the foundation for the context in which persons learn (Driver, 2002). At an organizational level, learning is incremental or radical, something that happens via small and continuous changes or something that requires discontinuous and radical change. What we are interested in here is how an organizational culture can maximize and celebrate the innate and human natural ability to continually learn, grow and develop and use it to its advantage. An understanding of learning theories is therefore important to this.

Within the concept of learning organizations, we have identified that there is a strong emphasis on *informal learning*, which, alongside education and formal training, is seen as the key to employability (Eraut, 1998: 37). Informal learning is an approach which emphasizes experiential, informal and self-directed learning, thus facilitating personal as well as organizational development. According to Eraut, the challenge of work itself remains the most important, yet undervalued, dimension of learning, in which formal education and training can be of only secondary importance. We will look at the debates about the credentialist approach to learning in the final section of this chapter. By credential-ist, we are referring to the idea that adult learning is not valued unless it leads to formal qualifications. It therefore disregards the value of experiential learning which may not necessarily lead to a qualification (Gorard and Rees, 2002: 106).

The notion of learning transfer or how this is evidenced is a less researched area. Learning transfer has been defined as 'prior learning affecting new learning or performance' (Marini and Genereau, 1995: 2). It incorporates various ideas, such as positive or negative reinforcement, and the building of new concepts from old ones using linguistic theories. Understanding how the transfer of learning exists in the literature is moving away generally from experimental psychology towards more psycho-social and cognitive theories of learning (Macaulay, 2000). Macaulay (2000: 5) talks about the 'active learner', where learning is an active process in which motivation is intrinsic and the centrality of the learner (as opposed to the learning task) has become a basic tenet of non-formal adult education. Within this learner-centred concept of learning, knowledge is not given but is actively acquired and interpreted by the individual. The transfer of learning will best be facilitated by creating a suitable climate in which the feelings and attitudes of the learners are as important as their cognitive strategies in dealing with the learning task. Therefore, helping employees to be self-directed, allowing time for reflec-tion and making connections between prior and present experiences are more effective than traditional top-down or didactic approaches. Thus: in social care organizations, these can be reinforced by the way in which change is managed or the way in which 'courses' or 'training' are com-missioned and delivered (See Chapter 6 where we also consider the importance of *creating* learning opportunities for employees).

LIFELONG LEARNING AND CREDENTIALIST APPROACHES

Our introduction to issues around workforce development in Chapter 1 and the strategies being deployed in social care to achieve this raised questions about different perspectives on learning and whether the competency based or qualifications approach is one that really reflects the objectives for learning. Hutton, when Minister for Social Services (in 1998), stated that:

> The attainment of higher levels of qualifications is a key government objective for the whole economy. Qualifications are a measure of the outcome of training which the public can understand, and which allow the staff concerned to demonstrate their competence and take pride in what they can do. (cited in TOPSS, 2000: 2)

Predictably, what we have seen in social care is a growing emphasis on education, assessment and the acquisition of formal qualifications. The picture that emerges is one where formal education is promoted as the key to high-quality standards, and credentials or qualifications provide the best evidence of this. The move towards credentials and qualifications reflects a modernization agenda that aims for evidencing professionalism through education and qualification that is here to stay. However, our brief overview of learning theory indicated that this is not necessarily the best and only way of ensuring quality and provision of relevant services.

A key challenge for organizations is to find a way to ensure that professional learning and professional qualifications genuinely enable employees to contribute to quality services and not assume that a piece of paper is in itself an indication of excellence. Research in the National Health Service, for example, has found that nurses and allied staff focused on gaining credits to improve job prospects or to increase earnings, rather than for any process and benefits of learning on the end user, the organization and increased skills (Hewison et al., 2000). Another recent example has been the tendency of social workers to supervise and assess social work students in order to gain the Practice Teaching qualification, after which many then cease to provide this ongoing learning and support role. This makes the provision of practice learning placements for social work education a very challenging task. Organizations should also aim to ensure that 'credentialism' does not exclude those very people who use or have used its services and who may wish to contribute in the workplace but who feel excluded from or unable to participate in formal education. Challenges in achieving diversity using learning will be further developed in Chapter 5 when we look at equalities issues in organizational learning strategies.

The challenge presented to any leader of learning is to ensure that professional learning and professional qualifications genuinely enable employees to contribute to quality services. In summary, learning at work should be accessible to all, and an effective learning culture will provide for different learning styles and abilities and recognize that the costs associated with providing formal learning and the pressure to deliver services will inevitably restrict the number of employees able to achieve formal qualifications. Ideas about learning that incorporate both formal and informal learning, and credited and experiential learning, are fundamental to lifelong learning. We will therefore conclude this chapter by outlining the concept of lifelong learning which is supposed to be for everyone and may, for our purposes, provide some insights into the policy instruments for lifelong learning present in the social care arena.

LIFELONG LEARNING AND SOCIAL INCLUSION

Lifelong learning has been defined as the 'continuation of conscious learning throughout the lifespan' (OECD, 1996: 98). The Organization for Economic Cooperation and Development has adopted a 'cradle to grave' concept of lifelong learning where the 'the whole spectrum of learning, formal, non-formal and informal is covered in this broad definition, as are active citizenship, personal fulfillment, social inclusion, professional, vocational and employment related aspects' (OECD, 2003: 7). Subsequently, there has been a set of initiatives ranging from individualized funding incentives for learners through to the creation of a new framework promoting basic literacy and numeracy and vocational qualifications to increase skills and knowledge in the workplace. There is also an assumption that those participating in learning should contribute either through finance or time to their own learning in partnership with the state. Lifelong learning is associated with modernizing western education and training systems to increase competitiveness and innovation at a time of intensifying global trading pressures by promoting investment in human resources across the lifespan and in a variety of settings (Field, 2001). These themes are echoed in social care where a national survey of employees in 1999 revealed that many people working in social care had either none or inadequate qualifications to work with some of the most vulnerable members of our society (TOPSS, 2000).

BOX 2.2   REFLECTION BREAK

What examples can you think of where policies of lifelong learning have entered the social care arena? You may think of these either in terms of the workforce or the community or society where learning is used to promote social inclusion.

Apart from learning and development policies and initiatives directly affecting the social care workforce, you may have also considered the social inclusion agenda, where there has been a number of movements to promote employment and independence away from welfare, the increasing use of 'Direct Payments' or 'Individualized Budgets', and the increasing development of social enterprises in the social care sector led by service user groups around issues that directly affect them. The increasing availability of web-based resources through the internet has given people much more information about their rights and access to a wider range of services. The increasing ability of members of the community to access knowledge and research around health, education and public services, and the dissemination of this through user-led or advocacy groups and the internet itself, has enabled learning to be linked to service delivery. This can have the effect of making public services more accountable and user-centred.

The demand for, and supply of, skills and knowledge in social care requires attention not only through learning programmes such as those arising from the National Training Strategy for Social Care (TOPSS, 2000), but also through developing learning for employability and to raise standards. There are practical implications resulting from this, such as the confidence and capability of those learners participating, as well as situational factors. These situational factors have been identified by Eraut et al. (2002) in their examination of the micro culture of the workplace and the process of how employees are managed. Eraut et al. (2002: 252) go as far as to say that 'of all the mechanisms used at organizational level to promote learning, the most significant is likely to be the appointment and development of its managers'. Eraut et al. were referring to the significance of management development and highlighting a need for longer-term strategies as well as those which are focused on meeting immediate skill shortages in professional education. This will be picked up again in the final chapter of this book. However, in the meantime, we have identified that it does not seem possible to discuss lifelong learning in social care without addressing issues of widening participation and access to learning and education.

There is plenty of evidence pointing to the relevance of social relations and social structures to the patterns of learning observed in social care organizations. One example is the role of women as carers and the constraints of social, material and cultural resources on women's access to certain opportunities in learning and employment (Coffield, 2000: 10). There are positive examples too, such as within social work education where going on to study for a degree in social work is one of the success stories of Access to Higher Education. Social work has also been identified as one of the few disciplines that recruit more former 'Access' students than any other areas of study (UCAS, 2003). Jones (2006) attributes this to the shared orientation of Access courses and social work training towards working with those perceived as socially disadvantaged. Both have adapted approaches that are underpinned by an emancipatory philosophy which acknowledges structural inequality in access to educational achievement (Jones, 2006: 488). This is why, in Chapter 4, we will be going on to look more closely at some of the specific challenges in social care in widening participation and in developing diversity of the workforce. This will pick up on themes around lifelong learning and its policy formation after introducing the broader concepts here.

All of these developments, however, should contribute to a wider appreciation of the social policy and welfare issues in social care which use learning and employment to rebuild or review the role of the state and promote the social inclusion agenda. Nevertheless, where opportunities for learning and career advancement are concerned, there is plenty of evidence that there remains an uneven playing field in workforce development in social care. In conclusion, working towards a learning organization *and* a learning society must inevitably take account of the structural inequalities reflected in the social care workforce and the subsequent measures required to address these.

LIFELONG LEARNING – VISION OR REALITY?

Finally, we might consider how far any of the concepts discussed in this chapter are actually measurable and the types of indicators used to demonstrate success in the area of organizational learning and development. This is especially difficult when we are looking at the process of development as opposed to the direct outputs of learning itself. Within the Performance Assessment Framework (PAF) there are already a number of performance indicators that were designed to demonstrate organizations' explicit commitment and achievement in areas of learning, such as practice learning placements within social work education or the numbers of staff achieving certain nationally recognized qualifications such as NVQs against the National Training Strategy. Some commentators have been less enamoured with the government's vision of a learning society, stating that individual behaviour and attitudes are at the heart of the new approach at a time when values of autonomy and independence are deeply embedded in our culture. At its worst, Coffield (2000) notes how this reflects a commonly-noted trend towards authoritarianism and compulsion, directed increasingly not only at benefit seekers and other marginalized groups but also at professionals and managers in the form of compulsory professional development and regulatory requirement. He asserts that in a learning society, 'the fact that individuals are treated as though they can acquire and understand the implications of new information about their wellbeing becomes in turn a justification for reducing the resources that are made available through public services' (Coffield, 2000: 9–10). According to Field (2001), although this can amount to a form of 'structural discrimination', it is one that largely passes unnoticed and unchallenged. Field asserts that by individualizing the characteristics which justify employees and others in treating people differently, the trend towards lifelong learning also helps fragment the excluded, and encourages a search for individual solutions:

> 'This pattern is reproduced through other areas of public life, as the welfare state switches its focus from 'passive support' to 'active strategies of insertion', the most significant of which include training, so that individuals can acquire the skills and knowledge required for them to take active responsibility for their own well-being'. (Field, 2001: 14)

We may conclude that the jury is still out on lifelong learning on the basis that it poses new and contradictory challenges to the policy community and community of practice that promotes and encourages learning throughout the lifespan.

With these critiques in mind, and to prevent getting bogged down into some of these pertinent yet very difficult challenges, we will conclude this chapter by reminding you of our overall purpose of this text, which is to facilitate the demonstration of leadership and good management skills in workforce development issues through your contribution to a learning culture. We reiterate that learning to learn and developing a culture of learning is a truly necessary pre-occupation of leaders and managers in social care. There are three key components which underpin these roles. First, resilience and the ability for sustained engagement in the process and for tolerating the frequent uncertainty that accompanies changes in the care sectors. Secondly, resourcefulness by employing a range of organizational and individual learning and development tools and strategies. These will involve us in developing our intellectual as well as practical skills, imagination, flexibility and intuition about the way in which people around us learn. Thirdly, developing a critical reflective approach that enables us to stand back from our roles and analyse the organization for any opportunities, by taking a 'synoptic reflexive view' (Claxton, 1999, cited in Coffield, 2000: 34). This is what we have been trying to do in this chapter on learning culture, which we have aptly titled 'a work in progress?'.

If learning organizations or cultures are to become truly effective, it is essential that leaders must engage with the language of empowerment. This is a sometimes overused term but one that captures the best approach that is needed for effective learning. The organization must become a community that recognizes its place in the wider community. Leaders must work towards a learning alliance between learners and the organization (Hay, 1999). You must be clear that this is not about lowering standards but rather, on the contrary, it is about raising standards. Remember that the objective is to minimize practices that tell adults unnecessarily what they need to learn and how to learn. Instead, the objective is to encourage a dialogue between learners, their leaders, managers and facilitators. This is by encouraging learners to actively consider their own learning needs, reflect and learn from their practice, to learn from each other and value experiential learning. Recognize the contribution that each other can make not only to their own learning and practice but also to others' learning, including out in the community,

In the remainder of this book we will be touching on different learning strategies or contexts for learning that will give pointers for this approach, for example by developing your own coaching and mentoring skills, using open learning materials, the use of reflection, evidence gathering and recording by keeping learning logs and actively seeking ways to accredit prior education, experiential learning and coincidental learning. We will also examine the tensions arising from widening participation in raising standards and succession planning.

CHAPTER SUMMARY

In this chapter we have tried to make sense of organizations as sites of learning and development. In our overview of the learning organization, we have considered how individual learning is related to organizational learning and the possible levels and purposes of aggregation. As a manager or leader of learning, one needs to consider the different levels, individual, team, section at which learning takes place, and how these relate to each other and the broader objectives of service improvement as well as improved outcomes for service users and carers. Fook (2004: 72) described organizational learning as 'learning about the political conditions under which individuals can function as agents of organizational action', providing a framework that links personal and individual learning with organizational practice and the wider political, social and economic drivers for these. Fook's model of critical reflection highlights the importance of leaders and managers in providing an environment within which reflective analysis can be guided. The critical reflective process should enable employees to construct and understand their place, position, purpose, role, practice and power within the organization in order to transform the ways they act and work within it.

The study and practice of learning and development is challenging because it is underpinned by so many different disciplines. In organizations delivering social care, the demands made on human or resource development often make it difficult to reconcile the needs of the business with the needs of the individual. This remains a challenge. Despite the achievements made by social care since the late 1990s there continues to be a significant gap between strategy and the delivery of learning and development. To tackle this gap, learning and development professionals need to work closely with managers to build and support learning cultures that will make workforce development plans come to life in the workplace. Frontline managers in particular need help in supporting their learning and development responsibilities as they come under many other pressures in organizations that are constantly changing and restructuring. Trying to develop practice-based career pathways for both qualified and unqualified staff, however, has been shown to be beneficial for staff retention and morale. This is why investment in learning should be used to maximum effect, underpinned by principles of lifelong learning and the philosophy of learning organizations.

Recommended further reading

F. Coffield (ed) (2000) *Differing Visions of a Learning Society* (Bristol: Policy Press). Volumes 1 and 2 of this book present the culmination of years of empirical work undertaken into lifelong learning supported by the Economic and Social Research Council's programme of research. Both volumes explore the ways lifelong learning can contribute to the development of knowledge and skills for employment and other areas of adult life, and provide evidence about what policies are or are not working. It also provides the basis for structural reform.

Social Care Institute for Excellence (2004) *Learning Organizations: A Self-assessment Resource Pack* provides a set of tools which are interlinked and give guidance towards creating a culture of learning in the workplace. They can be used during team days, management meetings and training sessions. Available on CD-Rom or as a series of cards from www.scie.org.uk.

Web-based resources

Learning and Skills Council (www.lsc.gov.uk) exists to promote the skills of young people and adults in the UK to ensure that the workforce is more competitive. The web-site provides updated information on some of the key initiatives to make learning provision more responsive to the needs of individuals and employers. It also produces a wide variety of publications, some for guidance, others for information, all of which are available in electronic form.

3 LEARNING AND WORKING INTERPROFESSIONALLY

This chapter explores:

- The current context of interprofessional working and learning
- The variety of definitions used in the arena of interprofessional learning and working
- The knowledge, values and skills required for interprofessional working
- Interprofessional teams and interprofessional learning
- The evidence base for interprofessional education
- Planning learning – should it be interprofessional or uni-professional?

INTRODUCTION

This chapter explicitly explores the links between interprofessional learning and interprofessional working for students, workers and managers in social care. The chapter uses the term 'interprofessional' to begin to explore the power dynamics between workers professionally qualified or not, users and carers and organizations. The prime focus and purpose is on providing best practice in the delivery of services. Interprofessional working and learning is one aspect of developing best practice across team and organizational boundaries. Users' and carers' participation is central to how successful interprofessional working is both now and in the future. We will explore the dynamics involved in interprofessional working using a range of definitions following which you may wish to draw your own conclusions.

BOX 3.1   REFLECTION BREAK

Reflect on one interprofessional learning opportunity you have undertaken. This may have been a course you attended at a university, or one within your organization or the team you work in. How successful was it? What did you learn? How did you put the learning into practice? What was successful/unsuccessful about your interprofessional learning experience?

THE CURRENT CONTEXT OF INTERPROFESSIONAL WORKING TODAY

In Chapter 1 we explored the developing managerialism and private sector ethos for social care developed in the 1990s. In 2005 the registration and regulation of social workers established social work as a profession (GSCC, 2002). Social care workers must also adhere to the *Code of Practice* but are not regulated as yet. Interprofessional working holds within it all the political ambitions of New Labour and previous governments since the late 1980s, when important concepts such as collaboration and the notion of 'seamless' services were introduced. Their meanings and the implications at strategic and operational levels for demonstrating and delivering good practice with users and carers have been rehearsed and debated (Whittington, 2003). Legislation and associated guidance has enshrined these notions within services in health and social care and education, with the purpose of providing more effective services that meet the needs of users and carers. Developments in legislation and policy relating to interprofessional working have previously led to the care programme approach in mental health for people with mental health difficulties, person-centred planning for people with learning disabilities, and the single assessment process with older people.

The current government wants professionals to work together more closely. This requires a change in professional identities to develop closer collaboration with users and provide more effective and sensitive services. For example, the Skills for Care *New Types of Worker Project* (2005b) was identified as a source of evidence in the Green Paper *Independence, Well-being and Choice* (Department of Health, 2005a). The aim is to achieve the development of new roles that are more person-centred. These developments will be taken forward by the *Options for Excellence* (Department of Health and Department for Education and Skills (2006) review of the social care workforce and the Children's Workforce Development Council (CWDC), where consideration is being given to new roles such as social pedagogues and the lead professional and personal development/transition workers.

ADULT SERVICES

The key issues for adult services identified in the Green Paper (Department of Health, 2005a) centre on meeting outcomes based on what people have told the Department of Health (DH) they want: 'Improved health, quality of life, making a positive contribution, exercise of choice and control, freedom from discrimination and harassment, economic well-being and personal dignity' (2005a: 10).

> 'The aim is to provide creative and holistic models of care, offering more control and choice to service users and carers. For example, the use of direct payments and developing use of technology will be extended and involvement of the broader community in caring will be explored. The attention to early preventative services is a clear focus and has implications for Fair Access to Care Services and eligibility criteria within limited resources and Best Value. Local government is expected to increase further its work in partnership with the Third Sector, with implications for different funding streams, for a common assessment framework for all workers that could be used with all people with complex needs. Managers and leaders need to develop a workforce that meets the challenge of these proposed changes, as with the move from social work to care management in the 1980s, and the split between 'purchaser' and 'provider'. This will mean radically different ways of working, redesigning of job roles and reconfiguration of services using 'a firm knowledge base'. (Department of Health, 2005a: 13)

An evidence base is an important factor when considering a refocusing of services but also when developing different models and methods of collaboration and interprofessional working.

CHILDREN'S SERVICES

Following the inquiry after the death of Victoria Climbie (Laming, 2003), *Every Child Matters* (Department of Health, 2003) and The Children Act 2004 (Department of Health, 2004b) legislation initiated a programme of reform for interprofessional working. *Every Child Matters: Change for Children* (Department of Health, 2004a) names five outcomes that mattered most to children and young people: being healthy, staying safe, enjoying and achieving, making a positive contribution and economic well-being. There is a focus on four main areas: supporting parents and carers, early intervention and effective protection, accountability and integration (locally, regionally and nationally) and workforce reform. Universal and target-focused services for children are being reorganized with a single focus. A Minister for Children, Young People and Families has been created within the Department for Education and Skills (DfES) with responsibility for children's social services, family policy, teenage pregnancy, family law and Children and Family Court Advisory and Support Service (CAFCASS), all of which have been brought within the umbrella of the DfES. A Children's Commissioner has been appointed as a 'champion for children'.

Most services fall into the Children's Trusts, with one local director of children's services and a lead council member for children, and for child protection the Area Child Protection Committees are replaced with Local Safeguarding Children Boards. Before these measures, the Labour government laid the foundations for developing improvements in children's services by introducing Sure Start initiatives and goals to raise educational standards. Many inter-agency and interprofessional initiatives are now evident within children's services, such as the extended schools service, increased spending in Children and Mental Health Services (CAMHS), alternatives to custody in the youth justice system, addressing homelessness and reducing the use of bed and breakfast accommodation for children.

Practice implications include the introduction of the common assessment framework, the introduction of a lead professional to avoid duplication, the improvement of information sharing through changes in legislation and policy, and multidisciplinary teams based in and around schools and children's centres.

The National Service Framework for Children, Young People and Maternity Services (Department of Health, 2004c) offers standards for health, social and educational services that need to be met over a ten-year plan, for example, tackling poverty and inequalities and delivering services that are holistic and meet the needs of the child. Again, discussion in the introduction of the document (Aynsley-Green, 2004) talks about 'how to ensure that children's services locally are coherent in design and delivery, with good coordination, effective joint working between and across sectors and agencies, with smooth transitions and in partnership with children, young people and families'.

The Common Core of Skills and Knowledge for the Children's Workforce (Department for Education and Skills, 2005b) has been developed as part of the *Every Child Matters: Change for Children* policy agenda. It identified six key areas: effective communication and engagement; child and young person development; safeguarding and promoting the welfare of the child; supporting transitions; multi-agency working; and sharing information. This document asks service managers to implement these common core elements as part of training and workforce development in order to 'support strategies for enhancing frontline practice but also help establish a greater shared language and understanding across different parts of the workforce' (DfES, 2005b: 4).

In summary, service provision for adults and children and families will need a radical reform of the workforce. 'We want to value the specific skills that people from different professional backgrounds bring, and we also want to break down the professional barriers that inhibit joint working, and tackle recruitment and retention problems' (Department of Health, 2003: 12). Key to this overall aim is the consultation and involvement of users and carers in the development and provision of joined-up, universal, preventative and targeted services to children in the context of their families and adults in need of services. This aim is to avoid a replication of assessments and offer continuity of worker contact.

The potential divisions arising from the different provision of adult and children services will have its own impact regarding interprofessional and inter-agency working together, particularly where there are risks to children from a parent perhaps through drug and alcohol misuse or mental health difficulties. Key worker systems for children and families will still need to liaise with adult services and vice versa. These issues have been analysed by Stanley and Manthorpe (2004) in relation to key inquiries concerning children and adults from the 1990s and explore the notion of the blame culture in social care. Reder and Duncan (2004) compare the findings of a series of meta-analyses of reports relating to Part 8 reviews, where a child has died or been seriously injured, or Public Inquiry reports spanning the last 30 years. They highlight 'particular clusters around: deficiencies in the assessment process; problems with interprofessional communication; inadequate resources; and poor skills acquisition or application' (Reder and Duncan, 2004: 96). Stanley (2004) explores the experience of women users of the mental health services where their child has died. She cites a number of inquiries where the woman user of mental health services was seen in isolation rather than within her family context, where she may hold multiple roles including that of mother. Lack of coordination across interprofessional and inter-agency boundaries led to difficulties in assessing risk for the mother and the child.

DEFINITIONS OF INTERPROFESSIONAL WORKING AND LEARNING AND THE INCLUSION OF USER AND CARER INVOLVEMENT

Over our years of working in education and practice we have noticed how many terms relating to interprofessional working and learning are used interchangeably by individual practitioners from a range of backgrounds, in policy documents and in legislation. It could be argued that it is a question of semantics, but in terms of professionalism and good practice we think it is important to understand the meaning behind the terms we use and then clarity can ensue in terms of service delivery.

BOX 3.2   REFLECTION BREAK

Identify in the section above how many terms relating to interprofessional and inter-agency working are used. What does each mean? Can you provide a working definition for each term identified? What terms do you use as a manager and educator?

Leathard (1994: 5) discusses the range of terms used with reference to what she terms as the 'terminological quagmire' across professions, sectors and organizations. She distinguishes between concept-based terms such as interdisciplinary, multi-professional, holistic and trans-disciplinary, process-based terms such as partnership, joint planning, team work, common core, joint learning/working and cooperation, and agency-based terms such as inter-agency, forums, and locality groups.

Rawson (1994) extends this discussion to identify differences between the terms 'inter' and 'trans' and 'multi'. 'Inter' 'denotes relationships between and among the elements and further implies some notion of reciprocal operations'. 'Trans' 'signifies relationships across or beyond but with no indication of mutuality'. 'Multi' offers 'composition but again does not immediately suggest any give and take' Rawson, (1994: 40). Moreover, the term 'professional' denotes a specialized practitioner who could also be a member of an exclusive registerable group with specialized expertise, for example GSCC (General Social Care Council), NMC (Nursing and Midwifery Council), BMA (British Medical Association) or COT (College of Occupational Therapy). The term 'occupational' offers a broader scope but does not include professional identity and career structures, whereas agency and sector terms simply refer to the organizations involved in the process, be it inter-agency, trans-agency, etc. The term 'disciplinary' simply refers to the body of knowledge used by workers in their practice.

In summary, there is plenty of debate about the different terms used when talking about interprofessional working and learning and so we now turn to the definitions for interprofessional learning in order to add clarity. The Centre for the Advancement of Interprofessional Education (CAIPE) defines interprofessional education as 'Occasions when two or more professions learn from and about each other to improve collaboration and the quality of care' and multiprofessional education as 'Occasions when two or more professions learn side by side for whatever reason' (cited in Barr, 2002: 6). Leathard (1994: 6) helpfully summarizes these in plain terms, that is 'What everyone is really talking about is simply learning together and working together'. This is helpful because it can include users and carers by definition. As we will see in our next chapter, users are involved in research, consultation, training, collaboration and controlling or leading services (Braye, 2000). It also addresses the need for the CAIPE definition to move to include users and carers and recognize that workers in the collaborative process are not always defined as professionals.

Users and carers and their expert roles within these complex relationships in providing best services are explored in a range of literature and policy documents written by users and carers (Begum et al., 1994; Carr, 2004; Begum, 2006), government and professionals. There are a number of pieces of legislation that require user participation in many dimensions of health and social care across adults and children and families services (e.g. National Health Service and Community Care Act 1990, The Children Act 1989, Best Value as laid down in the Local Government Act 1999 and Community Care (Direct Payments) Act 1996, Modernizing Social Services 1998, Health and Social Care Act 2006). Political campaigning from user and carer groups has challenged the *status quo* of the organization and the workers within it, who define themselves as being the experts and who hold the power to identify and deliver services. However, Carr (2004: 14) asserts that 'power issues underlie the majority of identified difficulties with effective user-led change. The message is that any user participation initiative requires continual awareness of the context of power relations in which it is being conducted.' She identifies key issues of representation, views of professionals about service users' capability in decision making and the impact of the power of different professionals, their language, values and assumptions on decision making processes. Jargon used verbally and in written records within professional groups and across organizations, such as the use of shorthand acronyms or referring to people as 'cases', can alienate and disempower service users. Thompson (2003) discusses how language is a vehicle for demonstrating our own values at a societal, cultural, professional, individual and personal level. Power can be used positively, promoting equality and anti-oppressive practice, or negatively through discrimination, lack of partnership and collaboration in practice.

SURE START AND PARTICIPATION PROGRAMMES

Two examples from adult and children and family services provide examples of different levels of participation in different ways by users with a range of professionals and agencies.

Sure Start programmes were aimed at children aged 0–5 and their families to address social exclusion and child poverty. They were designed to involve parents and a range of professionals from health, education, community development and social care in the planning, monitoring and delivery of the programmes. Parent forums were also a requirement, providing an example of inter-agency and user collaboration at a strategic and operational level. Key requirements for good partnership working have emerged from the National Evaluation of Sure Start (Myers et al., 2004) which replicate many of the themes prominent in this area of work, such as the need for openness and transparency, good communication, tolerance of different perspectives, accessibility for parents and carers to take part in decision making and the gaining of knowledge about professional roles.

In 2001 the government published the document *The Expert Patient* (Department of Health, 2001b). This offered 'a new approach to chronic disease management for the twenty-first century'. It identified a shifting emphasis following research and practical experience in North America and Britain showing that today's patients with chronic diseases need not be mere recipients of care. Central to the 'expert patient' is the concept that patients are key decision makers in the treatment process. By ensuring that knowledge of their condition is developed to a point where they are empowered to take some responsibility for its management, patients are encouraged into partnership with their health and social care providers, and are given greater control over their lives. [p. 5] Expert patients and carers can also be involved in teaching professionals about the nature of the disease and in developing suitable services across agencies. In Chapter 4 we identify and critique the eight different levels of Arnstein's (1969) ladder of participation, with information exchange at the bottom and delegation of power and control to facilitate citizen control at the top end. Now consider the following.

BOX 3.3   REFLECTION BREAK

How are users and carers leading/participating in developing the services outlined and in the services you provide? Make a list and define the level of participation? What could you do to develop participation with users and different professions together?

THE KNOWLEDGE, VALUES, ATTITUDES AND SKILLS REQUIRED FOR INTERPROFESSIONAL AND INTER-AGENCY WORKING

As a manager and leader it is important to consider how to measure workers' ability to work in an interprofessional and inter-agency context as part of supervision and appraisal. The methods used to measure such competency require some consideration. A competent reflective practitioner has the necessary skills, knowledge base and values to inform their practice. How often as a manager do you ask users, carers and other professionals and workers for feedback on this area of competence? In Chapter 7 we focus on work-based assessment and identify different methods of assessment that can be used to provide a range of evidence you can draw on to measure competence. Another area that has not been given attention in social care is the knowledge base that workers draw on to inform their practice. The values and attitudes of workers are now clearly linked to the GSCC *Code of Practice* (2002) and this can be used as a measure to inform competence.

Weinstein and Leonard (forthcoming) provides an exemplar set of collaborative competences to assess health and social care professionals that can be used by managers and leaders to guide appraisals and inform them about areas for workers' development. These are adapted from Barr (1998) and Weinstein (1998):

- Describe one's roles and responsibilities clearly to other professions and carry out your own professional role competently.
- Keep other professionals closely informed about work with people whom they have referred or with whom they are working.
- Communicate and negotiate clearly and without jargon, orally and in writing within small interprofessional groups, allied agencies and other organizations.
- Recognize and respect the roles, responsibilities and competence of other professions in relation to one's own, knowing when, where and how to involve those others through agreed channels.
- Work with other professions to review services, effect change, solve problems and improve standards.
- Work with other professions to assess, plan, provide and review care for service users and carers.
- Acknowledge and resolve interprofessional/inter-agency conflict or differences, openly and constructively.
- Encourage and facilitate the active involvement of users, carers, care workers or fellow professionals who, by reason of status, gender, race or other structural disadvantage, may feel less confident about their role or contribution.
- Facilitate or constructively contribute to interprofessional case conferences, meetings, team working and networking.

These competencies outline the evidence a manager or leader would be looking for in practice. The underpinning knowledge requires further thought. When considering the underpinning knowledge for developing competence there has been a gap in the explicit use of a range of theories from disciplines informing social care. We want to identify some key areas of knowledge that can be used for learning about inter-professional working. Networking theory, taken from sociology and applied to social care, allows us to explore the relationships between formal and informal networks in communities, families and with organi-zations and formal services. Payne (2000: 28) identifies 'systems theory, social exchange theory and cooperation theory' as the main source of knowledge underlying the concept of collaboration. Empowerment and organizational theories are often used to inform interprofessional prac-tice. Partnership working and the different levels continue to be devel-oped using research, models and guidance focusing on definitions, interventions and models such as task-centred practice (Marsh and Fisher, 1992; Department of Health, 1995; Frost, 2005; SCIE, 2006). Whittington (2005) explores three identity theories that can offer an analysis of interprofessional and team working. Social identity and self-categorization theories make the links between individual and shared group identity. Importantly, these analyse and 'address issues of iden-tity, rivalry, stereotyping, discrimination and the implications of status difference' (Whittington, 2005: 44). Discourse and narrative theories draw on the notion that our understanding and view of the world is socially constructed, based upon our own history and culture and how we interact with others and communicate this primarily through lan-guage. History, language and culture are important aspects of team and professional identities and can be structures that provide protection for these identities, maintaining status and expertise. The development of interprofessional teams and more equality in working with users and car-ers can challenge these shared values. Finally, there is the impact of late-modernity on the self. Colyer et al. (2005: 45) describes identity thus:

> The present era is distinguished from all preceding periods by the extreme dynamism of its institutions. ... Their dynamism is manifest in the runaway pace of change of such scope and profoundness that many pre-existing traditions and ways of behaving are questioned and displaced.

Late-modernity challenges the traditional definitions of a workplace and protected long-term professional roles and identities, and the specialist access to expert knowledge. The world wide web offers readily available knowledge to users, carers and professionals with less necessity for people to be together in time and space in work in order for them to communicate with each other (e.g. virtual interprofessional teams).

As we can see, there are some useful concepts and theories drawn from other disciplines. Some of these ideas are used implicitly in devel-oping everyday interprofessional relationships and provide an area ripe for explicitly extending the evidence and knowledge base for enhancing interprofessional working.

INTERPROFESSIONAL TEAMS AND INTERPROFESSIONAL LEARNING

We will now turn to the dynamics of interprofessional and inter-organizational working and what interprofessional learning may have to offer. Bashford (1999: 345) outlines 'perceived and actual' barriers to interprofessional learning that reflect the tensions of interprofessional working that are current today. These include:

- Difficulties in changing old patterns of uni-professional working.
- The need for strategic planning and an identified leader championing interprofessional working.
- Addressing the differences in organizational structures and culture and language.
- The threat and survival of professional identities.
- The potential impact on status and pay for professional workers (more recently illustrated by the NHS agenda for change where a range of staff have been regraded on their skills for the job rather than professional identity (Department of Health, 2004d)).

Interprofessional and multi-agency teams come in many forms. They may work together in teams in the community or across organizational boundaries remaining in their home base. More specifically, the Department for Education and Skills (2005a), recognizing the complexities of these ways of working and the changes needed, have published a toolkit for managers of multi-agency teams. It identifies specific issues for managers and leaders to address, such as who will be and is competent and confident to take the lead professional role, team location, differing pay and conditions with staff seconded from their home organization (e.g. social workers in health), health workers in the new Children Centres, and recruitment and retention.

Interprofessional learning builds on developing already defined structures. It cannot be seen as the total panacea to address difficulties in this area and defined areas of learning for teams need to be well planned and supported strategically and at operational level. Learning takes place in a number of ways and we will discuss this in the last section of this chapter. The first consideration is the need to design and provide an interprofessional team that is fit for purpose. Ovretveit et al. (1997) identifies five different team structures to assist workers and managers to understand their own roles and responsibilities in interprofessional teams and to consider the most suitable type of team to deliver services to a particular community. These five structures are:

1. **Profession managed structure** where professionals are managed by their own profession.
2. **Single manager structure** where all professionals are managed by one manager.
3. **Joint management structure** where there is an overall coordinator for the team, with team members relating to own professional manager.
4. **Team manager contracted structure** where the manager holds a budget to buy in professional services.
5. **Hybrid management structure** where the manager manages core staff and contracts in other workers and jointly manages other workers.

As a manager of staff in social care you could, for example, have a background in management, social care, health or education. The challenge for you as a manager, leader and educationalist is how to assist your staff members in sustaining their development in the context of constant change and reforming roles when you may or may not have similar qualifications. This involves careful consideration of the range of interprofessional qualifications, skills, attitudes, experiences and knowledge of each staff member. Payne (2000: 87) highlights the fundamental practical considerations of 'priorities, specialisation and workload allocation' relating to each worker's role. He includes within this the legal, procedural and organizational responsibilities (such as the approved social worker role) the lead professional role, the area of specialism as with a trained therapist and the assessment of risk in child protection inquiries. Payne also offers some helpful team work exercises to explore more fully the development of teams and their leaders and managers in this context. Most professionally qualified social care staff will be uni-professionally trained as a social worker with a range of professional qualifications from certificate (CQSW – Certificate of Qualification in Social Work) through diploma (DipSW – Diploma in Social Work) and now degree standard (BA/BSc). Alongside this, a number of academic qualifications will have been gained, ranging from a diploma to a masters degree.

However, social work training is now required to include interprofessional learning within the degree and this is delivered in a variety of ways with a variety of professionals across different courses (Department of Health, 2002a). Interprofessional working is also a requirement of the National Occupational Standards in Social Work (TOPSS, 2002). Users and carers are expected to participate in developing and designing courses and curricula, recruiting students, teaching and assessing practitioners. Clarity about the identity and role of the social worker/social care worker and the unique contribution offered are important in the context of reforms associated with job descriptions for new types of worker that include social work and social care, and that have health and education aspects to them. Social care workers have qualifications that range from other professional qualifications and work-based qualifications (NVQs) in care management, management and social care skills through to voluntary work and those workers with experience but no recognizable qualifications. There are other groups of staff that are dually qualified. For example, staff may have trained as a teacher, counsellor or nurse and then become a social care or social worker. Or they may have attended a degree programme that provides a nursing and social work qualification in three years. For example, London South Bank University and other higher education providers have offered a dual qualification in Learning Disability Nursing and Social Work since 1992 (Davis et al., 1999) and in 2006 validated a joint practitioner three-year degree programme in mental health nursing and social work.

If workers are multi-qualified, you need to regularly check that their professional registration is current for all the professions they have qualifications for and what is required for the job. Workers you are managing may need professional supervision from their own profession. As we will see later in Chapter 6, separate professional and accountable lines of supervision can to be structured into the organization of inter-professional teams. The links between these two forms of supervision, which may cross organizational boundaries, need to be made explicit and accountable, with confidentiality issues being addressed through written agreements. This process also needs to be linked into continuous professional development.

BOX 3.4   REFLECTION BREAK

Consider the five different team structures identified by Ovretveit et al. (1997). Can you identify a team you work in or work with? Does the structure provide fitness for purpose?

THE EVIDENCE BASE FOR INTERPROFESSIONAL LEARNING

Given the current government's investment in interprofessional education, one might also argue that evaluation will be required to legitimate this policy. 'Directive ... interprofessional education has become

managerially driven, resistance has become politically unacceptable'
(Glen and Leiba, 2004: 106). It is interesting to consider which major
policy initiatives have been based on evidence-based practice (EBP) and
those that are politically driven without an explicit trail of research evidence to inform such policies. Geddes (2004) discusses this very issue
in relation to the development of the Care Programme Approach (CPA)
in mental health services. The approach was recommended and supported as a logical best approach but was not actually based on any evidence for effective case management. Often with policy-driven changes,
it is only after the event that these changes are researched for their
effectiveness.

Definitions of evidence-based practice in social care and health build
from definitions for evidence-based medicine in the early 1990s. For
example, one definition often referred to is by Sackett et al. (2000: 246):

> The conscientious, explicit and judicious use of current best evidence in
> making decisions about the care of individual patients. The practice of
> evidence-based medicine means integrating individual clinical expertise
> with the best available external clinical evidence from systematic research.

There is an important link explicitly defined here between professional
expertise gained from personal and process knowledge, as defined by
Eraut (1994), and research and best evidence. Both are needed for
effective decision making. To illustrate the development and recognition of an evidence base to social work and social care, a more recent
review was undertaken by The Social Care Institute for Excellence
(SCIE, 2003). It identifies the 'main types of research, experience and
wisdom that combine to form the social care knowledge base' and how
to identify a framework for developing quality standards used in social
care (SCIE, 2003: 3). The authors summarize SCIE's work as 'better
knowledge for better practice' (p. 3). In answer to a basic question
about what evidence means, they identify five sources of social care
knowledge. Each source can learn from the other sources. The sources
are organizational, practitioner, policy community, research and user
and carer. This more recent and wider definition includes users and
carers as experts in knowledge and equal participants in research.
Sources of social care knowledge and their relevance to managing practice and learning will be examined in much more detail in Chapter 9.

Managers and leaders are crucial in providing a climate that explicitly and actively makes links between research and practice. At times
managers and leaders lack confidence in this area (Research in
Practice, 2003). There are a number of reasons for evidence-based practice to be attractive. These are helpfully summarized by Trinder and
Reynolds (2004: 3):

> Evidence based practice relays a devastatingly effective and simple message: the argument that practice should be based on the most up-to-date, valid and reliable research findings has an instant and intuitive appeal, and is so obviously sensible it is difficult to resist.

When deciding if interprofessional learning and working is effective, an important aspect we need to measure is the impact, both negative and positive, on the nature of the relationship between workers interprofessionally and inter-organizationally and each of their relationships with users and carers in providing effective services. Freeth et al. (2005) identify seven perspectives on how to judge the effectiveness of interprofessional education. These are:

- The manager's views of the benefits and costs to the service.
- The user's views about the impact.
- Whether the funding body sees it as effective.
- Views of the professional and regulatory bodies.
- The training provider.
- The tutor.
- The learner's views.

These may be similar or conflicting, depending on the focus of what is deemed to be successful interprofessional education.

Interprofessional learning is seen as one way of achieving better collaborative practice with the intention of improving outcomes for users. Barr et al. (2006) identify wide-ranging formats for interprofessional learning to take place. Interprofessional learning may be individual or group learning that is part of everyday practice or a short or long course, with or without a formal qualification, taking place in work or at a university. The mode of delivery may include interactive learning or didactic teaching. The course content may offer a common topic to be learnt by all or an understanding of different roles, responsibilities, perspectives and working together. Pre-qualifying learning offers opportunities for early learning together before workers become set in their uni-professional identity.

However, there is a need for more systematic research to relate better outcomes for users to increased collaboration. There are a number of reviews and publications that outline and discuss a variety of studies of interprofessional learning and education in health and social care in this country and internationally and a further review is being undertaken (Barr, 2002; Freeth et al., 2002, 2005; Mead et al., 2005; Barr et al., 2006). One key issue is the nature of the research. The Interprofessional Joint Evaluation Team (JET), of whom Freeth and Barr are members, has completed a number of reviews of the literature and research. The first was worldwide and led by Zwarenstein

(Zwarenstein et al., 1999). They confined their search to evaluations of interprofessional education based on randomized trials, controlled before and after studies or interrupted time series studies and outcomes affecting delivery of care to patients. None met both criteria so their second review used wider research methodologies of both qualitative and quantitative nature (Freeth et al., 2002). The studies identified were predominantly from North America. However, although the evidence base needed to be strengthened the writers are not saying interprofessional learning is not effective. A further review (Barr et al., 2005, 2006) widened the parameters of the first JET review. The JET classification of interprofessional education outcomes consists of:

- learner's reactions;
- modification of learners' attitudes and perceptions;
- learner's acquisition of knowledge/skills;
- learner's behavioural change;
- change in organizational practice;
- benefits to patients/clients (users). (Barr et al., 2005: 43)

This review was based on 353 papers, of which 54% of the studies were from the USA and 37% from the UK, with other studies from Australia, Canada, Sweden, Ecuador, Finland, Norway and The Netherlands. The studies were spread evenly between hospital and community-based staff. Most educational experiences reported in the studies lasted more than seven days, spreading over some months. Only 16% contributed to a higher education qualification or continuing professional development credits. 79% occurred at post-qualification stages. 58% of studies only considered the learners' experiences. 24% considered a patient/user perspective by questionnaire or use of secondary sources such as patient notes. There was 'a predominance of positive findings across all six of the outcome categories' (Barr et al., 2006: 74), and the authors identify three foci that contribute to making interprofessional learning effective. These included developing individuals (and there tended to be a focus in pre-qualifying training), developing organizational change and team and group collaboration within this. The latter did include service user participation but research methods often used secondary sources for service user feedback, as discussed above. Barr et al. (2005) propose a model that recognizes a dynamic and interactive link between the six outcomes to these three key foci. They need to positively reinforce each other and if aspects of the system fail, the momentum for the whole system is impaired and positive outcomes for interprofessional education can be undermined.

Newer research explores the experience of pre-qualifying students as this evidence becomes more available, following the expectation that interprofessional education is built into health and social care courses. For example, Miller et al. (2006) have recently published a study of four sites in the UK carrying out a variety of programmes of pre-qualifying interprofessional education in health and social care. This highlighted key areas for development and that one sort of learning experience does not suit all. The evaluation raised a number of issues outlining the positive and negative experiences of interprofessional learning, such as difficulty in measuring outcomes for users and carers, the role of medics, and stereotypes about them and their own behaviour which caused comment and attention. It was found that initiatives based on practice tended to promote more cohesion in the interprofessional student group and that the size of the student group was significant in affecting the learning experience as well as the role of the facilitator. Some students experienced dissonance if a different learning style was commonly used within their own professional group. The evaluation concluded that there is a need for sustainable infrastructures to continue and develop interprofessional education.

Glen and Leiba (2004) summarize some important features to consider when designing or sending workers on courses where interprofessional working and learning is a central outcome. Locally delivered task-focused and interactive practice courses with positive role models are more likely than university-based education to provide a positive experience for users and patients. Why? Potentially, local learning with professionals you will meet on a day-to-day basis can offer continuity of learning into practice and provide better professional relationships and, as a result, better services. These courses can offer time and space away from work for critical reflection and analysis in order to learn about different professional cultures and values.

The evidence base for the review outlined above, for example, may help you as a leader or manager in making decisions about commissioning interprofessional learning opportunities. Key areas for further research and development are identified, such as studies with a strong user or carer perspective. There is a need to broaden research across wider public services, to focus on team collaboration and to follow up studies that explore the impact of newer developments in pre- and post-qualifying education in health and social care.

DEVELOPING LEARNING OPPORTUNITIES FOR INTERPROFESSIONAL LEARNING – SOME FINAL WORDS

The complexity of interprofessional and interagency work requires that the gaps and conflicts between different professional perspectives and practices should not only be bridged but creatively exploited. ... This requires a high level of expertise in mediation and diplomacy used with pragmatism and authority. (Low and Weinstein, 2000: 216)

Leaders, managers and educators need to be able to use these skills well and the development of 'individual champions' (Department of Health, 1999) to lead organizational change in specific areas such as interprofessional working is one strategy that can be used. This role been developed by Skills for Care in the exploration of the characteristics of the people developing the New Types of Worker Project (Skills for Care, 2005b). When developing effective interprofessional learning it is important to consider first the other factors discussed in this chapter. These may include the changing socio-political context in which the learning takes place and any definitions of interprofessional working and learning used by the various agencies involved. It can also include the following:

- The required competencies to be achieved will define learning aims and outcomes.
- The knowledge and evidence base, for example research and theories reflecting one professional group, across all groups, inclusion of service users and carers' perspectives.
- The evidence base for different types of learning environment that can be provided. (e.g. university or work-based learning).
- The three foci relating to organizational change, team and group collaboration (including user and carer perspectives) and individual learning that contribute to effective interprofessional learning as defined by Barr et al. (2005, 2006).
- Whether uni-professional or interprofessional learning is going to be the most effective form of learning to achieve the competencies and outcomes required.

More recently, established patterns of workers attending one-off training courses and returning to work with little or no follow-up of their learning has been questioned in terms of effectiveness and the development of best practice. Strategies to review learning on courses or in other ways can be built into supervision and appraisals. The encouragement of workers to impart learning to other team members encourages a team learning culture. In health and social care, different types of interprofessional learning experience have been developed in order to encourage ongoing active learning that stimulates critical reflection and application to every day practice. Learning as a team or within a locality offers direct links with learning and practising together in the community. Work-based learning, e-learning, action learning sets, buddying, journal clubs, mentorship and coaching on a group or one-to-one basis have been developed in health and social care. Wenger (1998) identifies one social theory of learning which he terms 'communities of practice'. It adds another dimension to considering ways of creating effective learning environments. We are all members of communities of practice in our daily work and personal lives. As these change over time our roles will vary in different communities and our participation can be at different levels. The community does not have to be identifiable and boundaried; it can be flexible. We use everyday experiences in our teams and learn from these and the context in which we work. This will include formal and informal, peer and management relationships. Wenger (1998: 8) identifies that within organizations 'learning is an issue of sustaining the interconnected communities of practice through which an organization knows what it knows and thus becomes effective and valuable as an organization'. Communities of practice can be built for and with those people who are committed to the development of best practice in interprofessional working by coming together in a variety of ways, including online, video, conferences, and meetings.

With different sorts of learning environment for interprofessional learning there needs to be a range of differing styles of facilitation. Building on the experiences of Leiba and Leonard (2003) and Sims and Leonard (2004), facilitators need to be able to model co-working interprofessionally and with service users and carers. The ability to be inclusive, facilitate across professional/worker groups, establish clear working agreements, handle conflict fairly, challenge constructively, avoid getting 'professionally' defensive, take risks and deal with uncertainty are all qualities that need to be present in this complex arena.

CHAPTER SUMMARY

This chapter has analysed the principles of interprofessional working and learning in the context of the developing political agenda for collaboration between users, carers, workers and managers within and across organizational boundaries to offer quality holistic services. A variety of definitions have been identified and extended, using the principle that users and carers are central to this process. The role of service users as leaders and partners is further explored in our next chapter. The politically driven forces leading to collaboration and further organizational changes, such as the development of Children's Trusts and current changes to adult services provision, have been discussed in relation to the different identities and make-up of teams, comprising workers from a range of backgrounds and professions. We also explored the knowledge base used to work interprofessionally and the competencies required of workers. The evidence base for the value of interprofessional education contributing to better collaboration in practice has been used as an example of how to relate research to practice, with a discussion of different learning opportunities for interprofessional learning.

Recommended further reading

The *Journal of Interprofessional Care* aims to promote collaboration within and between education, practice and research in health and social care. It publishes a number of interesting articles about interprofessional collaboration in practice, and where this has led to improvements in the quality of care for individuals, families and communities. Contributors include service users, students, teachers, practitioners, managers, policy makers and researchers in education and there are about six issues each year. This journal is published by Taylor and Francis (www.tandf.co.uk/journals).

Web-based resources

Centre for the Advancement of Interprofessional Education www.caipe.org.uk – CAIPE promotes and develops interprofessional education as a way to improve collaboration between practitioners and organizations engaged in public services. It has a number of national and international resources from interprofessional education.

Sure Start www.surestart.gov.uk – a government programme which aims to achieve better outcomes for children, parents and communities by increasing the availability of childcare, improving child health and emotional development and supporting parents' aspirations towards employment through one-stop multi-agency involvement and projects.

Every Child Matters www.everychildmatters.gov.uk – provides a practical guide and toolkit for managers of integrated services.

4 USERS AS PARTNERS IN FACILITATING LEARNING AND DEVELOPMENT

This chapter explores:

- The growth of user participation
- The ingredients for promoting user participation
- Users as leaders, managers and partners in service development
- Users facilitating learning through awareness, reflection, drawing upon evidence, partnership working and evaluation

INTRODUCTION

Good leadership and improving the lives of people who use health and social care resources must go hand in hand. It is almost inconceivable to imagine that leadership development can evolve without the active participation of users. Since the early 1990s user participation has been fundamental to the reform of public services. There has been a plethora of legislative and policy developments placing user participation centre-stage in social care. This is not restricted to users commenting on the services they have received, but has gradually increased to incorporate all aspects of service and workforce development. As we saw in the previous chapter, user participation with varying degrees of success has become a common feature of formal learning, training and qualifying processes (both pre- and post-qualification). Most practitioners, managers and leaders will have had users involved in some capacity shaping their professional development. This may have been through contact and discussions with individuals about their personal circumstances or working at a strategic level with users and/or user controlled organizations.

> **BOX 4.1   REFLECTION BREAK**
>
> Think about a time when you had direct contact with users and note whether this was part of direct individual work, someone sharing their experiences at an event or part of a process of strategic planning and decision making. As you reflect on this consider the following questions:
>
> 1. What sort of impact did your experience have on you?
> 2. What (if anything) did you learn from this encounter?
> 3. What form of user input do you feel most comfortable with and what do you find most challenging?
> 4. How does this affect your learning?

Skills for Care (2006b: 1) points out that:

> leaders and managers must have a critical understanding of anti-discriminatory practice and the impact of exclusion and disadvantage on people's lives. Leaders and managers must be proactive in working with the diversity of staff, of people who use services and of carers, and in promoting social inclusion. ... Leaders and managers need to have vision which is informed by involving people who use services and other partners.

In facilitating learning through leadership and management it is important to recognize and work with the fact that different types of user participation are required and all have a valid role to play. However one needs to be wary of not being over-dependant on certain types of participation at the expense of others. For example, many people find that when users tell their individual personal stories it is very powerful and much more likely to leave a lasting impression than if users facilitate a teaching session on how to define and achieve strategic user-focused social care outcomes.

The challenge for those in leadership and management roles is to use a variety of organizational and strategic frameworks to embed user and carer participation, both formally and informally, into the fabric of learning and development. Skills for Care (2006b: 2) advocates that a model of leadership and management should, among other things, be:

- integrative and clear about the links between people who use services, carers, stakeholders, the organization, the team and the particular individual;
- based on shared outcomes, values and attitudes within a learning organization;

- capable of describing partnerships and networks; and
- dynamic and developmental.

This chapter demonstrates how users can have a critical role in facilitating learning and development in social care. The emphasis is placed on shifting away from learning approaches where users are merely called upon to tell their personal stories, to a model where users have an active role to play in a variety of ways as colleagues, leaders, managers and partners at a strategic level. We will argue that users have occupied leadership and management roles within social care over a long period of time and there is much to be learnt from this. Therefore it is necessary to challenge some of the inherent and covert messages that appear to place users in one camp and 'professionals' in another, thereby creating a 'them and us' situation. In social care the starting point for effective management and leadership of learning in social care must be that users are recognized as leaders, managers, colleagues and partners in service development rather than as an 'add-on' or some form of process that has to be gone through because of policy dictum.

DISTINGUISHING BETWEEN USERS AND CARERS

Traditionally, the distinction between users and carers has been blurred. The two groups tended to be viewed as synonymous with each other. Consequently, leaders and managers have used the same structures and approaches to promote participation with users as they have with carers. This means that the specificity of users' and carers' experience and expertise can be overlooked and disregarded. The focus in this chapter is on users but this does not mean to suggest that the perspectives and contributions of carers in facilitating learning are not equally important or significant. Indeed, many of the ideas and issues raised are also relevant to the participation of carers. However, the lived experiences of carers are often different (but not unrelated) from that of users and each need their own voice and contribution.

INGREDIENTS FOR PROMOTING PARTICIPATION

The terms participation and user involvement tend to be used interchangeably. Although there is a lack of consensus about the distinction between participation and user involvement, there is little doubt that they are both part of the everyday social care vocabulary. For the purposes of this chapter 'user involvement' will be treated as one component of participation. Robson et al. (2003: 3) define 'user involvement' as the 'participation of users of services in decisions that affect their lives (at an individual level) ... collectively, involvement can include participation in decision making, policy formulation, service development and in the running and controlling of services'.

Traditionally, user involvement has been seen as a linear process. Arnstein (1969) put forward a ladder of participation with eight different levels, associating information exchange at the beginning as part of the manipulation of citizens and at the top of the ladder delegating power and control to facilitate citizen control. Consultation and partnership working fall within the two ends of the ladder. Arnstein's ladder has been a valuable tool for beginning to develop an understanding of and promoting participation. Nevertheless, Beresford and Croft (1993) proposed a three-step version of the participation ladder. This included: 'information gathering exercises; consultations on plans already drawn up and users having a direct say in decision making' (Beresford and Croft, 1993: 49). Over the last few years the ladder of participation has been critiqued and further developed (Wright et al., 2006).

The notion that participation is a straight linear process does not accurately represent the simultaneous interaction of the different components. Participation tends to be organic and somewhat messy, so different elements of the ladder may be called upon depending on the environment and culture in which it is being used. Wright et al. (2006: 8) elaborate further by defining participation as:

- ... involvement in individual decisions about their own lives, as well as collective involvement in matters which affect them;
- a culture of listening which enables [users] to influence both decisions about the services they receive as individuals on a day-to-day basis, as well as how those services are developed and delivered for all [users] who access them;
- not an isolated activity, but a process by which [users] are empowered and supported to influence change either within an organization or by directly leading in policy and service development;
- not a hierarchy [as Arnstein (1969) suggests in the ladder of involvement] where the aim is to reach the top of the ladder ... different levels of participation are valid for different groups of [users] and at different stages of policy and service development.

Wright et al. (2006: 10) point out that effective user participation requires agencies to adopt a whole systems approach that focuses on four interacting elements:

- **Culture**: the ethos of an organization, shared by staff and users, which demonstrates a commitment to participation.
- **Structure**: the planning, development and resourcing of participation evident in an organization's infrastructures.

- **Practice**: the ways of working, methods for involvement, skills and knowledge which enable users to become involved.
- **Review**: the monitoring and evaluation systems which enable an organization to evidence change affected by participation.

Beresford and Croft (1993) argue that the key elements for successful participation include:

- resources;
- information;
- training;
- research and evaluation;
- equal access and opportunities;
- forums and structures for involvement;
- accessible language;
- advocacy (cited by Turner, 2005: 6).

Drawing on lessons learnt from involving users in social work education, Levin (2004: 17) points out that in addressing the process and practicalities of involvement the first steps to be taken include: 'securing resources; deciding who will take the initiative forward; defining users; thinking about the meaning and level of involvement; planning training and support; addressing payment issues; identifying, approaching and bringing together potential partners'. Effective participation must, in addition to tackling the practicalities of the process, include negotiating a joint agreement about aims and expectations, clarifying the parameters within which work is being undertaken, working creatively, using a variety of approaches and securing the support of leaders and managers within user-controlled organizations, statutory services and voluntary and independent sector providers. Some of the stickier and more complicated issues to be addressed include equality and diversity, user payments, capacity and support for user-controlled organizations and achieving appropriate representation.

EQUALITY AND DIVERSITY

Users are not an homogeneous group and one size doesn't fit all. Therefore not only do social care resources have to be used flexibly and adapted to achieve necessary social care outcomes, but also specific attention has to be paid to making participation appropriate and accessible for disadvantaged groups of users. Carr (2004: 21), reviewing the difference user participation has made to social care, points out that:

> attention to the diversity of users in terms of race, culture, sexuality ... was lacking in mainstream services and participation initiatives. This relates to both diversity within user groups and the relative lack of

knowledge about user participation for marginalised people. Users who are marginalised from mainstream can also be found to be under – or unrepresented – in the participation intended to develop those services.

The reasons why black and minority ethnic users and those who are lesbian, gay, bisexual or transgender are marginalized are vast and complicated. Therefore, to achieve effective social care delivery, it is essential to work with these constituencies to find methods of participation that are built on trust, a sense of safety (i.e. people's sexuality is not divulged without their consent or in an inappropriate way) and engagement techniques starting from their perspective. Begum (2006: 21) warns against relying on shortcuts or surrogates:

> ... there has been a tendency to substitute the direct experience of black and minority ethnic users with proxy representatives. Black and minority ethnic community 'leaders', voluntary sector workers and black and minority ethnic professionals have been seen as surrogate users and a conduit in terms of user participation. ... The reality is they have a role to play in advocating and representing the interests of black and minority ethnic users, they do not have direct experience of being social care users and are themselves not immune to holding stereotypical views of users and what they need. The message is simple: there can be no substitute for user participation and shortcuts are not the solution.

The path to promoting the participation of marginalized and disadvantaged groups is rarely trod and is littered with twists and turns. Nevertheless, when time, energy and resources are invested in engaging and supporting marginalized and disadvantaged groups, there are real opportunities for ensuring social care resources are used effectively to achieve valued and meaningful (to users) outcomes (Begum, 2006: 8).

BOX 4.2   GOOD PRACTICE EXAMPLES

ROOTS is a group of African Caribbean people with learning disabilities that came together 'to use direct experience, shared learning and good practice examples to promote positive change in the attitudes of staff working for local service providers and culture of organisations' (Singh, 2005: 10)

Equalities National, an organization for black and minority ethnic disabled people and carers not only directly provides services but also contributes to policy and service development at different levels (Begum, 2006).

USER REPRESENTATION

A recurring barrier in promoting participation is the thorny question of representation. There can be a temptation to involve individual users without serious thought and consideration being given to the support and training they may require. It is often erroneously assumed that these individual users can speak on behalf of and represent a whole group of people without attention being paid to how they can be held accountable to their constituency. Such participation is problematic because it is tokenistic in nature and bypasses the requirement to support users to make informed judgements and decisions based on networking with their peers. Also, if users are cherry picked to be involved without clear criteria and transparency about why and how they were selected, there is a danger that the whole basis of the participation work becomes undermined and discredited.

Arguments such as 'you are not representative of our users', 'it's the same old faces over again' or 'you're a professional user' are another way of agencies resisting participation on the basis of spurious notions of not being representative. This particularly seems to happen when users, through their experience of participation, become informed, skilled and articulate. Somehow the process of developing expertise and confidence in some aspect(s) of service development is at some level seen as quite threatening and is consequently used as ammunition to dismiss or undermine the contribution users have to make. Lindow explains:

> When users become 'competent and articulate', professionals start saying – it happens to me almost every week – oh you're just professionalized users. They use the word professional as a dirty word applied to us although they use it in relation to themselves as though it were gold. (cited in Morris, 1994: 49)

Accusations of unrepresentativeness should not be used as a barrier to participation. Beresford and Croft (1993: 28) illustrate the double-edged sword that users are faced with in relation to participation: 'When we agree with them, we are representative. When we don't, they say we aren't.' Of course the other charge that is often promulgated is that user organizations are not representative and therefore should not be listened to. This may be true of some user-controlled organizations in the same ways as some black and minority ethnic community organizations do not represent the direct voice of users, but that does not mean that the baby is thrown out with the bath water (Begum, 2006). Turner (2005: 17) explains user groups:

> may not be perfect, but they offer a better opportunity to accountability and representation than working through individual users who happen to be in the right place at the right time but have no links to other users.

This is a practice that would only ever be acceptable in an initial bringing together of interested parties to establish a formal structure for user involvement; it should never be the basis of continuing work.

CAPACITY AND SUPPORT FOR USER-CONTROLLED ORGANIZATIONS AND NETWORKS

User-controlled organizations and networks are an extremely valuable resource for enabling users to tap into and engage with a range of participation work. In addition to directly campaigning and providing services, user-controlled organizations are in a unique position to facilitate participation through advocacy, training, and briefing, networking with other users, dealing with practical arrangements and offering ongoing support. Inevitably, the wealth of knowledge and expertise embodied within user-controlled organizations must be resourced properly. This is about funding and supporting the establishment of strong infrastructures and capacity building. Access to training, meeting space, transport, library facilities, shadowing opportunities, secondment, coaching, mentoring and other structures or systems all play a role in building the capacity of user-controlled organizations and networks.

USER FEES AND EXPENSES

The principle of paying users' expenses and a fee for the expertise, time and effort contributed is generally accepted. It is one of the prerequisites that users and their organizations have clearly set out for engagement in participation. User fees and reimbursing expenses is an area of policy and practice that really taxes people. The benefits system can serve as a major barrier to users receiving fees and expenses. Also, there tends to be great variation in terms of how people are remunerated and the rates of pay (Turner and Beresford, 2005). Despite user fees and reimbursing expenses being a complex area of work to tackle, it is critical that leaders and managers lend their weight to ensuring that the difficulties are addressed and good practice is promoted (Department of Health, 2006b).

PARTICIPATION AS A MEANS TO AN END

In trying to understand the significance of participation it is helpful to perceive it as a journey to improve outcomes for users, but instead of professionals being in the driving seat, users and professionals collaborate to make the journey. There are many different routes that can be taken while promoting participation. It may be argued that the vehicle used for the journey is not as important as remembering why a particular journey is being made and where the final destination needs to be. However, for many users their experience of the process of participation is as important as the outcome. Beresford et al. (1997: 78 and 177) remind us that:

> ... there is a fundamental difference of perspective between service providers who are asking 'Am I providing a good service?' and that of users who are asking 'What needs to happen to improve my quality of life?'. Both the user perspectives, of desired outcomes, and the professional one, of ways to make those possible, are needed to form a joint and rounded view. ... Users ... judge the quality of services in two ways: they are concerned that services will help them achieve the outcomes they aspire to; and they are concerned that services are delivered in a way which empowers rather than disempower them. ... User involvement is not an end in itself but a means of effecting change both in the outcome itself and in the behaviour of staff.

BOX 4.3 TOP TIPS FOR PROMOTING USER PARTICIPATION

We offer the following tips if you are working to promote participation:

- Distinguish between users and carers.
- Address access issues.
- Sort out a clear process for paying users and reimbursing expenses.
- Ensure participation is fit for purpose.
- Jointly negotiate aims, expectations and constraints.
- Agree ground rules.
- Resource appropriate infrastructure.
- Invest in user-controlled organizations and relevant groups.
- Respect the contribution of all stakeholders.
- Value diversity both within and across different stakeholders.
- Establish clear lines of accountability.
- Have transparent decision making.
- Build in flexibility and adaptability with agreed review standards.
- Evaluate the impact and outcomes of participation work.

Source: based on Beresford and Croft (1993); Levin (2004); and Turner (2005).

GROWTH OF USER ACTIVISM AND PARTICIPATION

The user movement, which includes, among others, a whole range of disabled people, mental health system survivors, young people 'looked after', older people's networks and families living in poverty, has grown in prominence over the last two decades. This has been partly attributable to a rekindling of interest in human rights, citizenship, choice, empowerment, independent living, advocacy, consumerism and democratic/participatory approaches, but also due to the civil rights campaign and burgeoning 'self-help' movement. The mushrooming of the user movement and recognition of the necessity to reform public services, particularly the organization and delivery of social care, meant that involvement and participation became the foundation upon which the transformation of social care was built.

Barnes and Mercer (2006: 38), in documenting the creation of user-led services, explain that the 'failures and shortcomings in the organization and delivery of mainstream statutory and voluntary sector services have been a major stimulus to disability activism'. Indeed, the Independent Living Movement in the UK was born out of the experiences and actions of a group of disabled people working to move out of a Leonard Cheshire residential home and live in the community. Stemming from this and a sense of injustice and inequality, users organized and campaigned for advocacy, welfare reform, the adoption of a social model of disability, user-led training, user-led research and user-controlled services. Morris, in *The Shape of Things to Come? User-led Social Services* (1994: 9–11), highlights some of the keys factors that helped shape the growth of the user movement and the demand for user-led services:

> Protest is a key element of user-controlled alternatives to mental health services. ... User-controlled services have emerged out of people's desire to have more say, out of their anger, but the reality of why there's such an interest in user-led services is the government's wish to encourage consumerist perspectives.

As the user movement and user involvement agenda grew in strength and confidence, protest and anger became positive channels for change. There was a shift from solely being critics of the system to the creation of alternative services and different ways of doing things. The burgeoning of user involvement was undoubtedly helped significantly by the fact the messages and campaigns fell on fertile ground within social care organizations. As Higginson (1990: 100) reminds us: 'Most of us set out in a career in social work with some idea that we want to be instrumental in effecting change – in individuals, in communities, in society at large'.

Generally, within the social care workforce there is recognition that users must be involved at some level. This stems from feelings about what is 'socially just, morally right: professionals may be sceptical about government rhetoric about user choice but at least the rhetoric echoes what many social workers were trying to promote all along' (Morris, 1994: 12). As Marsh and Fisher (1992: 58) point out: 'To be on the child protection register or not to receive a home help can have a profound impact on people's lives. Having your say in this process is something most of us would accept is ethically right: it is, if you like, part of natural justice.'

USERS AS LEADERS AND PARTNERS

In order to facilitate learning through effective leadership and management it is an absolute imperative we stop thinking of leaders and managers as one breed and users as another. In reality, leaders, managers, staff and users are both learners and facilitators of learning. As we saw in Chapter 1, a key ingredient of good leadership and learning is the ability to work collaboratively with users, staff and other stakeholders to stimulate and bring about change. The particular model of leadership adopted is dependent on context, circumstances and the personal qualities of the individuals involved. However, in the twenty-first century we can never get away from the fact that users are not passive subjects or recipients who are invited along to help us execute our leadership and management responsibilities. The relationship between users, carers and leaders and managers is an intricate one that has to be built on mutuality, respect, shared power and a partnership that accords proper weight to each other's roles. Within the social care profession anecdotal evidence suggests that there tends to be an unspoken assumption that users can only be clients or customers and they are rarely our leaders, managers, practitioners or peers. The situation in terms of carers is slightly different. Because of demographic factors it is not unusual to find carers in a variety of roles and positions within social care. This may be attributable to the fact that, rightly or wrongly, carers can be much more 'invisible' and can be assimilated into an organization more easily than certain groups of users can. Undoubtedly, questions have to be asked about how alert social care employers are to creating an environment that is responsive to the employment requirements of users.

Much of the literature on leadership and management in social care fails to acknowledge the fact users have and continue to occupy key leadership roles. Yet the history and work of the user movement clearly demonstrates that the current context, policies, structures, processes and values within which social care operates have been strongly influenced by the leadership roles and activities users have adopted. Barrett and Rogers (2003: 6) point out that: 'Leadership occurs and is expected among groups of people, and groups of people collect and organize themselves'. Indeed, one only needs to look at the development of independent advocacy and self-advocacy to recognize that it was a collective response to the exclusion and 'voicelessness' of the most visibly disadvantaged users: mental health system survivors and people with learning difficulties living in long-stay hospitals, older people with dementia in residential care, children with 'challenging behaviours' in institutions and so on. Similarly, it was the self-organization of disabled people and their organizations that worked for and achieved anti- discrimination legislation (Disability Discrimination Act 1995), albeit a shortfall from the demand for civil rights legislation (Sang, 2005: 10).

In Chapter 1, we identified the link between leadership and managing change through learning. Fundamental to learning and leadership is communication, energy, focus, vision, direction and the use of one's power (individually or collectively) to influence or control people, resources or events to bring about change. According to Martin (2003: 5): 'Leaders work with others to visualize how change could make an improvement, they create a climate in which the plans for change are developed and widely accepted and they stimulate action to achieve change.'

Users have many of the characteristics and qualities that we associate with good leaders. The user and carer movements evolved through the initiative, determination, foresight, direction and vision of individuals coming together and bringing others on board to bring about change. A combination of leadership and management approaches were adopted to initiate, advance and oversee significant transformation in the way social care services were organized and delivered. Key activists as leaders within the user and carer movement 'identified a wave and rode it, while others persuaded us a wave was coming, went out of their way to appear the most visible surfers to onlookers and whose actions were regarded by onlookers as appropriate (and necessary) for leaders to take' (Grint, 1997: 9–10). Kotter (1992) differentiates between leadership being about transformation and management that is concerned with transactions. Sometimes this is alternatively described as leaders 'doing the right thing' and managers 'doing things right'. Whatever definitions are used, it is indisputable that both leaders and managers (sometimes one and the same person/people) within the user and carer movements have played a central role in the continued growth of self-help, user-controlled services, participation and the changing climate of social care.

Leaders in the user movement have tended to focus on developing and promoting a new vision, building relationships, motivating people, networking, communicating ideas, modelling good practice, providing direction and generating change in social care policy and practice. Whereas managers have dealt with the more thorny issues of fundraising, budgets, governance, premises, planning, human resources, problem solving, performance management and the everyday practicalities of running organizations and services. In reality, in the statutory and voluntary sector and within specialist or mainstream roles, users are leaders and managers.

BOX 4.4   REFLECTION BREAK

Are you aware whether there are any users among your peers, colleagues and seniors? Does the work environment and culture make it possible for users (with the relevant knowledge, skills, experience and abilities) to be in leadership and management positions in a variety of roles (so they are not restricted to specific user posts)?

If you are not a user, consider what difference having direct personal experience of being one might have on your professional role and identity. As a user, how important would it be to you to keep your personal life and experience private? What factors would influence your decision to share the fact you have direct experience of being a user with colleagues and/or your seniors?

Leaders and managers have a responsibility to model good practice and ensure that user participation is at the crux of their daily business. This is not motherhood and apple pie but an absolute imperative for facilitating learning and continuous improvement through leadership and management. Participation must be viewed as one of the essential cogs that keep the wheel of planning, delivering and evaluating social care policies and resources running.

Robson et al. (2003) conclude from research on working towards user-centred practice in voluntary organizations that the key enablers of change are: focus on users and users' priorities, vision and commitment, sustained leadership, quality of dialogue, resources, equality of opportunity and continuous monitoring and evaluation. These enablers of change are equally applicable in the statutory and private sector. Therefore it is important to turn our attention to how users in mainstream and specialist roles can lead or work with others to facilitate learning. Before doing this it is useful to revisit our earlier discussion of leadership and learning.

LEADERSHIP, MANAGEMENT AND LEARNING AND SERVICE USERS

Among other things, learning, like leadership and management, involves good communication, sharing vision, creating energy, understanding experience, developing insight, problem solving and facing challenges. It is a two-way process that users have to be integral to. Change cannot take place or be sustained without some form of learning at an individual, group or organizational level. As discussed in other chapters, learning is a constantly evolving process which comes in many shapes and forms. Sometimes it can be very formal and structured and at other times informal, loosely defined (if at all) and possibly unconscious. Inherent in leading and managing change is a responsibility to facilitate learning. Unless people's capacity to learn and progress is fully utilized, transformation, quality of performance and transaction will be limited.

An extract from a speech by Jesse Jackson, a compelling American political leader, provides a good metaphor in understanding the task of leaders and managers in facilitating learning: 'Truth, like electricity, is all around us, but we have very few conduits for it. What you do is plug the people into your socket, they give you the electricity, and you give them heat and light' (cited in Starratt, 1993: 48). Involving users in learning is like putting the plug into the socket to generate heat and light. Gould (2000: 586) refers to learning in social care 'as a process of purposive engagement with practice'. Connecting users into the process of reflection and engagement with practice is at the heart of building the confidence, empathy, expertise and vision of staff, while also improving social care outcomes.

USERS FACILITATING LEARNING

Users can facilitate learning in a myriad of ways and it is impossible to document all the possible approaches. New and creative approaches to promoting learning and development are constantly being developed, yet it is probably fair to say that in social care experiential learning is at the core of personal and professional development. Jarvis (1987: 8) defines learning as 'the transformation of experience into knowledge, skills and attitudes'. In thinking about how users may facilitate learning, it is worth considering some of the key elements necessary to create a learning culture. This, among other things, includes awareness, reflection, drawing on evidence, partnership working and evaluation.

AWARENESS

Both self-awareness and awareness of the experience of others are at the heart of learning. Indeed, being aware is often identified as the starting point for an experiential learning cycle (Martin, 2003). Merely making an observation of an incident or process does not amount to awareness. To develop awareness it is necessary to go a step further and identify patterns and relationships between oneself and the environment. Social care can rouse a lot of emotions and complex feelings. This is particularly true when power relationships and methods of working are challenged by the very process of participation. Therefore it is extremely important that leaders and managers are open about their own learning when working with users to plan and develop social care resources. Users have a long history of raising awareness of personal, professional and political issues through training, making presentations at events, contributing to team meetings and a variety of other methods. Sometimes the very fact users have a presence in the course of participation work generates awareness and learning.

Early on in the user movement a lot of the work was focused on user-controlled awareness training, but as collective action grew and the process of consciousness-raising evolved, there was a shift from 'awareness' training to equality training. There is an important distinction between awareness training and equality training; the former, as the name suggests, creates awareness but does not necessarily lead to a change in behaviour, whereas the latter places a strong emphasis on changing behaviours through exploring the consequences of particular attitudes and actions. Obviously, users can facilitate learning on an array of strategic and practice issues. Therefore, their input should never be restricted to awareness raising or equality training (although this is an important component).

REFLECTIVE PRACTICE

Reflective practice is deeply embedded into the learning culture of social care. Therefore it makes a lot of sense that users are in a position to support reflective practice whether they are in leadership and management roles or brought in to proffer specific expertise. As we will see in subsequent chapters, this might mean establishing mechanisms for users to provide group supervision sessions, non-managerial support, mentoring and opportunities to explore the material contained within reflective diaries or learning journals.

At this point some readers will inevitably have concerns about confidentiality running riot in their minds. However, it is important to remember that users who engage in supporting reflective practice will have considerable expertise and knowledge in this area. Also there is no suggestion here that users work with the individuals or teams that are involved in their care. Equally, there is no evidence to suggest that users are lax in terms of respecting confidentiality. Indeed, many will know only too well that confidentiality has to be at the core of everything and some will have had bitter experience of the consequences if confidentiality is breached.

The elephant in the room that may not be explicitly acknowledged or understood is that of the power dynamics if users are in a role supporting reflective learning. Some professionals may feel threatened or uncomfortable with a user facilitating reflective work because of an underlying and possibly unconscious fear that a shift in roles threatens their power base or professional status. However, rather than letting this militate against users' involvement in reflective learning, it is important to create a space that is safe enough for the underlying fears to be explored. There is as much to be learnt from exploring the barriers and power dynamics associated with users facilitating reflective learning as there will be from actually reflecting on practice.

EVIDENCE

The importance of drawing on evidence to inform learning and development cannot be understated. Leaders and managers need to utilize evidence to assist them in their task of instilling and managing change. Without drawing on evidence, it is difficult to challenge poor practice or persuade others to change what they do. There is a danger that if available evidence is not used by leaders and managers, then new ideas or proposed changes may be regarded as the whims of particular individuals rather than being considered and informed decisions based upon strong evidence.

In health settings, decisions about effectiveness of clinical interventions and how resources should be organized and delivered have centred on what the evidence indicates. A strong emphasis has been placed on rigorous scientific scrutiny, with the goal of trying to deal with the tensions between clinical certainty and uncertainty. Kitson (cited in Martin, 2003: 82) explains:

> The ongoing tension between certainties over uncertainty is the driving force of the evidence-based practice movement. Its central philosophy is one of never taking for granted one's own practice, and by using a structured, problem-based approach each practitioner can logically manoeuvre their way through the obstacle race of clinical decision making.

The endorsement and widespread use of evidence-based approaches in social care have only gained momentum over the last five years. Previously, there was reluctance towards scientific methodology which affected not only how interventions were evaluated, but undermined the development of sound theories and exploration of the nature of social problems. Also, a lack of political and fiscal support for improving the evidence base of social care, combined with organizational structures and cultures that did not facilitate evidence-based practice, meant that the use of evidence as a learning and service development tool was impeded. Nevertheless, in social care an expectation of interventions being subject to scrutiny and a strong track record of participatory approaches helped to shape a changing approach to evidence-based practice (Macdonald, 2000: 136).

In Chapter 9, we will be looking at how, over the last five years, the climate in social care has changed significantly. There is now a widespread recognition that evidence-based practice lies at the heart of improving social care outcomes. The Social Care Institute for Excellence (SCIE) was established to respond to the growing appetite and demand for evidence about the effectiveness of different approaches in social care (www.scie.org.uk). SCIE's remit is specifically to build up a knowledge base of what works well in social care and to use this to develop good practice.

User participation has to be at the crux of the drive to develop good practice based on available evidence. In practice, this means that users should not just be passive subjects of research but active partners in designing, conducting, analysing and publishing research. Equally, their perspectives should be reflected when reviewing literature. This might mean that it is necessary to draw on grey literature that might not otherwise be picked up in systematic reviews that have rigorous formal criteria which serve to exclude small and often qualitative studies. There is a growing body of research and literature produced by users that can be used to assist learning and development. User-controlled participatory research is exceptionally valuable in providing a wealth of knowledge for staff to draw upon when needing to shift towards a more user focused approach and perhaps change the direction of their work.

BOX 4.5   USER-CONTROLLED RESEARCH

A research project controlled and run by users sought to identify what people thought of the social care services they use. One of the key findings pointed to the value of outcomes:

(Continued)

Users recognised the value of evaluating services in terms of their outcomes, but they saw it as essential that users' views are primary in this process and that the evaluation included the subjective perspectives of individual users. They recognised that such work could be supported by an element of objective measures, for example, a mental health service user suggested that effective services could be measured in relation to spending on drugs and that effective support would lead to less spending on drugs.

Turner, M. (2003) *Shaping Our Lives–From Outset to Outcome: What People Think of the Social Care Services they Use*. York: Joseph Rowntree Foundation.

PARTNERSHIP WORKING

Following on from some of the themes in the previous chapter, a substantial proportion of our learning takes place through actually doing a particular activity or job. It could be worth exploring opportunities for working alongside users within user-controlled organizations. There is a great deal to be gained from practice- and work-based learning in organizations set up especially to provide user-led services driven by the demands of consumers.

BOX 4.6 USER-CONTROLLED SERVICES

Independent living centres

Direct payment support services are one of the many essential resources provided by independent living centres. The emphasis in independent living centres is that disabled people with direct experience and expertise are able to assist direct payments users (or potential users) through the process of applying for and managing a direct payment (including training and employment).

User-controlled organizations

User-controlled organizations, such as the Wiltshire and Swindon Users' Network, offer placements to students,

(Continued)

(Continued)

and these have been very successful. User-controlled
organizations demand of the students a willingness
to question their value base and attitude in a way that
is not possible within other placements. Issues of
empowerment, rights and responsibilities, and choice and
control are perceived differently in user-controlled
organizations, and the students acquire much learning
towards making a more balanced judgement in assessment.
(Levin, 2004: 39)

As the role of social care practitioners changes with the advent of
self-assessment, individual budgets, service brokerage and community
based provision, the likelihood is that the demand for the type of support
user-controlled organizations offer is going to grow. A consumer-driven
resource tends to be significantly different from that traditionally
provided by the large major charities and the statutory sector. For
example, People First, a network of people with learning difficulties,
has forced a major rethink in terms of advocacy and self-advocacy.
Therefore a practitioner placed within People First is going to be exposed
to a different approach and philosophy as to what may be offered in a
statutory sector day service.

EVALUATION

An important part of the learning cycle for both individuals and organizations has to be the process of evaluation. This is not the same as reflection, although the two can overlap. Evaluation suggests that an assessment
or judgement is made about the value and efficacy of certain interactions
and interventions. Mistakenly, evaluation is often thought about as the
endpoint, yet good evaluation processes are both ongoing and part of a
cycle of continuous improvement. Sometimes there is a strong argument
for embarking on an evaluation at the end of a project or intervention.
However, this does not negate the need for incorporating formative evaluation throughout a project or area of work. Evaluation should enable
staff to understand and learn more about the value of particular interventions or interactions by assessing outcomes, limitations, resource implications and challenges associated with particular work. Users can be
instrumental in undertaking evaluations and collaborating with others to
share the learning that may be yielded. Also, of course, as recipients of
services they are one of the key stakeholder groups that will feedback as

part of the evaluation. However, it is crucial that users are engaged directly in analysing findings and generating ideas for new ways of working as part of the evaluation process.

CHAPTER SUMMARY

This chapter has promulgated the argument that user participation is the vehicle for improving social care outcomes and the process of service delivery. This is not about 'motherhood and apple pie', but is an essential tool for facilitating learning and development. Users are leaders, managers, colleagues and partners in developing social care. The chapter has put forward a supposition that there has been a tendency to view users in a single-dimensional way, which reinforces a 'them and us' situation. There are a multitude of possibilities for consolidating individual and organizational learning through collaboration, co-determination and co-working with users and their organizations. This chapter has explored a few of the ways in which users can engage with instilling change through facilitating learning and development.

Leaders and managers have a responsibility to draw upon the expertise and experience of users. There are a number of practical and policy matters to be addressed when engaging users to facilitate learning, including putting in place necessary structures and systems. Repertoires of participatory approaches are at the disposal of leaders and managers. The appropriateness of any model employed has to be negotiated with the relevant users and their organizations. One needs to be cautious not to restrict user participation by an over-reliance on personal testimonies. User participation has to encompass a whole spectrum of learning, from awareness, reflection and work-based learning to active involvement in strategic planning and service delivery. 'User participation has been a revolution in social care. It has come a long way and achieved a great deal, but it is a revolution that continues for users, planners, providers and practitioners alike' (Turner, 2005: 2). The flagship of this revolution is the participation of users in facilitating learning and development. Leaders and managers have to nail the flag to the mast and make sure it does not waver in the wind of conflicting priorities.

Recommended further reading

The Social Care Institute for Excellence has produced a number of guides covering key research findings, ideas from practice and

(Continued)

(Continued)

details of relevant standards with guidance on how to involve different service user groups in developing and providing care:
Resource Guide 2: Involving service users and carers in social work education. By Enid Levin, March 2004.
Practice Guide 06: Involving children and young people in developing social care. February 2006.
Position Paper No. 3: Has service user participation made a difference to social care services? March 2004.
Report 14: Doing it for themselves: participation and black and minority ethnic service users. By Nasa Begum, July 2006.
Position Paper 05: Working together, Carer participation in England, Wales and Northern Ireland. By Alan Roulstone, Val Hudson, Jeremy Kearney, Ailsa Martin with Jon Warren, June 2006.
All of these can be obtained in accessible versions from www.scie.org.uk/publications.

Web-based resources

National Centre for Independent Living (www.ncil.org.uk) – is the national organization providing information, training, expertise and policy development on all aspects of direct payments and independent living. Its aim is to enable disabled people to have self-determination, choice and control, and equal access to economic, social and cultural life.

   A National Voice (www.anationalvoice.org) – is the only national organization run by and for young people from care. Everyone who is under 25 and is or has been in care in England is automatically a member and it welcomes all professional contributions. A National Voice gives help with tasks such as consulting young people, training for professionals and organizing events for young people as well as supporting members to do public speaking and presentations.

   The Princess Royal Trust for Carers (www.carers.org) – is the largest provider of carers' support services in the UK with a network of 122 independently managed Carers' Centres and interactive websites. The Trust provides quality information, advice and support services to almost a quarter of a million carers, including 13,000 young carers.

5 PROMOTING DIVERSITY AND EQUALITY THROUGH LEARNING

This chapter explores:

- The legal and policy framework to support equality and diversity in social care organizations
- Theoretical models influencing diversity management
- Promoting diversity through learning
- Applying a learning perspective within a whole systems approach

INTRODUCTION

Addressing discrimination and promoting equality and diversity in workforce development have been issues that have taxed policy makers, educators, regulators, leaders and managers within the health and social care sector for a considerable length of time now (King's Fund, 1990; McDougall, 1996; Department of Health, 2001a, 2005b; Stephens, 2001; Butt et al., 2006; Hafford-Letchfield and Chick, 2006b;). While the solutions might not be clear-cut or precise, there is little doubt that equality and diversity considerations have to be strongly connected to policy objectives and strategic action.

The Association of Directors of Social Services (2004: 4) unequivocally states:

> ... social care as a profession works with the impact of discrimination, and whatever the individual understanding, everyone within the profession is charged with the responsibility to deal with inequality and injustice ... equalities are therefore at the core of the social care value base and constitute a moral imperative. ... The business case for modernization and reform of the public services ... covers opening up areas of recruitment in an intensely competitive labour market, financial savings on disciplinary, grievance and tribunal costs, tapping into a vibrant voluntary sector

resource, and demonstrating that the (diversity) strategy adopted results in sustained and recent progress.

Within the context of social care (and allied professions) there has been a widespread recognition that anti-discriminatory practice and promoting diversity are key components of leadership and management tasks. However, what is less convincing is the ability of leaders and managers to incorporate diversity and proactively tackle discrimination through the process of facilitating learning and development.

This chapter will argue that the success or failure of ensuring social care practice leads to effective social care outcomes for all users and carers rests upon the ability of leaders and managers to actively support all students and staff to address diversity. Hence leaders and managers need to be well versed in the context in which different approaches to equality and diversity have emerged and be able to apply a model of working which embraces everyone's responsibility to tackle inequality, discrimination and social exclusion. Indeed, the Skills for Care statement for a leadership and management development strategy for social care (2006b: 1) draws specific attention to the fact 'leaders and managers must have a clear understanding of anti-discriminatory practice and the impact of exclusion on people's lives. Leaders and managers must be proactive in working with diversity of staff, of people who use services and of carers, and in promoting social inclusion.'

The challenge facing everyone in workforce development and social care is how diversity can be embedded into the very fibre of the profession. All staff should be appropriately equipped to entrench it into their practice rather than it becoming something that 'certain' individuals (often those from diverse backgrounds) have to take responsibility for. To explore how diversity and anti-discriminatory practice can be applied within a participatory learning and development approach, this chapter will start with a brief introduction to the legal and policy framework. It will then take an overview of the social care workforce and the impetus driving change in the workforce development. In order to understand the variety of approaches that leaders and managers can or have drawn upon to promote equality and diversity, the chapter will define what is meant by these two terms and consider the theoretical models that have informed the development of policy and practice. We will go on to make the case that one of the best approaches to promoting diversity that leaders and managers can adopt is one which is underpinned by an emphasis on a learning perspective (Lorbiecki, 2001). To expand on a learning-based model we will draw upon Comerford's learning through engagement framework as 'an ongoing, socially constructed, contextual process based in relational learning' (Comerford, 2005: 113). The final section will explore how learning through engagement can be applied within a whole systems framework, focusing on culture, structure, practice and review (Wright et al., 2006: 10).

In light of the fact that there is a dearth of research and literature around age, disability or sexuality-related discrimination in the milieu of social care, much of the discussion will be focused on supporting the learning and development of staff and students from black and minority ethnic communities and women (Annelies et al., 2002; Carter, 2003; Harlow, 2004). However, it is important to stress that many of the arguments and strategies highlighted will also apply to diversity in relation to disabled people, older or younger people and people who are lesbian, gay or bisexual studying or working in social care.

Much of the diversity management literature places a strong emphasis on improving corporate performance and creating more socially inclusive work environments by 'releasing desperately needed talents suppressed by mono-cultural organizations that label and stereotype on the basis of race, sexuality, disability and so on' (Lorbiecki, 2001: 346). While much of the focus within organizations has been on equipping leaders and managers to tackle discrimination and promote diversity, there is now a growing acknowledgement that this needs to be done in tandem with learning and development being explicitly at the core of promoting diversity.

BOX 5.1   REFLECTION BREAK

Think about diversity in your current environment and reflect upon the following:

- What strategies are in place for tackling diversity?
- What sort of leadership and management is in place to support the implementation of diversity?
- To what extent is everyone in the organization or team encouraged to address diversity?
- How does diversity affect your learning, practice and professional development?

LEGAL AND POLICY FRAMEWORK

There is now a significant legislative and policy framework not only making it unlawful to discriminate but also placing a statutory duty on (particularly public sector) organizations to put in place measures to cater for the particular needs of marginalized groups like people from black and minority ethnic communities and disabled people. Friday and Friday (2003: 865) argue that 'managing diversity is an active phenomenon, which involves directing what individuals bring to the organization to ensure its strategic goals are being fully and effectively met'. Indeed, the Audit Commission point out how 'the written and spoken commitment of leaders is not enough. It must be demonstrated by action and consistency of message' (cited in Association of Directors of Social Services, 2004: 5). Therefore it is no longer acceptable to pay lip service to diversity policies that never see the light of day or undermine the importance of incorporating diversity throughout professional practice by dismissing such work under some spurious notion of 'political correctness'. Leaders and managers have to be proactive in bridging the gap between espoused policy commitments and spearheading an agenda for action that builds a well-motivated and skilled workforce that can, in turn, provide good quality services and interventions reflecting the diverse needs of users and carers.

Traditionally, the legislative and policy framework has focused on gender, race and to a lesser extent disability. However, during 2006 legislation and regulations were introduced to specifically address discrimination on the grounds of religion, age and sexual orientation in employment. The former potentially has far-reaching implications in terms of the age structure of the social care workforce and recruitment and retention policies.

Whether sexuality, age, disability, religion, race or gender-related discrimination and good practice is being addressed, leaders and managers have a central role to play in terms of modelling good practice through their own work and ensuring that diversity-related issues are interwoven into the learning and development of all staff. Now more than ever, as social care faces massive changes in the profile of its users and carers and the workforce confronts changes in its demographic profile, the ability to proactively tackle and embrace the diversity challenge becomes much more central to the task of supporting learning and development (Equal Opportunities Commission, 2003; Owen, 2003).

FUTURE OF SOCIAL CARE WORKFORCE

For leaders and managers in social care, diversity has to be managed and promoted alongside a background of developing a workforce 'fit for purpose' (Department of Health, 2000, 2001a). As we saw in Chapter 1, this means combining policy objectives with an assessment of the future direction of service delivery, forthcoming expectations and needs of users and carers, the skill mix of current and future workforce, technological advancements and wider environmental influences. Strategies to meet the social care needs of the population and deal with inequalities have to be deeply interwoven with mechanisms for addressing workforce developments. There are some real challenges in social care associated with difficulties in recruitment, retention and skills improvement (Ward, 2004; Skills for Care, 2005a).

Leaders and managers are going to have deal with an increasingly diverse workforce both at entry level and in terms of continuing professional development. In addition, the imperative to improve the skill base and level of qualified workers has led to an increase in the levels of participation on qualifying and post-qualification courses. Inevitably, the widening access to social work education and employment has meant that the need to address diversity has gained considerable momentum. Before considering the implications for learning and development of an increasingly diverse social care student and workforce population, it is useful to look at some of the key characteristics of the social care workforce.

WOMEN AND SOCIAL CARE WORKFORCE

The Skills for Care report *The State of the Social Care Workforce* (2005a: 2) highlights that:

> 80%+ are female, increasing to 95%+ in certain sectors such as residential, domiciliary and early years childcare. The workforce includes people of all ages, but especially 35–49 year olds who account for approximately 40% of the total.

A growing number of women in the workforce are likely to be carers for parents and relatives who are ageing as well as having primary responsibility for their children. A combination of lifestyle and career histories means that the proportions of women in frontline or first-tier management are substantially higher than those in senior management or leadership roles. Equally, there are a larger proportion of women concentrated in the areas where workers are least likely to have a professional qualification (particularly residential, domiciliary or early years childcare).

BLACK AND MINORITY ETHNIC EMPLOYEES AND SOCIAL CARE WORKFORCE

Black and minority ethnic employees are in the least well paid segments of the social care workforce (Kenny and Field, 2003). Proportionately, they are in larger numbers in residential and domiciliary care where access to training and support tends to be more limited. The number of black and minority ethnic staff among the qualified and post-qualified workforce becomes smaller as the level of seniority increases. Black and minority ethnic workers constitute a vital component of a workforce where there are considerable difficulties with recruitment and retention, and pay levels compared to other public and independent sector are low. Recruitment from overseas has been one of the approaches taken to fill vacancies among qualified workers. The GSCC's International Recognition Service in 2003 (now superseded by social worker registration) issued over 2,500 Letters of Verification to social workers qualified overseas, to allow them to work in the UK.

Research suggests that black and minority ethnic managers receive less supervisory support, training and development opportunities and good quality feedback than other managers (Holmes and Robinson, 1999; Improvement and Development Agency, 2004). Black and minority ethnic managers are more likely to miss career progression and development opportunities. Although the comparatively early adoption of equal opportunities policies and ethnic monitoring and record keeping in social services departments and the comparatively high proportion of certain black and minority ethnic groups within the workforce can be viewed from some perspectives as showing a degree of success (Butt et al., 1991; Smyth, 1996), social care workers from black and minority ethnic groups still experience racism from both users and colleagues (Moriarty, 2004). These incidents varied in frequency and type, but a study done by Butt and Davey in 1997 shows that undermining participants' professional competence is one form of racism in social care and that many staff had little faith in the ability of their managers and employers to take action to protect them from tackling racism in the workplace.

DISABILITY, SEXUALITY AND THE SOCIAL CARE WORKFORCE

The evidence base in relation to workforce issues for disabled people and lesbian, gay or bisexual people is very scant. The National Institute of Social Work workforce studies are one of the few studies in which the experiences of gay and lesbian workers can be compared with heterosexual staff. The proportion of staff able to be open about their sexuality varied considerably by employer, and it seems likely that having to conceal their sexuality contributed to a sense of isolation for gay and lesbian workers (Moriarty, 2004). Compared with other staff, gay and lesbian employees are more likely to have experienced verbal and physical abuse, to feel that they had been discriminated against, and to have less sense of involvement in the organization (McLean, 1998, cited in Moriarty, 2004). At the time of writing, the Disability Rights

Commission is investigating the health criteria laid down in the General Social Care Council's registration requirements for Registered Social Workers (GSCC, 2006). However, it is important to remember not all disabled people will have problems. Equally, not all disabled employees will be users of social care services. Disability and being a user are not synonymous with each other although there may be times when the two overlap.

In terms of tackling discrimination on the grounds of sexual orientation, the difficulties in addressing workforce issues can be potentially the most problematical area in terms of promoting diversity. On the whole, work and learning environments do not create a culture where issues around sexuality are openly acknowledged or addressed. Organizational cultures and working practices tend not to facilitate a dialogue about sexuality and the potential impact or influence this may have on people's professional practice. Indeed, it is paradoxical that given the nature of social care, sexuality *per se* is often brushed under the carpet or is the poor relation in terms of tackling inequality. Only when sexuality as a broader issue in social care practice and workforce development is openly addressed will it be possible for staff who are lesbian, gay or bisexual to feel more comfortable about being open about their sexuality and the barriers that they encounter.

BOX 5.2   REFLECTION BREAK

How diverse is your work or team? How do you think difference within your group affects the way you learn or practice? If you are a member of a marginalized group on the grounds of race, religion, gender, disability, sexuality or age (or a combination of these), how do you think this affects your professional development and career prospects?

AN OVERVIEW OF CAREER BARRIERS IN SOCIAL CARE WORKFORCE

It is not my intention to discuss the career obstacles faced by marginalized groups in detail here, as there is an extensive body of evidence highlighting the types of barrier women and black and minority ethnic employees face (Annelies et al., 2002; Audit Commission, 2002b; Singh, 2002; Harlow, 2004; Improvement and Development Agency, 2004). Nevertheless, it is worth summarizing that power differentials, stereotyping, tokenism, informal and hidden promotion processes, reliance on informal networks, different values and management styles, failure to manage poor performance, lack of appropriate support, the proverbial 'glass ceiling' and ghettoizing are all factors that serve to undermine the career prospects of women, black and minority ethnic employees and other marginalized groups of employees in the social care arena.

While there is no standard prescription for managing diversity, it is crucial that current management profiles are not cloned (predominately white, male, non-disabled and heterosexual) as this is unlikely to provide the type of management and leadership that will lead to the delivery of appropriate and effective social care interventions and services (Singh, 2002: 3).

DIVERSITY AND EQUALITY

Leaders and managers have to create a climate within social care to encourage and advance diversity initiatives and facilitate organizational and cultural change through promoting learning from internal and external evidence-based good practice (Singh, 2002). In order to facilitate this learning and support the necessary change, it is important to start with an understanding of the distinction between equality and diversity. Equalities policies emerged during the late 1970s and 1980s to tackle discrimination and oppression. They have sometimes been construed as everything and everyone being treated equally. However, the intention was to ensure discriminatory practices that may favour one group or another were ruled out. The philosophy behind equal opportunities policies was underpinned by a recognition of the specific experiences of discrimination and oppression and the need to minimize the impact of policies and procedures that discriminate (directly or indirectly) against particular groups. Diversity has become common currency in public discourse over the last few years. Butt (2006: ii) defines diversity to mean 'taking account of the complexities of the lives of individuals and of groups of people, and the impact of these complexities on their experience of discrimination and disadvantage'. Such a definition avoids seeing staff, users and carers in relation to single equality groups, according to their gender, race, disability, age, sexuality and so on. The strength of this definition rests with the fact that simultaneous or compound discrimination and oppression can easily be accommodated and addressed. Nevertheless, critics argue that by promulgating the idea that all types of difference and inequality come under one roof, there is a danger that it waters down or diverts attention away from the specifics of the distinct types of inequality and what is required to tackle them. Moreover, the term 'diversity' (although often used interchangeably with 'race' 'equality', 'sex equality' and 'disability equality') fails to convey what has to be challenged and what needs to be achieved in the way that 'anti-racism', 'disability equality', 'gender equality', 'heterosexism' and 'race equality', among others, make explicit. The shift away from naming the specifics of the different inequalities people encounter to a more integral and diversity-based stance is reflected in the government's move to establish one single commission for equality and human rights entitled the Commission for Equality and Human Rights (CEHR). Ensuring that the different strands of equality and anti-discrimination frameworks (age, race, sexual orientation, disability and gender) are addressed within broader-based diversity approaches requires careful attention so that the specific experiences, concerns and requirements emerging from the different forms of oppression are not diluted or overlooked.

THEORETICAL MODELS INFLUENCING DIVERSITY MANAGEMENT

Diversity management has evolved from the influence of a number of different theoretical approaches. Without going into great depth, it is useful to briefly consider some of the key influences (by no means an exhaustive list) that have contributed to the development of diversity management at the time of writing. These can be summarized as follows:

- Awareness and consciousness-raising frameworks promoted the notion that initiatives like disability awareness, race awareness and multiculturalism (so that people understood other cultures, lifestyles and experiences of discrimination) were key to accepting people from diverse communities. The limitation of awareness and consciousness-raising approaches was that they may make people understand discriminatory behaviour and attitudes but this did not necessarily lead to a change in their actions or behaviour.
- The equality and equal opportunities model built on the idea that simply being aware of others people's cultures, lifestyles and experience of discrimination were not enough. Therefore, policy and legal frameworks were introduced to combat discriminatory policies and practices.
- The 'difference' model identifies the unfair treatment dealt to some groups, such as lesbian, gay or bisexual people, disabled people or older people, and designs interventions based on valuing and utilizing their differences. This is the model that drives the business case because it is believed that there is likely to be better decision making, more creative and better use of employees' potential if investment is made in a wider pool of staff.
- The 'capabilities' model works from the premise that everyone has the right to achieve their aspirations based on human rights entitlements and the freedom to choose the life they wish to pursue. The emphasis is very much on the capability of every individual to

achieve their goals. Arguably, this is not dissimilar to the much heralded 'American dream', where, theoretically, with enough hard work and commitment every American can attain their aspirations. The need to tackle discriminatory policies and practices is not a feature of this approach as it is individual effort and capability that determines one's destiny.

The affirmative or positive action model tends to be mistakenly associated with the idea of positive discrimination. The latter is illegal. Therefore, an employer cannot try to change the balance of the workforce by selecting someone because they are from a particular racial group, although it is lawful to put statements of encouragement on advertisements where certain groups are under-represented in the workforce. However, employers and others can take positive action to prevent discrimination. Where, over the previous 12 months, no one from a particular racial group, or only very few people from that racial group, have been doing a certain type of work or are concentrated in certain grades in the organization, then it is lawful to offer training only for people from that group or to encourage people from that group to apply. For example, management courses targeted at black and minority ethnic staff or women are permissible as positive action if used for training purposes and for tackling discrimination that prevents certain groups from reaching leadership and management positions (see Box 5.3) (Singh, 2002).

BOX 5.3   POSITIVE ACTION TO PROMOTE SUCCESSION PLANNING – A GOOD PRACTICE EXAMPLE

An 'aspiring managers' programme was offered by a local authority social services department to develop the management potential of staff from black and minority ethnic and other disadvantaged backgrounds within the existing workforce. Using positive action within the context of local strategic equality initiatives, staff were sponsored on to a specially commissioned in-house Certificate in Management in Health and Social Care. A scheme of work-based learning and a management mentoring programme provided practical support to develop participants' management experiences and skills. Within six months of completing the 'aspiring managers' programme, eight (out of 19) succeeded in gaining first-line management positions. The use of

---

(Continued)

mentoring and the direct involvement of participants' line managers in delivering specialist areas of the curriculum contributed to the quality of support, success and ownership of this positive action initiative (Hafford-Letchfield and Chick, 2006b).

Equality scheme model – The Race Relations (Amendment) Act 2002 places a statutory duty on all public bodies to: eliminate unlawful racial discrimination; promote equal opportunities; and promote good relations between people from different racial groups. The strength of the race equality schemes lies in the fact there is a duty to do equality impact assessments. More recently, the Disability Discrimination Act 1995 introduced in 2006 the Disability Equality Duty for public sector bodies. The legal duty provides a framework for achieving partnership between disabled people and public authorities to produce better services and more inclusive environments and communities. It requires public authorities to proactively look at ways of ensuring disabled people are treated equally rather than as a special add-on (Disability Rights Commission, 2006).

BOX 5.4   PROMOTING DISABILITY EQUALITY IN RECRUITMENT – A GOOD PRACTICE EXAMPLE

A national social care organization reviewed its recruitment monitoring statistics and noted that disabled people were not only under-represented within the workforce, but also that they were not getting through to interview stage. The recruitment paperwork was adapted to be more user-friendly and an independent employment advice service was contracted to support prospective disabled applicants through the recruitment process. The telephone number of the advice service was included in job advertisements. In addition, a guaranteed interview scheme was introduced to ensure disabled applicants who met the essential criteria were guaranteed an interview.

Learning model – As the name suggests this approach is constructed on the notion that individuals and organizations have to recognize that diversity is a multifaceted social construction. This is a complex phenomenon which sees people 'not in terms of what they look like, or where they come from but through incorporating their different, important and competitively relevant knowledge and perspectives about how to actually do the work, which is learnt from the experience of being members of different groups' (Lorbiecki, 2001: 346).

An alternative way of understanding the evolution of changing views on diversity management is to reflect on the shift from a resistance- or assimilation-based approach. This acknowledges discrimination and fairness (underpinned by equal opportunities philosophies). It addresses access and legitimacy through acknowledging difference and creating cultures where differences are valued (diversity model). Finally, the evolution of a 'learning and effectiveness model', where the focus on diversity is strategically linked to the activities and systems in an organization to diversify the actual work rather than concentrating on diversifying the workforce which may or may not meet organizational objectives (Dass and Parker, 1999; Lorbiecki, 2001).

PROMOTING DIVERSITY THROUGH LEARNING

> Practitioners need structured assistance to explore social identities and their construction to produce the knowledge and awareness that will prepare them for exposure to and engagement with others … the learning process must include emotional, cognitive, behavioural and spiritual dimensions. (Comerford, 2005: 133).

Leaders and managers have a key role to play in exploring and creating models of working where everyone in the delivery of social care is party to understanding both the problem and finding the solutions to addressing exclusion, oppression and diversity. Therefore, Comerford's definition of learning seems particularly apt, as she describes it as a 'mutual exploration process in which all on the journey are identified' (2005: 133).

The learning model proposed by Comerford (2005) has much to offer in terms of enabling practitioners to understand how difference and diversity are constructed and responded to through a process of active engagement with each other and with those that are different from them. Yet to capitalize on this it is important to acknowledge at the outset that in the same way as there is no standard or universal experience of discrimination or oppression even within certain groups (i.e. the experiences of a working-class lesbian are likely to be different from those from middle-class backgrounds), there is equally no singular approach to learning. To facilitate learning through mutual engagement there needs to be some recognition that learning styles may vary depending on gender, race or other experience of social exclusion.

LEARNING DIFFERENTIALS

It is generally accepted that there are gender differences in the way men and women learn. Women tend to acquire knowledge and understanding by going through different stages. According to Singh (2002: 20):

> Men tend to learn by applying analytical rules, logic and models to facts given to them by the teacher. In contrast, women often prefer to learn by reflecting on their own experiences, identifying often vicariously with others involved in the issue, applying their experience and then developing their own model with a deeper and wider understanding than the purely analytical.

Black and minority ethnic people's preferred mode of learning will depend very much on the context and circumstances that are brought to the table. For many learners from non-traditional backgrounds, particularly black students, the educational system has not been a place with many positives (Cropper, 2000; Johnson-Bailey, 2004). Also, the preferred learning style is likely to be dependent upon personality traits, experience of discrimination and the degree of comfort, trust and safety within the learning environment. Motivation to succeed and seek further educational experiences in adult life, particularly for mature students, can be determined by a variety of factors, including teacher, peer support, cultural values, and financial and family pressures, (Calder, 1993).

In light of differences in preferred learning styles, leaders and managers need to adopt a role which embraces individual and collective variations in learning and acknowledges the role of the learning environment. It is also important to ensure that learning occurs at both an individual and organizational levels, where employees experience the psychological benefits of feeling valued and are able to undertake interesting and challenging work (SCIE, 2004).

EXPERIENTIAL LEARNING AND ENGAGEMENT

It is important to recognize that learning is a complex, ongoing and evolving process that needs to be broadly defined. In Chapter 2 we considered what constitutes a learning organization. Gould (2000) points out that the learning process is pervasive and occurs at multiple levels within an organization. Leaders and managers who provide a shared understanding of the skills and competencies necessary can make staff equal partners in the formulation and implementation of diversity (and other) strategies.

To be able to use learning as a tool for addressing diversity across organizations and among individuals it is useful to consider Kolb's (1984) learning theory. This is by no means the only theoretical framework that is applicable, and the work of other theorists such as hooks (1994), Pepper (1942) and Rorty (1989) are also useful in providing a contextual framework. Nevertheless, the experiential component of Kolb's analysis provides a good springboard for opening up a framework that can be used to interweave good practice in relation to diversity within a learning culture.

Kolb (1984) proposes a learning framework where emotion and experiential learning are key ingredients for facilitating learning and development. Learning is contextual and shaped by a mediated understanding of the past and direct in the 'here and now' experience. Kolb defines learning as 'the process whereby knowledge is created through the transformation of experience' (1984: 38). The fact that cognitive and emotional dimensions are central to the learning process means that such a framework is particularly well suited to facilitating learning around diversity.

Arguably, a learning model that relies upon understanding and knowledge based on experiential encounters can be limited because it does not engage people sufficiently in the learning process. Indeed, there can be over-reliance on drawing knowledge and skill development primarily on the experiences of individuals who are members of socially excluded groups. Comerford (2005) draws a distinction of engaging with human diversity through learning and learning through engagement. The latter is much more effective for sustaining a long-term ability to bring about attitudinal and behavioural change in terms of diversity. Its strength lies in the fact that it sets diversity within an approach that is ongoing, socially constructed, acknowledges the context and importance of relationships and interactions between those involved.

Comerford puts forward a learning paradigm that stresses a model that 'finds life and meaning through group processes in which social structures and processes are interrogated using individual and group processes' (2005: 119). To capitalize on Comerford's learning model there has to be a combination of 'exposure, engagement, emotion, empathy, narrative, personal disposition, the learning environment and sense of self in relation to others' (2005: 113).

For social care practitioners, learning through engagement can occur through reflective journals, learning sets, team meetings, conferences, workshops, one-to-one supervision, reading and discussing literature, journal clubs, case reviews, formal or informal training sessions, guest presentations and material generated by the group. Comerford argues that learning about diversity is encouraged by such groups which provide a forum where unconscious appreciation for resilience and the resourcefulness of those disadvantaged by social structures can be valued (2005: 119).

Reframing an understanding of diversity and the strategies and actions necessary to promote it within a conceptual framework that emphasizes learning through engagement is very attractive, as it does not place responsibility on the shoulders of particular individuals or teams. Instead, diversity is a dynamic, live and ongoing matter, with which everyone is engaged, and is central to professional and organizational development. Nevertheless, it is important to remember that learning through engagement is a tool and not a panacea. Indeed, critics would argue that unless the learning process includes addressing the social and political contradictions that practitioners face, then it will be of limited value and possibly somewhat naïve (Lorbiecki, 2001). Also, within the context of social care, a careful balance needs to be reached in terms of concentrating on the emotional dimensions of practice and the focus on methods, skills and tasks (Lefevre, 2005). Inevitably, the relationship between group or team members, individuals and those in leadership or management roles is central to the process of learning and improving practice in relation to diversity.

APPLYING A LEARNING PERSPECTIVE WITHIN A WHOLE SYSTEMS APPROACH

In the same way as it was argued in Chapter 4 that to embed user participation within an organization a whole systems approach is required, it can be similarly argued that to effectively promote diversity it is essential to apply learning through engagement across the four interacting dimensions of culture, structure, practice and review. Therefore, each of these components will be considered in terms of how learning through engagement might be applied.

CULTURE

Leaders and managers have a key role to play in creating an environment where diversity is not viewed as something to be dealt with by certain individuals or groups of staff. Equally, it is important that leaders and managers create an ethos of staff engaging with each other so that there is an openness and readiness to learn about diversity and the implications for the work environment through discussion, debate, inquiry and reflection. As part of this process, leaders and managers must be prepared to demonstrate that they are willing and able to engage with and learn from the staff they work with as well as through learning from their peers, users and carers and other stakeholders. One of the main challenges for leaders and managers will be to create a culture where they are able to take responsibility for decision making, providing strategic direction and the impetus for change in terms of diversity. This should be done without stifling debate and a process of learning in the course of questioning, observing and engaging with each other and with others. A recurring problem in terms of promoting diversity is there being a culture of fear, intimidation, embarrassment and unease about addressing diversity because there is some form of prevailing notions that if one shows signs of uncertainty or lack of knowledge, then they will be perceived as 'politically incorrect' or homophobic, racist, sexist or whatever.

STRUCTURE

Embedding diversity into the structure of an organization using a framework of learning through engagement requires leaders and managers to set in place systems and processes which encourage interaction between and across different groups and teams of staff. For example, this might mean establishing structures such as learning sets and other forums where practitioners can engage with each other for mutual benefit and learning. Alternatively, it may be appropriate to arrange for regular meetings between staff at various levels of an organization and those in leadership and management roles to explore how particular strategic issues relating to promoting diversity can be progressed. The advantages of such systems are that leaders and managers can learn from different groups of staff how policies can be put in practice and what sort of difficulties or opportunities may arise.

Allocating human, financial and technological resources to support the development and implementation of diversity work is central to ensuring the effective achievement of progress and change. Therefore leaders and managers need to engage with staff to be able to put in place the necessary infrastructures required to promote diversity. This means they have to be prepared to learn through working alongside staff to identify what resources are required and how they should be employed to support the implementation of diversity policies and procedures. It is important that dialogues about delivering effective diversity work should start during the policy formulation stages rather than be presented as a *fait accompli*.

For some leaders and managers, a significant structural issue that will have to be addressed is whether diversity work should have targeted specific resources or be integrated into the mainstream business of the organization. The decision will be dependent upon a number of different variables. However, in many cases, there will need to be a combination of specific and mainstream activity. Whatever the balance of the work might be, leaders and managers should actively involve staff in exploring and learning from each other the merits of different approaches. In the process of engaging with staff to promote diversity, leaders and managers should remain alert to picking up any resistance or attempts to potentially sabotage the implementation of diversity work. Leaders and managers should be able to explore group dynamics and any barriers presented through engaging staff in a process of learning. This can encourage staff to reflect upon what is happening and to use their knowledge and skills to solve problems and identify new opportunities.

PRACTICE

Learning through engagement can be promoted in a myriad of ways. Reflecting upon and engaging with others to explore the experience and issues emerging from direct work with users and carers is an invaluable tool for social care professionals to address diversity and improve anti-discriminatory practice. Leaders and managers have a role to play in ensuring that there is a range of one-to-one and group-based forums to facilitate learning through engagement in relation to diversity and anti-discriminatory practice.

An essential aspect of promoting learning through engagement is the commitment and ability of leaders and managers to be part of the process and learn alongside their staff and peers rather than expecting others to change their practice and remaining aloof. This means leaders and managers must be open to exploring with their peers and other staff (where appropriate) the content of their own professional practice as well as being able to engage with their staff in promoting diversity and anti-discriminatory practice. Indeed, the ability to lead by example and model good practice in promoting diversity has to be one of the qualities that leaders and managers must be able to demonstrate. This means being prepared to have one's work open to scrutiny and a willingness to make changes based on both the learning acquired through interacting with others and drawing upon the contribution and expertise of staff working at various levels within an organization.

REVIEW

One of the areas often overlooked by leaders and managers in promoting diversity is that of actively engaging staff in using evidence generated from monitoring and evaluation to improve future practice. It is important that leaders and managers support staff not only in collecting and monitoring information or being part of evaluation exercises, but they must also be part of the process of trying to understand the implications of what the data reveals. For example, leaders and managers ought to involve staff who are routinely engaged in collecting ethnic monitoring data to use the collated figures as a basis for learning through engagement by enabling staff to explore the implications for their professional practice and consider how improvements can be made. Similarly, if leaders and managers encourage staff to contribute to the evaluation of changes in policy and procedures or new initiatives by drawing upon their knowledge and expertise, then there is a greater chance not only that will changes be better informed but also that there will be a greater degree of cooperation in implementing any recommendations.

CHAPTER SUMMARY

In light of the fact that the learning through engagement paradigm and diversity are complex evolving phenomena, it is important to recognize that leaders and managers need to draw on a portfolio of approaches which can be tailored to the requirements of the individual or organization. There are some quite specific strategies and actions devised for offering leadership and management around diversity (i.e. positive action programmes, gender-friendly working policies and specific employee support groups for lesbian, gay or bisexual workers) which are valuable and valid. However, these need to be utilized as part of an armory of approaches within a whole systems framework. Leaders and managers have a pivotal role to play in ensuring that learning through engagement is integrated in a variety of ways within the culture, structure, practice and review mechanisms of an organization.

Careful and specific attention has to be paid to the pros and cons of the repertoire of diversity promotion strategies and actions that are available. Whatever approach is adopted for tackling exclusion and diversity, there has to be dialogue, debate and review mechanisms so that all those engaged with the approach and others are able to continuously improve their practice and professional development through a mutual process of learning through engagement.

Recommended further reading

J. Butt (2006) 'Are we there yet?' Identifying the characteristics of social care organisations that successfully promote diversity. In J. Butt, B. Patel and O. Stuart (eds), *Race Equality Discussion*

(Continued)

Papers (London: Social Care Institute for Excellence. Available in print and online from www.scie.org.uk). This discussion paper considers the steps needed and evidence base for promoting diversity effectively in social care organizations and addresses the overall response to diversity in all its complexity.

J. Fish (2006) *Heterosexism in Health and Social Care* (Basingstoke: Palgrave Macmillan) develops a theory of heterosexism to conceptualize LGBT oppression and provides examples from everyday health and social care environments.

Journal of Learning in Health and Social Care is an international journal that contributes to the growth of knowledge about approaches to the facilitation of individual, team and organizational learning in a variety of professional environments and provides research-based evidence on key learning issues in relation to diversity.

Web-based resources

Higher Education Funding Council for England (www.hefce.org.uk) – provides advice and guidance on good practice for promoting diversity in higher education which can also be relevant for and transferable to other institutional settings. Particularly recommended is J. Powney (ed.) (2002) *Successful Student Diversity: Case Studies of Practice in Learning and Teaching and Widening Participation* (Glasgow: University of Glasgow, The Scottish Council for Research in Education).

6 ASSESSING AND CREATING OPPORTUNITIES FOR LEARNING

This chapter explores:

- The manager's role in helping others to link personal and professional motivations to learn and develop themselves
- The use of supervision and appraisal to support staff effectiveness at work
- Dealing with difficult issues and the role of learning and development in managing poor performance

---

INTRODUCTION

So far within this book we have been mapping out the demands for learning, education and staff development in social care within its social, economic and policy context as well as examining the imperatives for learning linked to organizational change. Against this backdrop, the demands for professional knowledge, skill and expertise have never been greater and the requirement for managers and practitioners to have deep and critical knowledge and expertise in their field is self-evident. We have already established that actively helping staff to get better at their jobs is an important aspect of the work of managers and one of the most cited features of effective managers is the way in which they allocate their time to this and how well they review the performance of their staff (Martin, 2003). Line managers have also been cited by practitioners as the most important source of personal support to them, yet many managers express a lack of confidence in this area and describe their role predominantly in terms of directing staff instead to other resources (Buxton et al., 1998). Staff development is not just an episodic task but should be reinforced through the support and encouragement and feedback given day to day in the practice environment.

Active staff development requires skilful and thorough scrutiny of how the worker is currently performing against criteria set for each expected outcome of social care services. This should be done in a way that links management and practice, which can so easily become polarized into opposite and competing positions. The opportunity for both parties to question and to discuss practice openly and honestly should culminate in an agreement about any gaps that exist in a member of staff's knowledge and skills, followed by regular and joint examination of the range of possible actions and changes that could be undertaken by both parties to address and progress towards closing the gaps identified. This usually takes the form of an agreed personal learning and development plan which specifies the way in which staff members' development can be implemented, reviewed and evaluated. These processes may already be familiar to many of you in your role as managers and staff developers in social care, and are reflected in traditional activities such as training needs analysis, supervision, performance appraisal and personal development planning. In this chapter, we are going to look at aspects of these activities that can increase your effectiveness and leadership in learning. We will begin by looking at some of the prerequisites for staff development, for example how you might go about assessing learning needs in your service area, and the use of supervision and performance appraisal to draw up individual learning plans for staff. We will then give an overview of formal and informal learning strategies that can be developed to implement these. We will conclude this chapter by looking at some of the specific challenges presented by staff where agreement about their performance and learning needs is not so straightforward or can become disputed.

ASSESSING LEARNING NEEDS AND DEVELOPING LEARNING STRATEGIES

The diagnosis of learning needs is a process of information gathering and analysis. A common method used to identify the knowledge, skills and abilities of the individual or team is via supervision or the performance appraisal process, but how much of this process has *maintenance* elements and how much has *developmental* elements is often questioned (Leat et al., 1997). The performance appraisal process is being increasingly utilized for reviewing employees' past efforts and for setting new performance objectives. At the same time, this process is employed to assess current training and developmental needs, and consequently challenges how effective the appraisal process can be as a realistic or accurate determinant of future developmental needs. We will look at the actual process of appraisal later on, but will continue here to look at the three levels in which you might be involved in contributing to or undertaking learning needs analysis. These can be undertaken at the individual, organizational and partnership level (see Table 6.1).

ASSESSING INDIVIDUAL TRAINING NEEDS

At an individual level, staff must play an active part in their own training and development:

> As a social care worker, you must be accountable for the quality of your work and take responsibility for maintaining and improving your knowledge and skills. This includes meeting relevant standards of practice and working in a lawful, safe and effective way. (GSCC, 2002: para 6)

Early identification of an individual's learning needs begins at recruitment and selection followed by rigorous induction. Induction is the process which helps new members of staff settle into the organization and their new job, but established staff also need an induction to any new roles they take on. This is more than preparing and handing new staff an induction pack and inviting them to read it. It should include the staff members' first experiences of learning and development, where managers and other staff can help them to match the skills and abilities they bring to the post from their past experiences and to identify what support will be needed to meet the requirements of the new job. Managers should be able to discuss with staff the expected competence and accountability level of their new post and how continuous professional development (CPD) can help them reach this. Induction also signposts to staff in new roles the level of support they can expect, such as supervision, team and peer support and how these will help them integrate into the organization by keeping them informed and supported. Coaching and mentoring can provide useful tools in the induction period by using more informal development tools. Research evidence shows that organizations providing effective induction for staff are more likely to retain them for a longer period than organizations that do not (Audit Commission, 2002a). At an economic level any improvement in an organization's ability to retain staff will be reflected in the saving of expensive resources if further recruitment is required.

Looking at an individual's job description is a good place to start and a well-written job description sets out the skills, knowledge and competencies needed to carry out a role. In terms of professional development, managers provide a personal point of contact for staff within the organization and mediate between the requirements of individuals and

Table 6.1 Analysing staff development needs at different levels

Level of development required	Individual	Organizational	Partnership
Implementing and doing things well	Staff competent at the level of existing requirements • Achieved national qualification • Satisfying service user/carers' needs • Participating in regular supervision and appraisal	The organization is meeting its current objectives • Minimum standards being met, for example using the national minimum standards	Working together to achieve existing standards • Structures, policies and procedures in place for interprofessional learning
Improving and doing things better	Staff using evidence systematically to improve in skills, knowledge and practice • Staff have opportunities to monitor and evaluate their own personal learning and progress towards development targets	Setting higher objectives and reaching them • Evidence of research-informed practice • Using benchmarking or setting and devising local standards to meet local needs • Innovative approaches to supervision such as group/team supervision	Continuous improvement in team working, systems and processes • Setting learning objectives outside the national minimum standards • Sharing a set of skills, knowledge and behaviours for staff working together • Consulting services users/carers on practice developments
Innovating and doing new and better things	Developing new and creative ways of working, with a shared sense of purpose • Taking a leadership role in developing others • Disseminating and promoting evidence-based practice • Diversity of staff involved in leading practice	Changing objectives and strategies and achieving excellence • Strategies in place to support succession planning • Accreditation and awards for excellence • Participation of service users/carers in assessment	Creation of strategic learning partnerships involving managers, commissioners, providers of learning and service users/carers. Working across boundaries to create new relationships and new services • Innovative practice across professionals • Active 'community of practice' • Leadership from service users and carers in learning

those of others in the work group or team (Peel, 2003). Professional development can be defined as meeting one's professional responsibilities at various points throughout their career as well as harmonizing these with the needs of the organization and service development. This suggests that the professional development of an individual also has a wider function and is influenced through the changes to the professional landscape, such as those we identified in Chapters 1, 3 and 5. As we will see later on, this is where it is important to clarify the role of supervision and appraisal, and to work as an advisor, arbiter as well as an educator in this respect.

ORGANIZATIONAL FRAMEWORKS

At the organizational level, a framework is required to assess and support staff learning and development and should describe each person's role and responsibility within it. Such a framework would ideally contain the following:

- A set of aims, objectives and principles stating what the organization is trying to achieve modelled in the context of the national and local context for social care.
- A statement about how staff can access learning and development that is firmly based on equality and equity and recognizes diversity in the approaches adopted, including the appropriate use of positive action.
- A code of practice that different groups of staff will need to abide by and which integrates the GSCC *Code of Practice* (2002) for social care and other professional codes where appropriate.
- A model for implementing learning and development with opportunities to 'step-on' or 'step-off' or to transfer skills and knowledge to different areas of practice using a 'skills escalator' approach (Department of Health, 2002b).
- Clear policies and procedures supported by accessible documentation and training which facilitates development planning, for example induction, supervision, appraisal systems and succession planning.
- The standards and objectives that the organization strives to meet and a transparent and agreed method against which staff learning and development will be benchmarked. This should include best practice and not just the minimum standards.
- Access to learning from a range of sources, such as formal structured accredited learning, in-house formal training, resources to support self-directed learning, experiential learning through job swaps, acting up, project work and other direct workplace experiences.

- Support systems for work-based learning, including mentoring, coaching and assessment.
- Clearly defined outcomes for individual and organizational learning that are focused on achievements and reflect learning in terms of the impact and benefits for the users of the service.
- Guidance and processes for registration and re-registration with the appropriate regulatory or professional bodies.
- Monitoring and evaluation of staff development systems and processes which inform a review of the framework overall.
- Celebration of staff achievements and accreditation schemes which recognize excellence in learning and practice.

In considering the learning needs of your team or service, you will need to keep your own personal and professional knowledge up to date, particularly around relevant legislative and policy frameworks and in keeping in touch with the profile and issues of the community being served. This can help to establish what skills, knowledge and behaviours are needed for development and to build on any strength in these areas. Learning opportunities should be based on developing individuals' practice throughout their career in a way that encourages transferability between different organizations and uses a common language or systems that can be understood by all stakeholders. Learning opportunities also need to be flexible enough to relate to work but provide wider opportunities to help prepare people for new roles or their next job. Finally, as we saw in the previous chapter, any learning and development framework should build on creativity, encourage diversity and enable people to contribute and influence practice knowledge and development.

ESTABLISHING LEARNING NEEDS AT THE PARTNERSHIP LEVEL

At the partnership level, the evolvement of multi-agency services and interdisciplinary teams will lead to establishing new roles for staff and making new connections. Different skills, knowledge and behaviours may assume greater importance as services mature. Some of the challenges are likely to include a much greater knowledge requirement for some staff of different policy and legal frameworks as well as the individual requirements to take on new responsibilities as career paths change over time. It is likely that there will also be more overlap with different professional groups as well as more specialist roles. The transition for a provider-led approach to one where service users and carers are increasingly empowered to be partners in making priorities means taking account of users' and carers' specific learning and development needs so that they can be truly involved. Both individuals receiving direct payments and service user organizations and support workers should be included. Working effectively alongside these stakeholders need to be approached in a holistic and strategic way, including training and learning together. Beresford and Croft (2003) talk about giving support for users' personal development to increase people's confidence, expectations, self-esteem and assertiveness as well as organizational development and training costs to support collective action.

BOX 6.1   REFLECTION BREAK

What national or local drivers are there for learning in your workplace? How do you take a holistic approach that accounts for personal as well as professional needs for staff development? What learning and assessment methods can or do you use to allow and value the development of staff you supervise over time?

MEETING IDENTIFIED LEARNING NEEDS: FORMAL OR INFORMAL LEARNING METHODS?

In Chapter 2 we discussed the concept of 'learning organizations' and learning cultures in social care, and it was acknowledged that the workplace is the optimal setting for learning activities. Research shows that most practitioners build their expertise through learning in and through practice where they polish their skills, hone their professional capacities and hence develop expertise (Cole, 2004: 2). The active encouragement of work-based learning departs from traditional models of how education is undertaken. The capture, measurement and accreditation of learning common to formal education does not easily lend itself to workplace learning. One way of addressing these issues would be to encourage practitioners to maintain a portfolio in which they keep a continuous record of both formal and informal learning. The advantage of keeping a portfolio is the continuous record, analysis and plan for learning which helps individuals gain a better insight into their own capabilities and establish a better perspective of routes to further development (Smith and Tillema, 2001). This can be electronic or stored in a ring binder. The types of evidence or contents within a portfolio might contain a selection of direct work with users or project work to show or portray an individual's skills, knowledge and understandings as well as highlighting their creativity, strengths and abilities. These might include: a certificate or record of any formal learning undertaken; reflections on practice; notes from supervision or appraisal, focusing on particular learning achievements; or verifications from work-based assessment and feedback from users, carers, colleagues or external partners on practice. This is not an exhaustive list but can be used within supervision or appraisals to get an overview of different forms of learning and learning styles.

Kirkpatrick (1967) identified the following factors as conducive to informal learning:

- Sufficient task variation in job, participation in temporary groups, opportunities to consult experts inside and outside the workplace, changes in duties and work roles that stimulate learning (Eraut, 2000).
- Work roles that allow for peripheral participation in communities of practice (Lave and Wenger, 1991) and facilitation of informal communication, problem solving and innovation within such communities (Brown and Duisguid, 1991).
- Structures and incentives for knowledge sharing, job mobility and autonomous jobs (Marsick and Watkins, 1999).

In Chapter 7 we will be looking at the process of assessment of work-based learning and how this can give an insight into a person's level of competence and capabilities to help establish a better perspective of routes to further development. Using methods to capture and record learning that arise out of practice is one of the functions of supervision and performance appraisal, and to acknowledge practice and learning as one and the same thing. Organizational and contextual factors can promote or impede informal learning and those that expose employees to the external environment, with flatter hierarchies and more widely distributed managerial responsibilities and high involvement of employees in service and process development have been found to be more conducive (Kirkpatrick, 1967). Access to learning resources to enable people to cope, give advice and guidance as well as a reward are also important.

FORMAL LEARNING

Formal programmes of study, particularly those that lead to accreditation and qualification, or in-service training courses are both widely recognized as a key mechanism through which employee performance may be either regulated or improved in the workplace. The importance placed on formal training in social care organizations and the money invested in such training raises a fundamental question as to just how effective they actually are. A number of research studies

(Stevenson et al., 1992; Clarke, 2001) have shown that although training programmes can often be found to produce positive results in terms of trainees' reactions to training (i.e. their satisfaction), training in itself may not result in demonstrable changes in either behaviour or performance back in the workplace, and this is often exacerbated by either poorly defined, over-ambitious or particularly diffuse training objectives accompanied by little thought as to how training content and delivery is expected to result in achieving specific outcomes (Clarke, 2001). Stevenson et al. (1992), for example, have suggested that trainees may require a period of time spent practising skills and integrating various content areas into their assessment practice before demonstrable improvements can be identified.

The success of any training may therefore be dependent upon a far more complex interaction of variables than those relating purely to the design of training programmes themselves. The more attention is paid to the diverse mediating variables that determine whether individuals can successfully transfer training to the job (i.e. personality attributes of trainees, training design and work environment), the more it seems that a comprehensive approach to training evaluation is required. Carpenter (2005) has identified four levels of outcomes from formal education (based on the work of Kirkpatrick (1967) and Barr et al. (1999)) that provide a helpful benchmark tool to use with staff when evaluating their learning and helping them to transfer this back into the workplace (see Box 6.2).

BOX 6.2   EVALUATING OUTCOMES FROM EDUCATION AND LEARNING EVENTS

The best known and most widely used classification of educational outcomes was devised by Kirkpatrick (1967). Kirkpatrick's model defined four levels of outcomes and was elaborated by Barr et al. (1999) for a review of interprofessional education in order to include the modification of attitudes and to address the relevance of outcomes to both individuals (service users) and organizations.

Level 1: Learners' reaction – these outcomes relate to the participants' view of their learning experience and satisfaction with the training they received.

Level 2a: Modification in attitudes and perceptions – outcomes here relate to changes in attitudes or perceptions towards service

(Continued)

users and carers, their problems and needs, circumstances, care and treatment.

Level 2b: Acquisition of knowledge and skills – this relates to the concepts, procedures and principles of working with service users and carers. For skills, this relates to the acquisition of thinking/problem solving, assessment and intervention skills.

Level 3: Changes in behaviour – this level covers the implementation of learning from an educational programme in the workplace, prompted by modifications in attitudes or perceptions, or the application of newly acquired knowledge or skills.

Level 4a: Changes in organizational practice – this relates to wider changes in the organization or delivery of care, attributable to an education programme.

Level 4b: Benefits to users and carers – this final level covers any improvements in the well-being and quality of life of people who are using services, and their carers, which may be attributed to an education programme.

Sources: Based on Kirkpatrick (1967) and Barr et al. (1999), cited in Carpenter (2005: 6)

MANAGING LEARNING THROUGH SUPERVISION

Supervision has been a core activity for social work and social care in the last decade, particularly since the focus on public inquiries which have raised its profile largely from a defensive perspective (Morrison, 2002). As a pivotal activity in delivering social care services, supervision is key to achieving quality assurance but has a particular role in developing a skilled and professional workforce. Professional supervision provides a bridge between first-line managers and practitioners. Recognizing the different roles and needs that supervision may be asked to meet is essential for any manager, and the use of contracts and structures for individual supervision are essential to establish the supervisory relationship on a clear and secure footing. Practice suggests that putting high-quality supervision, consultation and support in place helps practitioners to:

- become more self-aware in terms of their approach and evidence base;
- understand their role in assessing and identifying need;
- know how to respond to concerns raised by service users and carers, other practitioners and the community;
- recognize their limitations and when to call on the expertise of others;
- be familiar with current legislation, policy and guidance;
- know how to manage issues when they have concerns about service users and carers;
- understand procedures for making referrals and involving others; and
- be clear about what information to share with whom and when. (Department for Education and Skills, 2005a)

The supervision literature generally identifies four key functions to supervision:

- the **managerial** function, where accountability and performance is scrutinized;
- the **supportive or restorative** function, where staff are given personal support and their well-being is considered;
- the **mediation** function, where managers engage individuals with the organization and its objectives; and
- the **developmental** or **educative** function, which ensures continuing professional development that equips staff to do their job.

As this book is about learning, we are going to focus more on this latter aspect of staff supervision. According to Rogers (2002), the facilitation of significant learning rests upon certain attitudinal qualities that exist in the personal relationship between the facilitator and learner. He cites such qualities as realness or genuineness, prizing, acceptance and trust. When we looked at Kolb's learning cycle in the previous chapter, we noted that further elements that establish a climate for self-initiated, experiential learning include empathic understanding and trust in the capacities of the individual to develop their own potential. The role of the facilitator is to provide the individual or group with the opportunities for choice and self-direction in the learning process. These have also been identified as aspects of emotional intelligence (Goleman, 1998). The giving and receiving of critical constructive feedback has an important place in educational supervision and flourishes in an atmosphere of learning and self-improvement where there is a strong sense of security (Tsui, 2005). Becoming aware of your own style of giving feedback is an art and needs to be practised regularly and based on clear ground rules. Negotiating how and when feedback is given leads to a common understanding about its purpose in supervision and should be agreed in your supervision contract. This highlights the importance of preparation and the opportunity to acknowledge or consider any differences in power, for example what personal or cultural differences may be present when undertaking this activity and whether you are prepared to receive as well as give feedback within your supervisory relationship.

There may also be other motives for giving feedback than to encourage and develop learning, and you should make yourself aware of this as well as considering the consequences of not giving feedback. This will enable you to focus on how welcome feedback will be actually received. For example, before giving feedback to supervisees, always include an opportunity at the beginning of the session for them to express their own views about how they think they have done, as this is a more empowering approach. Giving feedback should occur as soon as possible after the event you are giving feedback about, and attention to creating the right environment for active listening is essential. Similarly, feedback should be as objective and concrete as possible, and based on observed behaviour rather than perceived attitudes. It should use lots of specific statements beginning with 'It was good when you... because...' or 'I didn't find it helpful when you ... because...' (Kadushin and Harkness, 2002: 160–1). This 'keep/change' rule enables the individual to receive affirming statements about themselves as well as issues offered tentatively for consideration and discussion between you both. The individual's personal limits need to be recognized and respected and any feedback given should be tied explicitly to what you think the supervisee can learn. Similarly, don't invite the supervisee to do this and then follow up any self-assessment with your own opposing appraisal as this can be more damaging than helpful (Doel et al., 1996). Tsui (2005) and Doel et al. (1996) remind us that we should review the feedback process to demonstrate positive practice in receiving feedback as well as giving it, and to report on any changes brought about by feedback and how this has influenced the learning achieved and the role of feedback in supervision.

The literature on the developmental stages of supervisors is scant (Tsui, 2005). One reason for the poor image of supervision generally is its lack of integration within a management framework and a lack of culture, expectations, processes and skills within organizations to do this effectively (Audit Commission, 2002a). Training and support for supervisors and supervisees is a vital mechanism needed to integrate supervision within an organizational context. It is also useful to be aware that national minimal standards for all regulated social care services for children and adults have requirements for supervision such as Standard 21 of the Domiciliary Care Standards, Standard 36 of the Care Homes for Older People and Standard 28 for Children's Homes

(McDonnell and Zutshi, 2006a). It is noteworthy that there is a disparity between the detailed attentions given to those practice assessors supervising social work students and the attention given to managers as supervisors. There is also a lack of focus on the issues arising from managing expert and specialist practitioners with more advanced or different skills than the manager. While acknowledging that student supervision is not the same as management of practice, qualified practice assessors can offer a potential body of expertise for the organization to draw on for managing practice.

Having said all that, on a more positive note Hawkins and Smith (2006) offer us some key principles on which to base the design and development of supervision skills programmes. They recommend teaching basic skills and techniques in the most lively way possible, using demonstrations, illustrative stories, engagement and trainees reflecting on experiences from their lives. Supervisory development programmes should start with a focus on self-awareness, using experiential learning processes and teaching theory only when this is underway, combined with practice and reflective evaluation on supervisors' own practice.

Research has described managers as not only the most stressed workers within a social services department, but also the ones who consider themselves to be least well-prepared and supported to do their current job (Balloch et al., 1995). Having identified the complexity of roles within supervision at the beginning of this section, the sub-roles most often include that of teacher, monitor evaluator, counsellor, coach, colleague, boss, expert technician, and manager of administrative relationships (Hawkins and Shohet, 2006). Much of the conflict around the role of supervisor emerges from difficulties in finding an appropriate way of taking authority and handling the power inherent in the role. This can result in games played to either abdicate or manipulate power and is particularly challenging within interprofessional supervisory contexts.

INTERPROFESSIONAL SUPERVISION

The notion of interprofessional supervision was introduced in Chapter 3 and is an important practice and theoretical issue for a number of reasons. As we discussed there, the evolving nature of public services means that it will be commonplace for specialist and generic workers within them to be made up of professionals from different backgrounds and disciplines. Multidisciplinary team work and collaboration have been identified as essential prerequisites for effective provision, functioning and delivery of services, but also as being advantageous to the well-being of team members (Ovretveit, 1993). From the perspective of the service users, interprofessional work can facilitate the bringing together of skills and information that provides continuity in care and the apportionment of clear responsibilities and accountabilities (Townend, 2005). As a manager or supervisor, it enables better coordination to plan resource allocation to deliver expert resources for the benefit of people using services. Interprofessional aspects of supervision creates rich opportunities for learning and practice development, but at times difficulties can occur due to differences of status, values, language, theoretical orientation and approaches to practice, which provide a personal and professional challenge to leaders in this area.

Townend (2005) defined interdisciplinary supervision as two or more workers meeting from different professional groups to achieve a common goal of promoting the well-being of users and carers. This, he said, could be achieved through a process that enables increased knowledge and skills, and an appropriate attitude and values towards maintaining professional competence. In Townend's own research with people working in interdisciplinary teams, he identified the following 'helpers' and 'hindrances' to interprofessional supervision:

Helpers:

- Different perspectives on an issue or situation
- Increased creativity
- Wider knowledge base
- Less likelihood of becoming complacent
- Critical thinking

Hindrances:

- Professional status and differences in training
- Absence of shared theories and language
- Absence of empathy for organizational issues
- Anxiety
- Fear of revealing weaknesses

Townend therefore makes the following recommendations for good practice in supervision:

1. Supervisors and supervisees ensure that they are familiar with each other's professional role, codes of professional conduct and values.
2. Supervisors and supervisees ensure they have enough knowledge about each other's background and training to recognize how previous training experiences are likely to be playing a role in forming assessment, conceptualization and decisions about care.

3. Supervisors and supervisees acknowledge any differences in status and incorporate in their supervision agreement how these will be addressed in supervision.
4. Supervisors and supervisees agree to work to a common theoretical or practice model within supervision or, if not, at least discuss and be aware of both the similarities and differences in preferred ways of working.

In conclusion, whether your supervision relationships within multidisciplinary groups are led, peer or part of a working team, their effectiveness will depend to a large extent on the ability of its members to be aware of, and process, the group dynamics that prevail. Any training for managers to be educators within the supervision or team/group contexts should also be supplemented by regular updates on research and promote a culture of reflection within the profession which will stimulate and promote the desire to know more. We will now turn to this latter, frequently cited skill in social care by looking at the potential of reflection in maximizing learning within the educative supervision function.

CRITICAL REFLECTION

We have already touched upon the concept of critical reflection several times in this book so far. There is an increasing interest in the way that critical reflection may be used as a technique to enhance personal and professional learning by encouraging a change in thinking or to develop a critical edge to an individual's practice. Contemporary contexts, in which social care services operate, highlight the need for staff to be empowered to both identify and solve complex problems as well as to constantly improve performance. Reflective practice may offer a framework through which practice can be critically examined and improved by challenging normal routines and enhancing professional growth and dynamic approaches to problem solving. Reflection in the context of learning is a generic term for those intellectual and affective activities in which individuals engage to explore their experiences in order to lead to new understanding and appreciation (Boud et al., 1985). It is a highly personal process, often triggered by an experience which creates and clarifies meaning in terms of self and which results in a changed conceptual perspective (Boyd and Fales, 1983). There are many key theorists on reflection, writing from different professional backgrounds, but essentially there are several key stages identified in any reflective process as illustrated in Figure 6.1.

The potential for encouraging reflective practice as a tool for learning and developing staff is enormous. Schön (1983) has highlighted the

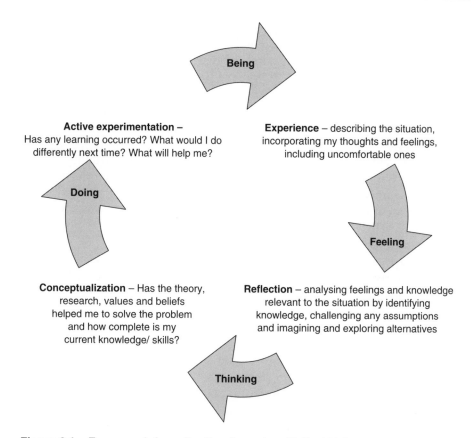

Figure 6.1   Framework for reflection (based on Kolb, 1984)

uncomfortable dissonance which practitioners experience when theory and technique grounded in research does not seem to quite apply to situations they are faced with on the ground or frontline. Building critical reflection into daily practice, supervision and appraisal is one way of addressing this dissonance and can help practitioners to articulate the specific nature of social care as well as to illuminate and access the knowledge and theories that are needed. The concept of reflection, however, has been criticized for not taking account of wider socio-political factors that have a major impact on both process and outcomes (Postle et al., 2002), and it is this tension that managers have to try to balance. There is also the naïve assumption that reflection can be taught and contained to using a checklist approach. Boud and Walker (2002) remind us that the very nature of reflective activities are such that they may lead to serious questioning and critical thinking in which the learner challenges assumptions of managers or the practice context in which they are operating. This can throw up ethical dilemmas related to the practice of experienced professionals and result in learners focusing alternatively on personal distress and oppressive features of the practice environment. If you are working to encourage critically reflective approaches with staff but are then not supportive of at least some of the wider exploration provoked, this can contribute to intolerable tensions between managers and staff. As outlined in the model above, reflection is not solely a cognitive process and emotions are central to all learning. When we discussed diversity and equality in the previous chapter, we recognized the importance of the affective dimensions of learning and for those facilitating in taking responsibility for creating a climate in which the expression of feelings is accepted and legitimate. This is also an important aspect of supervision and team communication.

Having to manage the conflict between demands for learning and busy workplace commitments can easily put staff supervision and development down the bottom of the agenda. Yet it is invidious to place blame with line managers for not releasing or being fully supportive of staff development because this only serves to shift the resolution of conflicts and contradictions between espoused commitments to staff development and actual organizational practice from senior to middle management and, in turn, to frontline staff. This is a well recognized feature of managerialism (Dominelli, 2002) and a lack of visibility and accountability in the very nature of supervision and what it stands for has made it vulnerable to managerialist approaches. We have seen above, however, that the best characteristics of supervision are vital to the management of practice. This includes the understanding that effective practice requires both a sense of disengagement *and* reflection.

USING TEAMWORK TO DEVELOPING EVIDENCE-BASED PRACTICE

We have already referred to the importance of evidence-based practice during our earlier discussion on interprofessional learning. The tentative move within social work and social care towards evidence-based practice highlights some of the issues discussed in earlier chapters about how people in social care learn best. Evidence-based practice or knowing 'what works' in delivering care services successfully is also underpinned by a performance management framework in social care which enshrines the principles of measurement and evaluation of what work is done and how these stand up to scrutiny against any aims or objectives set.

Evidence = research findings + interpretation of the findings (Marsh et al., 2005)

Knowledge = evidence plus practice wisdom and service users' and carers' experiences and wishes (Lewis, 2001, cited by Marsh et al., 2005)

According to Skinner and Whyte (2004), where staff are carrying out individual or group work with service users, this requires setting clear objectives for their work with each service user or group of service users. For managers, this requires setting objectives for each managerial task or project in a way that is explicit and SMART, that is:

- **S**pecific – clear, straightforward and understandable;
- **M**easurable – where progress towards them can be measured;
- **A**chievable – challenging but within reach given the resources available;
- **R**ealistic – based on accurate information; and
- **T**imebound – with specific dates and times set for achieving targets.

Therefore, the context or environment to support this process is very important, and should be one where the organization has a clear commitment and process for enabling leaders and managers not only to set standards but to access a range of activities for learning to support this and ensure transparency and consistency about what is expected. Establishing and setting a culture that allows practice to be evaluated against national and local service standards can sometimes be compromised by political and managerial pressure for more instant or unrealistic changes and this requires a developmental approach. The importance of senior managers in social care creating a climate that recognizes the value of developing evidence-informed practice will determine how decision making is influenced by the prevailing organizational and team culture.

'Professional confidence can only come from a belief that what needs to be done is worthwhile and from knowledge that an effective contribution can be made' (Skinner and Whyte, 2004: 368). Managers who are supported by their organizations in exercising leadership for staff to develop critically reflective practice based on evidence rather than on past or current patterns of practice are able to consciously build capacity for learning in their teams and service areas. Leaders in this area are those people who challenge and experiment with practice and consciously use a series of interpersonal and group skills to help people change their attitudes, habits, skills, ways of thinking and working (Kitson et al., 1988). This has to include collaboration across professional, role and organizational boundaries in order to share and learn lessons. Effective intervention in the frontline requires the use of evidence that is derived directly from practice concerns and offers solutions designed and tested to be feasible in practice (Marsh et al., 2005). However, resistance within the organization can be affected by factors such as the size and complexity of the evidence base, how it conflicts with other information, a reliance on personal experience and a natural tendency to retain practice patterns as well as contextual factors such as high stress levels and risk aversion (Haines and Haines, 1998).

In previous chapters you were introduced to Wenger's (1998) 'communities of practice', where learning is embedded in particular social and cultural contexts and happens outside formal settings and in more local terms. A community of practice is a term for how people learn naturally in their work communities. It emphasizes practice over theory and the social learning over individual learning, which lead to providing a good environment for the development of evidence-based practice. Within any 'community', members will have different interests, make diverse contributions to the activities that go on within it and will hold various viewpoints. Participation in learning takes place at multiple levels in a community of practice and is a shared responsibility by those within it, whether they are in virtual or co-located groups. A community of practice may not necessarily imply co-presence, a well-defined identifiable group, or a socially visible boundary. However, it does imply participation in a system about which participants share a common understanding about what they are doing and what this means for the team as a whole and the communities they serve:

> Any complex system of work and learning has roots in and interdependencies across its history, technology, developing work activity, careers and the relations between newcomers and old-timers and among co-workers and practitioners. (Lave and Wenger, 1991: 61)

In summary, because knowledge ultimately belongs to a community of practice, issues around learning must be addressed within the developmental cycles of that community and provide access to a wide range of information, resources and opportunities for participation. Managers can nurture these cycles by using opportunities for group supervision, team building through team learning activities and encouraging other team members to take the lead in sharing their expertise. This takes us back to the need to not only look to pedagogy as the source of learning (i.e. formal knowledge and teaching), but also to combine these with participation in practice, where staff have a stake in developing their own knowledge and expertise as well as the expertise of their service users and colleagues. Research and evaluation are both integral elements that are core to this process, and encouraging research by practitioners, actively collaborating with people producing research and making time available for practitioners to share their learning are features of leadership in evidence-based practice. We shall be exploring this further in Chapter 9.

APPRAISAL AND PERSONAL
DEVELOPMENT PLANNING

Systems of appraisal and their use vary between, and even within, organizations and are seen as a sign of good modern management practice. They have many enthusiasts and defenders and are characterized as a key management system by which the effectiveness of individuals are assessed and developed. Appraisal is a process that enables people to reflect on what has been achieved and to identify future development needs incorporated within a personal development plan (PDP). Personal development planning usually combines three aspects of staff development: job performance, career planning and motivation. The key areas of development are likely to be:

- **Knowledge** – acquiring and updating knowledge in vocational and professional practice and organizationally specific developments.
- **Skills** – demonstrable application of knowledge and the use of skills in workplace situations.
- **Behaviours** – awareness and demonstrable use of appropriate values, conduct and relationship skills in workplace situations.
- **Reflective practice** – continually review and reflect using feedback on learning and development activities.

There are certain conditions that make PDPs successful and help to embed them within the organizational culture. By ensuring that everybody has a PDP, the process is mirrored through the organization from senior managers right through to the most junior staff. PDPs are tools that spell out clearly identified learning needs in priority order. They also define how the learner will learn (e.g. by coaching, shadowing an 'expert', visiting another resource, job swap, reading, training course, distance or open learning) and by when. The manager needs to take responsibility for setting this up and monitoring the plan, and provides structure and time to make it realistic and workable. The plan should be regularly reviewed to ensure that the learning needs have been met. The employee could keep a learning log, reflective diary or portfolio of evidence to demonstrate what has been learnt and for reviewing purposes. At an organizational level, the outcomes of learning need to be identified, reflected upon, recorded and where appropriate accredited.

From an appraisee's perspective, appraisal is the means by which their achievements are recognized. Appraisees can communicate with more senior staff and appraisal gives them a sense of progress and movement within an occupational or professional role. There can be some problems with performance appraisal where poor implementation can result in inconsistent, divisive and over-individualistic implementation that detracts from effective team work. Failure of the relevant parties to see performance review management as a continuing process limits the benefits, particularly if this is unnecessarily bureaucratic and fails to communicate its value through inadequate consultation and preparation with those reviewing or being reviewed.

Organizational objectives and definitions of effectiveness must also be clear if appraisal is to be used to determine pay or progression prospects alongside individual targets. If there is no action as a result of appraisal, for example learning needs exceed resources, then staff may become cynical and detached about it. Appraisal can likewise easily become an end in itself, detached from aspects of organizational planning. At its worst, the one-to-one confessional aspect of appraisal is one important way in which people learn to internalize, or at least be aware that their performance and behaviour is constantly being monitored. We noted in Chapter 2 that whichever way systems are operationalized, they represent cultural artefacts that send out clear cultural messages about the way in which staff are valued (Pattison, 2003), and the real intentions to promote their learning needs and support for development against any stated vision of the organization to those 'out there'. These criticisms aside, we have provided below some basic guidance for managing performance appraisal with staff.

TOP TIPS FOR MANAGING PERFORMANCE APPRAISAL WITH YOUR STAFF

USING APPRAISALS TO SET STANDARDS AND OBJECTIVES

Employees cannot develop, nor can managers take an active role in their development, if they do not know what is expected of them. For each area of practice you are reviewing there must be a clear purpose of why it is done, an agreed task which lists the duties and responsibilities involved in implementing it, an agreed level about the performance expected within the resources available, and an indicator of how performance can be measured (either qualitatively or quantitatively).

PREPARING FOR THE INITIAL REVIEW MEETING

Both the reviewer and employee should be given training and preparation for the process. Details of your department's scheme and appropriate documentation should be made accessible and available. Sufficient notice should be given in order to plan the review date. At least a couple of weeks before the initial meeting, the employees should be asked to complete some initial information and thoughts about how they think they are doing and what they would like to achieve. This provides them with a planned opportunity to reflect on any helpers or hindrances to their performance. This should provide the basis of an agenda for the initial review meeting and the reviewer should follow a similar process, depending on the individual requirements of the scheme.

CONDUCTING THE INITIAL MEETING

This should be held in a location with no interruptions and be conducive to creating an atmosphere of open and honest discussion. The reviewer should explain the purpose of the scheme and use the documentation to cover the following areas:

- Clarification of the key accountabilities and objectives for the employee, linked to organizational and service plans.
- Identification of the performance indicators being used to measure progress.
- Agreement about the key objectives for the next review period and identification of the employee's training and development needs using motivational techniques.
- Consideration of equality and resource issues.
- An agreement recorded in the form of a personal development plan using SMART indicators which both parties will sign and both will retain a copy.
- A clear date for a mid-way and full progress review.

CONDUCTING THE 'PROGRESS REVIEW' MEETING

This is a formal meeting to review and assess whether the employee achieved the goals and targets. Time should be spent on considering, for example: What has been achieved and what evidence supports this? What has not been achieved and the reasons? What changes would help improve performance? A written record of this meeting can also help to provide information for more strategic training needs analysis.

MANAGING THE PROCESS

We identified earlier the principles of giving and receiving constructive feedback which are necessary skills to make the process go as smoothly and respectfully as possible. Listening and acknowledging feelings are important as well as the use of open questioning and a relaxed style throughout any appraisal process. Time limit the review and do not allow it to go over 90 minutes. Give it a structure and summarize frequently during the meeting. This will help you to manage the over-all process.

A suggested structure for an appraisal might be:

- **Opening** – give an introduction as to the objectives, structure and benefits of the meeting and establish rapport.
- **Closing** – summarize, check and give commitment. Review against the opening objectives and end on a positive note.

SELF-MANAGED APPRAISAL

The above model is very much based on a traditional top-down model much used in social care organizations. The appraisal process however can be one of the most disempowering tasks that managers and their staff endure (Bell, 1994). The challenge is to connect day-to-day work with performance improval without creating an environment which puts managers in the role of judge and jury and creating a lot of anxi-ety. Alternative methods to the above model can include self-managed appraisal, along with upward feedback and including feedback from team members, internal customers and most importantly service users and carers. In facilitating self-managed appraisal, Bell (1994) recom-mends collecting simple data on the following areas from colleagues and users and carers, and giving equal emphasis to the environmental factors that affect practice:

- What do you consider I do well when we work well together?
- What do you think reduces my effectiveness?
- Is there anything you would like to know more about for us to work together more effectively?
- Is there anything more you think I should know about your require-ments or capability?

Similarly, 360-degree feedback is based on the simple notion that to get a more accurate picture of individual performance, people who know the person from different perspectives are asked to contribute to any feedback obtained. From an organizational point of view, this is seen as a way to encourage a culture of openness and honesty, and provides a great opportunity to involve service users in giving feedback on staff performance. As we all know, in the busy workplace, it is difficult for practitioners to listen to other people's experiences of oppression and to critically reflect on these.

BOX 6.3   REFLECTION BREAK

If you were to implement more employee or service user-led performance assessment in your team or service area, how would you go about convincing the staff you supervise who are sceptical about the process? How would you ensure confidentiality during the process? Who would have access to the information or how might it best be used?

TROUBLESHOOTING AND WORKING WITH DIFFICULT SITUATIONS

Underpinning any discussion about learning and staff development is often the assumption that everyone is motivated and willing to learn. We know from change management theory (Clegg et al., 2005) that change fatigue can result from the increased presence of power and authority that go with the number and range of instructions flowing from management when implementing change. Resistance and resentment can develop, stemming from perceived loss of power, additional workload, and loss of income, job insecurity or fear of being unable to learn new skills or work behaviour. It is important, therefore, for those leading change to anticipate possible reactions, resistance and barriers to changing practice. Time- and communication-poor managers can also provide obstacles.

Harrison (1994) advocates a counselling approach to staff development, particularly in rapid change environments, to help manage the uncertainty, anxiety, pessimism and feelings of helplessness that change engenders. For staff that may be 'stuck', this may be due to chronic denial or difficulties in coping with change, where fear and frustrations lead them to cope incompetently and emotionally with their work. In these situations, a counselling approach, as opposed to a more behavioural approach, can help mangers when faced with the uncomfortable task of getting people to change their behaviour. To be able to do this outside the managerialist approach means drawing on counselling skills which can enable real learning to take place. Although counselling in its broadest sense can encompass anything from psychoanalytical to affective theories, the client-centred approach, based on Rogers (2002), is probably the most generally accepted definition in the UK and describes a process through which a person attains a higher state of personal competence. Its goal is to help people explore problems so that they can decide what to do about them through their own actions and self-empowerment in the face of a seemingly intractable and hopeless set of circumstance brought about by people, systems or events that are apparently or actually beyond the employees' control. A strong connection between counselling and active staff development is therefore assumed.

Argyris and Schön (1990) talks about helping and supporting the capacity of others to confront their own ideas to create a window into their own unsurfaced assumptions, biases and fears. He promotes the use of models of self-reflection and self-examination without causing people to become so upset that they lose their effectiveness and their sense of self-responsibility and choice. These approaches can build on the deployment of counselling within supervision and staff development. Gentle probing by maintaining neutrality of questioning, combined with unconditional positive regard, provides some examples of skills that can be used. Empathetic managers who let staff know that they understand their frame of reference, and can see the world from the staff members' point of view while still remaining separate from it, are also said to be demonstrating qualities of emotionally intelligent leadership (Goleman, 1998).

BOX 6.4   REFLECTION BREAK

You are engaged in a review discussion with Sanjit, a member of your staff who accuses you of being too demanding and unsupportive. Sanjit complains of feeling stressed and your talking about objectives is only adding to the pressure he feels. You feel this is unfair as you believe that you have been available and supportive but also have a lot of demands made on you. There has also been a complaint about this member of staff from other members of the team who feel they are 'carrying him'.

   How do you think you can take this situation forward? What support will you and Sanjit need to resolve the situation?

With any issues relating to poor performance, it is easy to jump straight to a defensive position, resorting to formal or disciplinary procedures. Such procedures, along with competency procedures, of course have their place but should only be used in particular situations after all other avenues have been explored and where there is no identified or explicit risk to service users and others. Evidence of poor performance may not be easy to find if standards have been left to drift or issues have been left unresolved. Acting openly and promptly is always advisable when tacking performance problems and gives a message to the whole team about what is expected. It also creates a fair and honest environment.

Similarly, it is easy to think that sending a member of staff on a training course will resolve their learning and performance difficulties. Ultimately, the responsibility for developing a member of staff who is practising poorly is a shared one, where partnership between yourself and the worker needs to be fostered, possibly using good role modelling. You may want to refresh yourself by looking at the equality issues in learning and developments explored in Chapter 4, and identify any steps that could be taken to reduce the potential for either individual or institutional discrimination. Motivating staff who are discouraged and disillusioned is hard work and you need the support of your own peers and manager to improve ownership of the task.

To conclude this chapter, Box 6.5 looks more at some of the other types of dynamic that can develop when working with staff who are thought to be 'struggling' to provide the standards of services expected. This example identifies the dramas that can be played out in these situations. If we do not analyse or grapple with these dramas, they can divert us from adopting some of the more positive approaches.

BOX 6.5   USING DRAMA AND WINNER'S TRIANGLES TO ENHANCE PROFESSIONAL LEARNING AND AWARENESS AND TO ASSIST APPROPRIATE RESPONSIBILITY-TAKING IN INTERACTIONS

Burgess has adapted models derived from Transactional Analysis to develop a framework that he has been using to work with managers. This framework offers manoeuvrability when stuck with issues of complexity, disempowerment and boundaries in work relationships. Using the Drama Triangle (Karpman, 1968) and Winner's Triangle (Choy, 1990) as tools for accelerating awareness of people's interaction with others, the strength of Burgess's framework lies in the way it helps to facilitate individuals in taking 'appropriate responsibility' and therefore helping people to become more 'response-able' (Burgess, 2005: 98).

The **Drama Triangle** describes three positions – victim, persecutor and rescuer – that people can take in any interaction. Burgess argues that adopting any of these roles prevents people

(Continued)

(Continued)

taking appropriate responsibility for themselves. The fluid dynamic between all three positions, where one can flip from one position into another, pushing, and/or being pushed by others in the game, allows people to stay in the destructive dynamics of the triangle where, despite rapid shifts between the different positions, no positive outcome is achievable.

The **Winner's Triangle**, on the other hand, has three corresponding positions – Assertive, Caring and Vulnerable – and taking a position in this triangle makes it more difficult for others in the dynamic to continue in the Drama Triangle. Burgess argues that people in any of these positions are faced with a choice of, first, awareness, and then of change (2005: 104) as the three positions deny manipulation. Even the perceived weaker model of being 'vulnerable' can lead to unexpected empowerment by being true to ourselves at a given moment and being who we really are in a way that does not disempower another, while being in tune with what is right for ourselves. Burgess likens this state of effectiveness with emotional intelligence, and the experience of daring to be Vulnerable, Caring or Assertive can lead to options and outcomes that are more creative than anything that might be planned beforehand. This, he believes, appears to happen simply through the opportunistic synergy that is freed when people respond to one another courageously as themselves, without defences and games.

Burgess concludes that using the Drama and Winner's Triangles can be a facilitative tool to provide a shared language and accessible understanding in the building of emotional intelligence and the behaviour it leads to. These collaborative qualities can be a useful model in supervision or consulting individuals as well as groups to explore why they are stuck in destructive patterns of interaction at an individual level. Further, this has implications for wider organizational learning and effectiveness. 'Emotional intelligence can be learned by individuals, while fine-tuning the interpersonal dynamics that make groups smarter requires the organisation to prioritise its values in training and development and performance evaluation' (2005: 111).

Source: Burgess (2005)

CHAPTER SUMMARY

Leadership and management are important in providing learning and development in your teams. They have a major role to play in changing environments and multi-professional teams where new cooperative working methods need to be supported and encouraged. We have seen that there are quite a few factors challenging us in this respect, for example: administration of the process in ensuring policies and procedures are in place for supervision and appraisal; assessing and planning to respond to staff development needs; capitalizing on any opportunities that promote work-based learning; and managing conflicts with staff in teams or organizations. You will need a working knowledge of learning and development strategies alongside effective change management in order to promote the values and standards required.

In embarking on leadership of a particular staff development project, you will need to attend to three key aspects of leading development work in this area: first, collaboration as a key to managing change; secondly, gathering and using appropriate evidence and being creative enough to experiment with practice; and thirdly, using critical reflection to encourage employee and user-led approaches to development.

This chapter has looked broadly at the manager's role in building capacity within a community of practice, whether this be a single discipline in social care or multidisciplinary. Common elements of this process include using evidence from practice to support a clear rationale for change or implementing a policy or procedure to support staff development. The core skills to develop staff must involve listening and providing opportunities for questioning and dissent and working sensitively and flexibly within set deadlines. Partnership approaches to staff development are crucial so that you are planning and evaluating together and, where possible, identifying and building on good current practice. Above all, leaders of learning should lead by example and be approachable and supportive in relation to informal as well as informal advice. If you are proactive about your roles and responsibilities in this area, you will already have ready-made materials and strategies to manage any changes that are needed.

Recommended further reading

Tony Morrison (2002) *Staff Supervision in Social Care: Making a Real Difference for Staff and Service Users* (Brighton: Pavilion) is a

(Continued)

(Continued)

practical guide which looks at the role of supervision in facilitating reflective and user-centred practice with practical exercises and materials that helps supervisors and supervisees deliver high-quality supervision.

Ming-sum Tsui (2005) *Social Work Supervision: Contexts and Concepts* (London: Sage) provides a comprehensive review of the historical development, theories and models used in supervision combined with advice on the practice of supervision, including specific formats and structure for supervision.

Web-based resources

Research in Practice www.rip.org.uk – provides some helpful exercises in how to use research in supervision.

Learning Resource Centre Network www.lrcn.net – contains a number of resources for people working around Practice Learning. Access to the Black Practice Teachers network can be granted via Gurnam Singh g.singh@coventry.ac.uk and is a good example of a 'community of practice' where practitioners can share ideas, expertise and resources for facilitating learning in relation to equality issues.

7 WORK-BASED ASSESSMENT

This chapter explores:

- The concepts and purpose of work-based assessment
- Methods of assessment and the key ingredients of fair and transparent assessment techniques
- The contribution of teaching, learning and reflection to the assessment process
- Matching work-based assessments with academic requirements for staff following qualifying and post-qualifying programmes
- The concepts of 'good enough practice' and 'fitness for practice', and the evidence requirements

---

INTRODUCTION

We have been looking at some of the broader and specific aspects of the practical applications of developing staff. Work-based assessment is a specific skill that merits closer attention. It is an everyday activity for any leader or manager responsible for staff development and is an important aspect of formal learning strategies. The purpose of this chapter is to provide an overview for leaders and managers of the principles and concepts of work-based assessment in order for themselves, or the workers they manage, to undertake fair and thorough evidence-based assessments of workers. This will be related to the relevant literature.

THE PURPOSE OF ASSESSMENT

The purpose of work-based assessment in social care is to provide a competent reflective worker who is fit for purpose. Work-based assessment is core to the demonstration of competence of professional and vocational qualifications in social care. A number of authors have discussed work-based assessment, particularly in relation to assessing students on social work courses (Shardlow and Doel, 1996; Sharp and

Danbury, 1999; Parker, 2004), in a wider context of assessing professional practice (Eraut, 1994), within nursing and social care (Jarvis and Gibson, 1997), and nursing (Downie and Basford, 1998), and nursing, school teaching and social work (Evans, 1999). Qualifications in social care can be gained through attending courses or collecting evidence for assessment through everyday work experiences with support from a tutor. For example, the National Vocational Qualifications (NVQs) routes encourage the latter.

Social work itself has encouraged a mixture of work-based claims and course attendance at a university to gain pre- and post-qualifying awards. This sort of assessment is usually part of an holistic assessment of the worker's competence and makes up part of a portfolio of work demonstrating evidence of actual work undertaken and the knowledge and values informing the work. In order to demonstrate the knowledge and values as well as the actual work observed, the worker usually prepares a portfolio of work, including a reflective commentary explaining and analysing the work presented. In this way the worker can demonstrate their thinking behind their interaction with users and carers and other colleagues. The knowledge base will be defined by the qualification requirements and these will relate to external frameworks such as the GSCC *Code of Practice* for all care workers (GSCC, 2002), the GSCC *Post-qualifying Framework for Social Work Education and Training* (GSCC, 2005a) and the *Guidance on Assessment of Practice in the Workplace* (GSCC/TOPSS, 2002).

The purpose of assessment is to see whether learning has taken place and if this has reached a certain level. This can be to measure competence in a practice environment and academic level at a university. Before a worker enters a formal programme of learning to gain an NVQ, diploma, degree or masters level qualification they must be assessed as suitable to begin with. There will be a set of entry criteria that needs to be met and which demonstrates that the worker has the potential to start and complete the period of learning successfully. Assessments therefore begin at this level and can consist of a range of requirements, for example assignments, presentations, observations of practice, placements. They can be diagnostic, in order to identify learning at the beginning of a learning episode, or continuous, involving formative assessments at distinct points during the learning episode which are used to inform future learning and development. Summative assessment takes place at the end-point, resulting in making a pass/fail decision.

Any learning provider team in relation to a programme of learning will bring together the work-based assessment and required academic work to provide an holistic picture of the worker's competence. They will monitor validity and fairness through arrangements for internal and external assessors/examiners in order to ensure all learners reach similar levels of competence to pass or fail the programme.

DEFINITIONS OF ASSESSMENT

First, let us explore some of the definitions and concepts of assessment used in education. Assessment is an essential way of judging whether learning has taken place. According to Rowntree (1987: 4): 'Assessment in education can be thought of as occurring whenever one person, in some kind of interaction, direct or indirect, with another, is conscious of obtaining and interpreting information about the knowledge and understanding, or abilities and attitudes of that other person.' Knight (2001: 3) talks about 'summative assessment providing "feedout" in the shape of a warrant to achievement or competence (for example, a degree certificate) and in the form of information that can be used as performance indicators in appraising the work of teachers, departments, colleges and national systems for education'.

The first definition offers us information about the context of the assessment and allows for the dynamics of the encounter between the assessor and worker to be recognized and explored. Assessment is not a value-free activity and both parties bring to the assessment relationship their own personal values and beliefs about 'what is evidence of fit for practice and purpose' and what is 'good enough' alongside external expectations from users and carers, educational bodies, professional bodies, employers and tutors. These are embodied in a set of outcomes or competencies. The second definition focuses on the outcome of the assessment and the differences between assessment and evaluation. However, both definitions offer important insights.

We will first clarify the differences between assessment and evaluation. Evaluation considers how the programme can learn from the educational experience of the learner. This focuses on a range of dimensions that can include gaining feedback from users, learners, work-based assessors, leaders, managers, employers and teachers about their experience. Questions considered are the suitability of the learning environment, and whether the course meets vocational, professional and academic requirements and levels. Is the learner learning what they need to be better practitioners and fit for purpose? Are the teachers competent? What is the drop-out rate of learners and why is this?

THE NATURE OF THE RELATIONSHIP
BETWEEN WORKER AND ASSESSOR

Many work-based assessments take place within a one-to-one relationship. The assessor's role may be to assess a learner on a one-off basis following a period of learning or the assessor may be part of developing the learner's competence through a teaching facilitator role as well as assessing their performance. With this type of assessor role it is important to consider the direct links between teaching and facilitating, learning and assessment. The assessor needs to provide feedback and learning opportunities for the worker to develop their competence by the end-point of the assessment period. To undertake an assessment task only could involve setting a worker up to potentially fail and would be unfair. The assessor needs to provide a learning climate that addresses the power dynamics in the relationship, builds trust and openness and provides the opportunity for learning and reflection to take place. There needs to be transparency in the assessment criteria to be met and methods to be used. In both examples, the assessor needs to have clarity about what they are assessing and how they will do this. This needs to be shared with the learner and recorded in a learning agreement.

Knowles (1984) identifies the key components for an androgogical learning contract between the facilitator and learner. This consists of setting a positive physical and psychological climate for learning that involves the building of collaborative relationships where trust can be built and support given. The facilitator needs to involve the learner in actively planning and identifying their own learning needs. This is done by identifying their learning objectives and matching these to the external assessment requirements, and by designing and implementing a plan to meet these and evaluate their own learning through self-assessment using critical reflection. In addition, visible and invisible similarities and differences need to be recognized and discussed (e.g. 'race' ethnicity, age, gender, disability, sexual orientation, religion, class). The professional value base of the assessor needs to be made explicit to the learner and ground rules for keeping within an anti-oppressive framework developed. This should include how discrimination will be addressed if issues arise, and acknowledge the power of the assessor role.

CRITERIA USED IN ASSESSMENT: COMPETENCIES AND OUTCOMES

This brings us to the exploration of criteria used in work-based assessment. Terms used commonly are 'competencies', 'key roles' and 'outcomes'. We want to define these clearly as this helps any work-based assessor understand the underlying principles they are using. These are behavioural concepts and assume an objective reality that is value free and not dependent on social context (Kemshall, 1993). All of these focus on what a student knows, their abilities and how this is demonstrated at the end of a period of learning, rather than how or where they learned it. Learning outcomes are generally determined by academic tutors designing the educational programme. They cover a range of academic, vocational and personal learning expectations and include measuring the knowledge, skills and values required to meet specific programmes of learning.

BOX 7.1   MEASURING COMPETENCY

What are the knowledge, values and skills you need in your role and for the workers you lead/manage? Some examples are listed below:

Values

GSCC Code of Practice, e.g. involving service users and carers in decision making, confidentiality, managing risk, working within an anti-discriminatory framework, treating people with respect, being open and honest.

Skills

- Communication skills – engaging, empathising, empowering.
- Information gathering and assessments.
- Accessing services.
- Recording skills.

Knowledge

- Legislation.
- Policies.
- Research informing practice.
- Theories and concepts in social care, e.g. theories of empowerment, partnership crisis, loss, attachment, transition and change.
- Methods of intervention, e.g. task centred practice, cognitive behavioural therapy, partnership working.

It is important that the assessment methods need to measure the outcomes defined for each period of learning. Competencies focus particularly on work-based evidence. They provide an independent set of criteria against which performance is measured and recorded (Wolf, 1995). Therefore the work-based assessor must provide evidence relating to these competencies or outcomes rather than relying on informal measures. Examples of informal measures might be where the assessor bases their assessment of competence by comparing the worker to their own performance when they were being assessed at that level, or against informal criteria within the team as to what is a competent worker. The key roles of a job such as in social care work, as a social worker or manager, are broken down into tasks and then the measure of competence is defined. In social care there are differing levels of measurement of competence against set criteria. Box 7.2 demonstrates how this is constructed.

BOX 7.2 THE COMPETENCY FRAMEWORK

Key role

Units of competence – the main functions of a particular role
Elements of competence – each function is broken into
specific tasks
Performance criteria – is used to measure/assess competence

Box 7.3 demonstrates the different levels at which the NVQ framework operates.

BOX 7.3 NVQ LEVELS

The following definitions of NVQ levels provide a general guide and are not intended to be prescriptive.

Level 1
Competence, which involves the application of knowledge and skills in the performance of a range of varied work activities, most of which may be routine or predictable.

(Continued)

Level 2
Competence which involves the application of knowledge and skills in a significant range of varied work activities, performed in a variety of contexts. Some of the activities are complex or non-routine, and there is some individual responsibility and autonomy. Collaboration with others, perhaps through membership of a workgroup or team, may often be a requirement.

Level 3
Competence which involves the application of knowledge and skills in a broad range of varied work activities performed in a wide variety of contexts, most of which are complex and non-routine. There is considerable responsibility and autonomy, and control or guidance of others is often required.

Level 4
Competence which involves the application of knowledge and skills in a broad range of complex, technical or professional work activities performed in a wide variety of contexts and with a substantial degree of personal responsibility and autonomy. Responsibility for the work of others and the allocation of resources is often present.

Level 5
Competence which involves the application of skills and a significant range of fundamental principles across a wide and often unpredictable variety of contexts. Very substantial personal autonomy and often significant responsibility for the work of others and for the allocation of substantial resources feature strongly, as do personal accountabilities for analysis and diagnosis, design, planning, execution and evaluation.

Source: QCA (2006)

You will find that the key roles and the assessment criteria are very broad and open to interpretation as to how much evidence in terms of breadth and depth is required and at what level the learner is deemed competent. Therefore, it is important, as discussed earlier, that there is a standardization process for the programme of learning to determine the level of learner competence in the workplace required. Secondly, the assessment process is standardized so the assessor knows what the methods of assessment are, how these match the required competencies to be measured, how frequently they will assess, where this will take place, over what time scale. The assessor also needs to be able to interpret the evidence collected and provide a meaningful response to the worker and the programme in order to be accountable for their assessment (Rowntree, 1987).

The introduction of a competency-based framework for social work led to much debate about how this framework could lose focus on the process of experiential learning and the principles of reflective practice (Issitt and Woodward, 1992). Writers such as Yelloly and Henkel (1995), Jones and Joss (1995) and Wolf (1995) argued successfully for a more holistic approach to learning and assessment of competency that includes the model of the reflective practitioner. Kemshall (1993) criticized the social work competency framework following the implementation of the first set of core competencies for the Diploma in Social Work in 1992. These competencies were written with large local authority social services departments in mind, and reflected much less of the work of smaller voluntary and private sector organizations, often working with marginalized groups in society. Therefore, one important aspect of defining competency criteria is to think about who is writing them and for what purpose?

Kemshall (1993) argued the need for a diversity of people to be represented on assessment panels to enhance fair decision making. As outlined previously, there are many competing views as to what makes base-line competency (e.g. user's experience, work-based assessor, college, professional and employer perspectives alongside team cultures of what makes a competent worker). These are all opinions influenced by our own personal and professional values and organizational cultures. Biased views can lead to discrimination and oppression of the learner. Reference to a learner who is 'fitting in' with the local team well might, on the surface, appear to contribute to their competence, yet on closer examination this is not a competency requirement whereas working within organizational frameworks usually is. The point being made here is that we do not need to like learners personally for them to pass. While a competency framework attempts to avoid bias and discrimination by providing explicit and detailed external criteria for measurement, this can still remain open to interpretation. The more general and less contextualized criteria are, when filtered through our own values, experiences and biases, then the more discrimination is likely to occur.

What is deemed as competence can change over time and, as Barnett (1994: 73) succinctly comments, 'we live in a changing society. Today's competences are not tomorrow's'. There is a need to evaluate what we define as competences and revise them in line with changes in current role expectations and new demands. For example, the views of users are now much more prominent in the National Occupational Standards (TOPSS, 2002) for social work. This document begins with what users and carers want from social workers. The introduction of *Codes of Practice* (GSCC, 2002), occupational requirements within social care and for leaders have brought changes to the required competences as a result of political demands and legislative changes.

HOW DO WE MEASURE COMPETENT REFLECTIVE PRACTICE – KNOWLEDGE, VALUES AND SKILLS?

This brings us to the tricky question of how we measure knowledge, values and skills? These represent the different domains of learning and are referred to in the Box 7.1. The outcomes and competencies used in work-based assessment in social care expect evidence from all of these domains and it is the assessor's job to help the worker identify and evidence these as well as make these explicit in their own assessment report. The GSCC *Codes of Practice* (GSCC, 2002) now offers a framework for measuring values, within which is an expectation of anti-discriminatory practice. This is quite general and stops short of actually naming specific marginalized groups. Confirming the underpinning knowledge from a learner of what informed their observed practice and skill base while working with users is important, and a reflection session or oral assessment covering key questions afterwards can allow the learner to provide such evidence to the assessor.

We also need to consider the different levels at which we are assessing. Is the person being assessed at an NVQ level 3, as an advanced practitioner or as a senior manager? Bloom (1956) provides a taxonomy for the cognitive domain that identifies different levels of learning, beginning with remembering and understanding knowledge through to application and higher-level analysis, such as evaluation and creativity. Some of the literature offers models of assessment that allow us to identify different levels of competence and using these may contribute to reaching a transparent, holistic assessment.

These models all consider ways of identifying levels of competence from novice and beginner stages through to competence at a basic level and beyond to proficiency and then on to expert practitioner status. Dreyfus and Dreyfus (1986) concentrate on skills-based acquisition and identify the use of tacit knowledge and intuitive responses, and how this develops as practitioners become more expert in their role. Benner (2001) applies this model comprehensively in relation to nursing.

However, criticisms by Eraut (1994) relate to the concentration on learning from experience and the emphasis on practice with little consideration for self-evaluation and learning from theoretical frameworks. How tacit knowledge that is built from experience and based on intuition is used in day-to-day practice and decision making is a useful concept to explore with practitioners in order to assess their competence. The use of only tacit knowledge can be challenged at a time when courses of actions and decisions made by practitioners need to be transparent and evidence-based.

In summary, any work-based assessor needs to consider how a practitioner demonstrates reflective practice and continuing professional development as part of the process they engage in to meet competency. They need to demonstrate how they use knowledge, including evidence-based practice, and work within professional value-led frameworks when working with users. If they are working in an intuitive way, then they need help to be able to make conscious the frameworks they are applying.

METHODS OF ASSESSMENT

Much of the literature is concerned with different methods of assessment and how to develop these (Knight, 2001). First, different assessment methods suit different learners and so a variety will meet the needs of a diverse group of learners and help them to succeed (Race, 2001). Secondly, the assessment methods used do need to measure the intended outcomes of the programme of study or work-based competencies required. For example, a written exam will not measure direct communication skills with users but it can test the learner's knowledge base. Brown (1999) discusses the range of instruments to assess practice within the context of university courses, including competence checklists, critical incidents, oral assessments and portfolios.

Evidence can be collected in a variety of ways and may be directly observed by the assessor or rely on indirect verifications by way of feedback and testimonies from users, carers, colleagues and managers, for example. We will explore the different methods of assessment but, first, it is important to summarize the principles of assessing competency. The assessment process needs to be fair. The principle of triangulation assists us through a process of cross-referencing a variety of evidence over time with the assessment methods designed to measure the required competencies (Shardlow and Doel, 1996). Validity is important so the process tests what it is supposed to test. It needs to be sufficient, up-to-date and authentic. Can you be sure the work you are assessing is the learner's work? Is the testimony/written feedback from the user their own freely given feedback? How do you know? How can you verify the evidence of practice? The range of assessment methods need to be used over time for consistency and the information gathered compared and contrasted, with consideration of the weight given to each source of evidence. For example, if the assessor is gaining evidence of competence during observations, then is this supported by other methods of assessment? Such as file reading and evidence from users and carers, and other workers and managers, within and across work and professional boundaries. If this is the case, then it is more likely that the learner is competent. A variety of positive and negative feedback from a range of sources will identify strengths and areas for development. Box 7.4 outlines the principles of fair assessment.

BOX 7.4   COMPETENCY-BASED ASSESSMENT

Competency-based assessment must be fair. These are the principles underlying any assessment:

- **Valid** – tests what it is meant to test
- **Reliable** – it can be trusted over time and across assessors
- **Authentic** – it is that person's work
- **Sufficient** – is it enough?
- **Current** – up to date

BOX 7.5   REFLECTION BREAK

How many work-based methods of assessment can you think of? Check yours against Box 7.5).

The work-based assessor is usually provided with an outline of the frequency and methods of assessment required and the competencies the worker is expected to meet. The methods used need to be explicitly discussed, written into the agreement and the assessment process planned for. Now you have an idea of the range of assessment methods that can be used, we will look more closely at several of these.

BOX 7.5 WORK-BASED METHODS OF ASSESSMENT

- Direct observation of practice
- Video/audio recordings
- Written work (e.g. records, reflections, critical incidents, logs)
- Portfolio of work
- Competence checklists
- Oral assessments, examining knowledge and values underlying observed practice
- Oral presentation
- Reflection and discussion
- Setting specific tasks
- Use of feedback to aid development, by other people apart from the named assessor
- Feedback by team members and other professionals
- User feedback
- User and carer trainer assesses competence through observation/assessment of portfolio work
- Carer feedback
- Self-assessment
- Manager feedback

HOW USERS AND CARERS MAY BE INVOLVED IN ASSESSMENT

Users and carers receiving a service from the worker could be asked beforehand if they agree to give feedback on the service received or relating to a particular event (e.g. after a direct observation of practice). This can then be formally agreed through a signed consent form that addresses issues of confidentiality. How feedback will be recorded needs to be agreed with the user or carer. What are their preferred communication styles? Are they agreeable to giving verbal feedback? Will they write this down in a letter or a pre-defined questionnaire, for example, or do they have particular needs where verbal and written communication needs to be reconsidered, such as through sign language, communication boards, working with an interpreter? Chapter 4 provided us with many examples of how organizations now have service user groups who advise on service delivery and provide training to staff on good practice. There may be members of the user groups in your organization who could provide an ongoing role in work-based assessments by providing user expertise in this area. Training and payment, monetary or in kind, would need to be considered to avoid tokenism and exploitation.

DIRECT OBSERVATION OF PRACTICE, ORAL ASSESSMENTS AND PORTFOLIOS

Direct observation of practice is a key method of assessment of practice. Planning for the observation is a shared task between the worker and the assessor. Areas to be decided and planned for are:

- Signed permission from the user or carer or worker (if a management/leadership/educator course), including asking if they will provide some feedback to the assessor verbally or in another recorded form.
- How the assessor will record during the session to provide specific evidence of competence.
- Identification of the key competencies to be assessed.
- Agreement that the assessor will only intervene if the level of practice is unacceptable.
- Discussion of when and where the observation will take place and the seating arrangements.
- Making clear the timescales for feedback – immediately for some verbal feedback and longer-term for reflective discussion and written feedback.
- Identification of indirect evidence to be seen to support the direct observation evidence (e.g. files, written records of supervision, teaching plans).

Many other methods of assessment test competence indirectly, for example through reflective records, assignments and case studies. Often it is only the user, carer and work-based assessor who can provide direct evidence of a worker's practice. The observation would usually be followed up with a session where the worker is asked questions to assist them to focus on the knowledge and values used to inform the practice that has been observed. This can be called an oral assessment.

Portfolios of evidence provide a range of evidence using different assessment methods. One of these is usually a series of observations of practice, additional evidence may consist of user feedback, other workers' feedback, reflective records and evidence of written records and reports used in practice. The portfolio is read alongside assignments and case studies where knowledge and values are evidenced through reading relevant literature, and reflection and analysis.

USE OF FEEDBACK

Feedback is an essential part of the assessment process. In the last chapter we looked at the principles of giving feedback in the supervision and appraisal context. Doel et al. (1996) talk about the specific and important use of language for negotiating feedback and use terms such as 'affirming feedback' and 'challenging feedback'. They also talk about the importance of receiving feedback by being aware of your own response when receiving it, and asking for feedback for yourself in order to model good practice. This modelling would include the principle of not becoming defensive but of responding to unfair feedback by listening, clarifying, considering and replying. Finally, it is always good to talk about the process in order to review both parties' position and to renegotiate the ground rules if necessary.

Overall, within the context of work-based assessment, feedback needs to be given specifically and regularly, both verbally and in writing, if the assessor role continues over a set timescale. It needs to be given in time for the worker to make improvements before the next formative or final summative assessment, and to include specific detail of competencies met and those that need to be evidenced with suggestions of how this may be done. This makes the process transparent and fair. It is also important for the assessor to encourage feedback to them on the worker's experience of being assessed and allow challenge and discussion from the worker to the assessor.

REPORT WRITING

What has been evidenced by the assessor then needs to be summarized in a report containing examples specific to the programme in order to provide verification that competence is met or unmet by the worker. Written formative assessments and feedback to the worker can be used, alongside other material required, to provide detailed evidence, with specific examples, in a written summative assessment report in the required format. Reports by work-based assessors provide work-based evidence of competence to an assessment panel linked to an assessment centre, university or education provider. The overall markers of the assessed work rely on the work-based assessor for evidence. Therefore, specific examples, demonstrating the principles of triangulation already discussed, need to be given.

Key points to remember in writing a report are:

- Ensure that there is a clear introduction setting the context of the learner's experience while being assessed (e.g. any reorganizations, changes in team, personal circumstances (if agreed), access to supervision, etc.).
- Explicitly address and acknowledge the power dynamics in the relationship in any introduction.
- Tell the person marking or assessing the content of the report what support and areas of development you assisted the worker with.

- Provide a sense of learning over time.
- Identify what the worker *can* and *cannot* do.
- Be specific about competency and the level met by providing examples. They may have done three complex assessments in practice but still need to develop these skills in more depth with a variety of users.
- Be clear about the learner's ongoing professional needs.
- Remember it is easier to pass someone than fail them.

Practice competence is usually assessed on a pass/fail basis rather than ascribing academic marks to this work. The reality of these assessment decisions is that it is often very clear to the assessor if a learner is exceeding the base-line well or if they fall well below this line. It is the borderline decisions that test the assessor's own competence in making an holistic assessment as well as defining evidence and competence for the different criteria (Wolf, 1995). Box 7.6 is a set of case scenarios that you can work through to help you consider how to apply the themes of good practice in work-based assessment outlined so far. Work through each scenario and jot down a plan of what you might do if...

BOX 7.6   CASE SCENARIOS

Scenario 1
A learner has to meet the defined work-based competencies or outcomes for meeting the post-qualifying award in Child Care at the specialist level (GSCC, 2005b). The assessor assesses that the learner is able to communicate well with users, both children and adults, but is not able to keep their chronology or records up to date and that the records do not provide a sense of who the child is, relevant information of the child's progress, or their wishes and feelings.

Questions to consider
How much flexibility is there for context (e.g. a very busy social work team with no workload relief and a number of crises which take the learner away from their core administrative tasks). How many chances do you give the worker to complete the records if they are not satisfactory? What advice and direction do you give? What competencies and values are being met/not met?

(Continued)

(Continued)

Scenario 2

You are assessing a worker who has been given positive feedback from users of the services but negative responses from other professionals and the manager.

Questions to consider

Would you require a further assessment? Does the programme of learning allow further assessment? What are the competencies and values required?

Scenario 3

The worker is required to provide evidence of feedback from users of the service. You are unsure if one of the feedback sheets actually reflects the views of the user and you think the worker may have made it up.

Questions to consider

Do you speak to the user yourself? Was this part of the learning agreement? How else can you check the validity of the evidence?

Scenario 4

A learner competently undertakes administrative and follow-up tasks, and works in partnership with carers and adult users, but the user is not seen in a truly confidential setting from the carer on the one observation you undertake.

Questions to consider

Does the assessor ask for a repeat observation or seek further information from the user? How many opportunities is the learner given and is that the same for all learners on that programme?

Scenario 5

The worker has planned a session with a young adult. This session lasts 20 minutes and covers many issues.

Questions to consider

Is this one observation of engaging with a young person sufficient or does it need to be longer? Even though the session was not very long, was the depth and quality of the interaction sufficient to demonstrate competence? Can this be verified by a secondary source, such as the manager, and are you confident with this, or are both needed to provide consistent evidence of this skill over time? What are the programme requirements for the length of time of the assessment observation?

(Continued)

Scenario 6

The learner is observed to empower and communicate and plan the service they will provide but is unclear of the knowledge base they used in the post-observation oral assessment.

Questions to consider

Do you give the learner another opportunity? How much help do you provide? Do you consult the tutor as to how many opportunities can be given? Do you liaise with the manager and the learner so they may get help to perform again through supervision? Can you consider outlining the competencies not met and get the worker to address these in subsequent oral assessments, if this is at an early stage of the assessment?

Scenario 7

The practice educator spends much of the session addressing the items they brought to the agenda rather than the student, telling the student what to do, and is unable to consider how to use open questions to draw out the student's own learning and development and link theory and values to practice.

Questions to consider

How will you give feedback? What would you say and what would you write down? Is the assessment developmental? If it is, how can you make sure the learner changes their style to be more facilitative if this is early on in the assessment?

PRINCIPLES OF GOOD PRACTICE WHEN WORKING WITH 'BORDERLINE' WORKERS

Making the decision to fail a worker is very difficult and occurs relatively rarely. In our view, it can sometimes be harder to fail a borderline practitioner than to pass them. The assessor needs to be confident that they have undertaken a fair and transparent assessment and that they have evidence of both competencies met as well as those not met. If there is a breadth and depth of unmet competency, then the decision may be more clear-cut. It is when the worker has met some competencies but not others, and these all cluster around the pass/fail borderline, that the decision becomes more difficult. As discussed earlier, the competency framework offers the opportunity to break down the social care roles into discrete parts. It is at the time of the summative assessment that the evidence for the discrete competencies is used to make an overall assessment of competency and reach a final decision. This can be hard to gauge when you are assessing one person or have not assessed for this particular award or accredited learning programme before. It is important to recognize our own values, responses to the learner and any discriminatory or prejudicial stereotyping as part of our own professional development in making fair assessment decisions, as they can influence how we identify what is competent or not. We can have skewed views and this can lead to what we see and what we record and collect as evidence. This means that at times a more positive or more negative assessment of the learner is made.

We recommend the following key principles in these situations:

1. At the beginning of the period of assessment obtain a sense of the weight given to the work-based assessment, whether a second chance is allowed, and the standard required from the assessment centre, university or education provider.
2. It is important throughout the period of the assessment to liaise with the programme tutor to discuss the standards of competency required and inform them of the learner's progress and of any concerns both verbally and in writing.
3. Consider seeking the advice of an expert assessor to talk through the issues and to explore the evidence you have in order to consider if this is balanced, triangulated, valid and reliable, with specific examples, and how you are relating it to the relevant competencies and GSCC *Codes of Practice* (GSCC, 2002).
4. The context of the assessment is important. What are the factors that may be disadvantaging the student in the workplace? For example, is there a lack of supervision and guidance from the manager or assessor in what is required? Is there a need for extra planning and preparation to identify the knowledge and value base of the work undertaken to the assessor?
5. Return to the learning agreement to review how the relationship has developed, the positives and negatives of the power dynamics and the impact of similarities and differences between the assessor and worker. Revisit how the worker learns and identify whether feedback or your facilitation style needs to be varied to meet the worker's learning needs.

CHAPTER SUMMARY

In this chapter we have explored the role of the work-based assessor in social care and the links to assessment centres, universities or education providers. Attention has been given to defining terms such as evaluation, diagnostic formative and summative assessment and the complexities of measuring competence and outcomes across the three domains – knowledge, skills and values. We considered the methods of assessment used in the workplace. These include a range of tasks and a variety of people who may be involved in this process. The role of observation, reflection sessions, user and carer feedback and the input of other professionals/workers across organizations were particularly highlighted as important methods for consideration when assessing the knowledge, skills and values domains. Triangulation as a concept was introduced to ensure the fairness of assessment through reliability, validity, sufficiency and authenticity of the assessment methods used. The use of learning agreements that include an explicit discussion of the power dynamics between the assessor and worker, explicit recognition of the worker's learning styles and a discussion of how to give and receive feedback were encouraged as models of good practice. Hints on report writing were also offered as well as a discussion of the principles of good practice when working with workers who may be at risk of failing.

Recommended further reading

GSCC/TOPSS (2002) *Guidance on the Assessment of Practice in the Workplace* (London: General Social Care Council) offers national guidance on best practice for assessing work-based learning and is recommended as an underpinning document in qualifying and post-qualifying social work frameworks.

G. Singh (2005) *Developing and Supporting Black and Minority Ethnic Practice Teachers and Assessors* (Leeds: Skills for Care) is written by an experienced academic and practice teacher. This text takes specific account of the issues in an area of potential discrimination using a clear anti-oppressive framework.

The *International Journal of Social Work Education* publishes articles of a critical and reflective nature concerned with the theory and practice of social care and social work education at all levels. It presents a forum for international debate on important issues and provides an opportunity for the expression of new ideas and proposals on the structure and content of social care and social work education, training and development. There are approximately eight issues per year.

Web-based resources

Practice Learning Taskforce (www.practicelearning.org.uk) – was set up to increase the quality, quantity and diversity of practice learning for the social work degree. The taskforce commissioned and published a number of practical documents in a series called 'Capturing the Learning', which aims to disseminate the learning and thinking that has gone on during the Taskforce's lifespan and much of it is based on work-based learning for different stakeholders.

Qualifications and Curriculum Authority (www.qca.org.uk/) – the QCA maintains and develops the national curriculum and associated assessments, tests and examinations. It accredits and monitors qualifications in colleges and at work.

8 COACH MENTORING AS A DEVELOPMENTAL TOOL IN THE WORKPLACE

This chapter explores:

- Coaching and mentoring and the differences between these approaches
- The benefits of coaching and mentoring from an individual and organizational perspective
- Developing a coaching and mentoring scheme
- The coaching culture
- Examples of the practical use of coaching and mentoring in social care

---

INTRODUCTION

This chapter specifically investigates how the skills of coach mentoring can be utilized as a tool for the continuous professional development of the workforce. A modern social care organization exists in a climate and culture of constant change and development. To meet the demands of twenty-first century social care, leaders and managers must ensure that all employees, including volunteers, are able to identify opportunities and are empowered to respond positively to any challenges. This chapter explores how the skills of coaching and mentoring can become a powerful, effective but economic device in the modern developmental manager's toolbox. It identifies the origins of coaching and mentoring and investigates the differences and similarities between these two disciplines. It explores how the skills and practices of coaching and mentoring can be blended and utilized by social care managers and supervisors as a management and developmental tool that can engage the greatest number of social care staff in reflecting on their practice, addressing their own learning needs and developing learning on and off the job. This chapter will demonstrate how coach mentoring can become an holistic learning strategy that enables managers, supervisors and colleagues to learn from and with each other. It recognizes that everyone has developmental potential and all managers and supervisors can learn the skills of coaching and mentoring.

EXPLORING COACHING AND MENTORING?

Both coaching and mentoring have long histories that can be traced all the way back to Greek mythology, classical Greek literature and Greek culture. Homer's *Odyssey* is an example of the well-known interpretation of mentoring, when an older person takes charge of supporting the development of a young person. Odysseus leaves his son Telemachus to the care and direction of his old and trusted friend Mentor before setting sail on his epic voyage (Clutterbuck, 2001). In the real world, coaching has strong roots in sports in general and can be traced back to the Olympics in ancient Greece right through to the present-day games. Clutterbuck (2001) suggests that the modern, business, concept of mentoring has its roots in apprenticeships. When Guilds ruled the commercial world, the road to the top in business began with an early apprenticeship to the master craftsman, a trader or a ship's captain. This older and more experienced individual would pass down knowledge on how the task was done or how to develop a craft. They also helped apprentices to operate in a particular business and in the commercial world (Clutterbuck, 2001).

Throughout this chapter we will refer to real case studies from our own experiences, although the names and some of the references within the case studies have been altered to maintain confidentiality and anonymity. These case studies have been carefully chosen to demonstrate how the use of coaching and mentoring skills and techniques can enable someone to reflect and learn and take control of their own learning. These case studies should also demonstrate how coaching and mentoring can be used to both support and embed diversity in the fibre of social care organizations, as Chapter 5 suggests.

BOX 8.1   CASE STUDY: CHALLENGING STAFF POTENTIAL

Jenny is a 21 year-old black woman recently arrived in the UK. She has taken employment in a social care service as an Advanced Modern Apprentice in an administration role. Jenny applied for the modern apprentice role as a route into employment in the UK. She holds a 2.1 science degree and therefore she was not enthusiastic that her apprentice role

(Continued)

required her to undertake an NVQ in Administration. Jenny very quickly became disaffected with her job role and what she perceived as her low status as an administrator and apprentice. She felt unchallenged by her job and the NVQ, which she felt did not meet her learning aspirations.

Jenny's manager, who was a coach mentor, suggested that she might benefit from being matched with a coach mentor outside her employing organization. Jenny accepted the suggestion and she was matched with a coach mentor from a National Health Service Trust.

The relationship lasted for approximately eight months and during that time her coach mentor supported Jenny in identifying her career aspirations and objectives, worked with her on identifying her learning needs and supported her in undertaking additional complex duties and projects at work. Jenny developed project leadership skills, organizational skills and helped to design and co-facilitate adult learning courses, something she realized she was particularly interested in. Jenny completed her NVQ and was re-graded from the modern apprentice to permanent status, with a pay increase. She enrolled on to a masters degree in Human Resource and Personnel Development and applied for, and was promoted into, a learning and development role.

Jenny reported that her coach mentor challenged her to stretch herself, to identify her strengths and weaknesses. She explored what she enjoyed doing and what she aspired to do. She clarified her work, career and learning objectives. She felt enabled to work and learn outside her comfort zones. She felt able to talk confidentially about her experiences, concerns and, importantly, how unmotivated she had felt in her day job. She felt she discovered new skills that she had been unaware of, was able to explore what she wanted to do, and make this a reality rather than a daydream. By attending regular coaching and mentoring sessions, she was motivated to keep on track and celebrate her achievements.

She felt that she eventually reached a point where she had achieved as much as she could in the relationship and felt able to 'stand alone'. Jenny reported that coach mentoring had empowered her to 'keep going'. Her sessions provided her with a valuable sounding board and offered guidance and a place to test things. She said she would recommend coach mentoring to everyone and felt that it definitely did what it said it would do. She felt that it gave her the boost into the job and salary she felt was more appropriate to her skills and abilities.

Learning and development is fundamentally what both coaching and mentoring are about, and perhaps the strongest philosophy behind coaching and mentoring is that everyone has some potential to learn, grow and develop.

BOX 8.2   REFLECTION BREAK

A good starting point when developing any coach mentoring relationship is checking out 'why are you here? What do you hope to achieve? Where are you at now? Where do you want to get to? And then explore how to get there.

Why not practice the 'GROW model' on yourself?

The GROW model

G – Goal, what is it you want to achieve for yourself?
R – Reality, what is the current situation?
0 – Options, what is it possible to do?
W – Wrap-up, what are you going to do?

(*Source*: www.mentoringforchange.co.uk)

Michelangelo is quoted as saying that 'beneath every ordinary block of stone is a beautiful statue just waiting to break out; it just needs some help in removing the bits of stone that disguise it'. Coaches and mentors are both concerned with helping the potential of individuals to break out, and both disciplines help this process by using very similar methods. Parsloe and Wray (2000) offer a very useful definition of both mentoring and coaching. They suggest that a mentor is concerned with building an individual's self-confidence, self-awareness and self-esteem. The higher the levels of confidence, awareness and esteem, the higher the learner's motivation to seize learning opportunities and to take responsibility for improving their levels of performance will be.

BOX 8.3   CASE STUDY PROMOTING SELF-ESTEEM

John, a gay man, came to mentoring because he was feeling highly stressed at work. He identified that his objective was to manage his stress better. He was an acting manager and believed that his status was, in part, the cause of his stress because he felt that he was trying too hard and was afraid of failure. Through using enquiring questioning and active listening, the coach mentor was able to encourage John to reflect on his self-esteem and confidence, and on his behaviours at work. John talked about how he felt he had lost confidence in his skills. He acknowledged his anxieties and stress levels, and that these had, in part, contributed to a dip in his self-esteem. This, in turn, had impacted on his stress levels. John was caught in a difficult cycle. John reported back that having an

(Continued)

opportunity to talk about and reflect on his feelings and behaviour in his coach mentoring sessions had helped to relieve some of his immediate feelings of stress. He said that it was a classic case of 'a problem aired is a problem shared; a problem shared is a problem halved'.

John undertook to conduct a time management audit. He also decided to ask for formal feedback from his manager and two of his colleagues about their opinion of his work performance. He decided to manage the feedback by requesting that they give specific examples, and he asked for positive comments as well as suggestions for any areas of development. He also made a commitment to book some time off and to leave work on time every Friday. John remained in coaching and mentoring for only four sessions. He experienced difficulty taking time out from his busy workload to attend the sessions. He reported back in his evaluation that the experience of talking to his mentor was extremely helpful and positive. He had got feedback from his manager that proved helpful. In particular, he had learnt that his manager's perception of his performance was better than he feared. He was successful in his job application to the post he had been covering. John had not successfully managed to block time out for annual leave and was not always successful at leaving work on time.

Significantly, John reported that he felt that his stress was reduced. He felt that he was more confident about his skills and abilities, and he believed that his self-esteem had improved. He recognized that he still had more work to do, particularly in relation to time management, and would probably return to coaching and mentoring in the future. He also said that he was conscious of regularly reflecting on his practice and felt he learned and benefited from doing this.

Parsloe and Wray (2000) point out that mentoring is most often oriented towards an exchange of wisdom, support, learning or guidance for the purpose of developing and achieving career and strategic business goals and personal, spiritual or life growth. Coaching, on the other hand, is typically result-, performance-, success- or goal-directed, with an emphasis on taking action and sustaining changes over time. Coaching is often used to improve performance in a specific area and is often more practice- than theory-driven. For mentoring to be truly successful the relationship should be strictly voluntary, and published guidelines warn against any financial connections. Coaching is very often provided on a fee basis. Both coaching and mentoring are usually provided on a one-to-one basis, but they can also be provided on a one-to-group basis, in peer groups, via email, telephone and even through video conferencing.

Peer group mentoring can be successfully utilized as a blended learning method in an adult learning programme. 'Blended learning' means using a variety of learning strategies that all combine to help development and learning. Blended learning could include face-to-face tutoring or workshops, reading complementary literature, online learning resources, independent study, action learning, etc. Although the term 'blended learning' seems relatively recent, the practice itself is not. In fact blended learning is something that most adults in the UK will have experienced during their school education and in further and higher education.

BOX 8.4   REFLECTION BREAK

Develop a list of learning strategies and resources that you might be able to use to develop yourself and that you might also be able to signpost learners to when you begin to coach mentor. These might be useful websites, online questionnaires and assessments, useful self-help books, learning on DVD, etc.

Zeus and Skiffington (2002) point out that the terms 'mentoring' and 'coaching' are used interchangeably, and Britnore Guest (1999) takes this further by suggesting that coaching and mentoring are looked upon as disciplines and practices that blend and overlap. Most coaches and mentors would probably agree that a good coach will also mentor and a good mentor will also coach, as appropriate to the situation and the relationship. In considering the best fit, therefore, the two approaches should be regarded as synergistic and complementary, rather than mutually exclusive (Britnore Guest, 1999).

At this point it might be worthwhile taking a moment to reflect back on some of the points raised in Chapter 6 where we explored how managers can use personal development plans (PDPs) to identify learning needs and how learners can learn most effectively, and that coaching can be a learning strategy. It is worthwhile adding that coaching and mentoring are not something that always have to be seen as being external to the manager and employee relationship. Coaching and mentoring techniques are a valuable tool that all managers should learn to integrate into their daily people management practices and to utilize in their face-to-face meetings with their employees. Doing so will enable them to make the most of their supervisions and PDPs with employees.

Coach mentoring techniques are used to develop congruence and rapport. They pull on many techniques that are classically linked to therapeutic relationships, such as active listening, reflective feedback, problem solving and empathy. While there may be therapeutic aspects to coaching and mentoring, for example the highs or lows a learner may experience because of a critical incident of learning, it is important to be clear that coach mentors are definitely not counsellors or therapists. Coaching and mentoring have strong links with action learning because they are focused on problem solving and a continuous process of learning and reflection.

Reflective practice is important because it engages us in actively being self-analytical. It encourages us to take responsibility for ourselves, our learning and for our own actions. It encourages continuing personal and professional development, discourages blame and encourages creativity, problem solving and continuing aspirations to raise quality and standards. In Chapter 6 we referred to the model of reflective and critical thinking from Kolb (Figure 6.1), which you may wish to revisit to consider how you might use these skills to develop your coach mentoring style. The most effective model of coaching and mentoring and action learning is that a learner is supported in getting things done. Action learning ultimately results in individuals learning with and from each other by working on real problems and reflecting on their own experiences (McGill and Beaty, 2001).

COACHING AND MENTORING IN PRACTICE

In order to ensure a proper focus during sessions, coaching and mentoring relationships should involve a proper contract of engagement or learning agreement. The contract or agreement should set clear parameters and boundaries around the relationship, for example where to meet – sessions should take place in a comfortable, quiet and private place – when and for how long to meet and over what agreed period of time–coach mentoring sessions will usually run for an hour and no longer than an hour and a half and usually for a minimum of six months and no longer than a year. Built into any contract should be an agreement to hold regular reviews and evaluations so that goals or objectives can be measured and the relationship continues to be effective. The parameters of the relationship should also be clear. For example, there would not usually be any contact between coach mentoring sessions except, for instance, to change times or cancel a session. An effective session should be focused, challenging and empowering. The skills of an effective coach or mentor are wide ranging and include:

- self-reflection and reflexivity;
- self-awareness;
- a commitment to one's own learning;
- an interest in developing others;
- empathy;

- congruency;
- empowerment and enabling approaches;
- active listening;
- open and enquiring questioning;
- good eye contact;
- open body language;
- assertiveness, honesty, and the ability to give meaningful and effective feedback;
- active respect and the valuing of difference and diversity.

Although this is a comprehensive list, all these skills and competencies should be employed by social workers and social care employees every day in their work with service users. Perhaps the most important competency of any coach mentor is the strong commitment to their own learning because this ensures that the experience of coaching and mentoring is a two-way learning process. A dedicated coach mentor should not be a personal friend or a direct line manager. This distance ensures that professional boundaries, impartiality and honesty are more easily maintained.

In previous chapters we have learned that the term 'leadership' is open to many different interpretations. Through the practice of coaching and mentoring we are able to demonstrate that leadership is about more than encouraging people to follow. It is about developing innovation, enabling people to walk alongside and eventually empowering them to walk past and become leaders themselves. Leadership in the context of coaching and mentoring, as we saw in Jenny's story, is about facilitating development, standing back and letting the other person fly without taking any of the credit. Coaching and mentoring is a powerful tool for succession planning, for developing the next generation of leaders and managers, and for supporting diverse learners to move up to and beyond the iniquitous glass ceiling (Hafford-Letchfield and Chick, 2006b).

BOX 8.5   CASE STUDY: PROACTIVE LEARNING

Elizabeth, an African Caribbean woman manager, was embarking on a course of study in the area of leadership and management. In her first coach mentoring session she reported that she was not sure that she could study at the academic level required. She felt undervalued and lacked confidence in herself as a manager. The objectives she set herself were 'to develop confidence, assertion and stress management and to develop greater political awareness and trust of others as well as self-respect'. With her coach mentor she developed a personal learning plan that included writing reflection notes about her learning. She carried out a time

(Continued)

management audit that enabled her to develop an effective study plan and carve out time to leave work on time at least once a week, not to take work home but to take time out to both relax and study. Elizabeth conducted a survey of her colleagues to get feedback about her performance at work. She read a book on assertion skills for managers and wrote a personal skills audit. After each session she completed a reflection note and developed personal learning and action points. She mapped her success at completing the tasks she set herself and reviewed these at the beginning of each session. Elizabeth always came to her session with a prepared agenda. Elizabeth often talked about her learning and her progress in the workplace and on the leadership course she was studying.

After five sessions Elizabeth reported feeling more confident and less critical of herself. She said she felt more assertive in the workplace and that a bonus of this was that she felt she was becoming more assertive in her personal life and she was able to give practical examples where she had used assertion skills. After eight sessions she reported that she felt greater respect for her practice and skills and that she felt there was also evidence of this from her team members. Elizabeth went on to achieve a leadership and management qualification and overcame another fear – she gave a presentation in public. Elizabeth is now a coach mentor.

A leader, manager or supervisor can utilize the skills and behaviours of coaching and mentoring to enable, empower and develop their employees. Rees and Porter (1996) suggest that it may be sometimes more effective for managers to coach an employee on the job rather than for such training to be provided off the job. They also suggest that by using coaching skills managers may be enabled to treat mistakes as learning opportunities rather than occasions for censure. Coaching and mentoring powerfully supports change, personal and professional development and learning, and organizational learning.

BOX 8.6   CASE STUDY: MANAGING CHANGE

Julie, a white woman senior manager in a local authority, was coach mentored for over 18 months. Throughout this she was involved in managing a team through extensive organizational change. Julie originally came to her sessions dubious that coaching and mentoring could offer her anything. She used her sessions to talk about the challenges of trying to motivate

(Continued)

(Continued)

disaffected employees during a period of difficult change. She discussed her anxieties about conflict and her guilt feelings about trying to balance her work and her parental role. She had little support from her own managers. It very quickly became clear for Julie that a valuable aspect of coaching and mentoring for her was having space to share her anxieties, concerns and fears. Rather than feeling judged, she felt listened to and believed that her confidentiality was assured and that she was given impartial and honest feedback. She was able to reflect in coach mentoring sessions on the process and management of change using management and leadership models of change to assess where she felt she, her organization and colleagues were at.

Julie was emotionally intelligent and she used her coach mentoring sessions to explore the benefits of this intelligence style and how to use this to her benefit. Julie very practically used her sessions to reflect on her management style, practice her responses to conflict, test out her approach to managing difficult team meetings and staff supervisions. She explored her guilt feelings about being a working parent and the difficulties she felt about leaving work on time in order to meet her parental responsibilities while her colleagues continued to work frenetically. Significantly, Julie started to practise coaching and mentoring in her own supervisions with her staff. She faced up to many of those difficult and challenging conversations she needed to have with her own manager and colleagues, and felt supported in doing this through her coaching and mentoring.

Coach mentors are not teachers. Instead, they facilitate and enable learning. It is important to note that coach mentors do not do the work for learners. Rather, they encourage and coerce the learner to take responsibility for their own behaviours and actions and then keep them focused and on track through questioning. Coaching and mentoring is not about sympathy but, through active listening, it is about demonstrating empathy, understanding, appreciation, support, encouragement and empowerment. Ultimately, coach mentoring is about enabling someone to find their own way and to make the changes that they want or need to make. A coach mentor will always be honest and will never makes promises about positive outcomes. Unlike therapy and counselling, a coach mentor will be impartial and non-judgemental. A coach mentor can provide a mirror to enable a learner to study and explore their aims, objectives, hopes and fears, and then through this reflection they are enabled to explore options for change. A coach mentor will always aim for complete congruence.

Coach mentors in a business context will not specifically focus on a learner's personal life but will rather focus on their professional life. However, as the case studies in this chapter demonstrate, the personal cannot always be avoided in coach mentoring sessions. Where the personal is a factor, the coach mentor will always aim to steer the conversation back to how the personal may affect the professional. Coaching and mentoring should not be confused as a passive role. A coach mentor will be challenging and hold learners to account for their behaviours and actions. But they are not directive. Their role is to create personal responsibility and enable people to identify the way forward – to map out where they want to get to and then get there.

COACHING AND MENTORING IN THE ORGANIZATIONAL CONTEXT

Coaching and mentoring promotes and supports organizational development and learning in a variety of ways:

- Supporting new employees into the organization and during induction.
- Supporting learners engaged in professional academic education or work-based learning.
- Helping employees identify and work towards achieving career aspirations, objectives and goals.
- Supporting individuals or teams through change.
- Helping to identify and develop leadership and management skills and behaviours.
- Supporting the development and advancement of black and other minority ethnic employees and other employees who may be most at risk of disadvantage.
- Promoting, nurturing and developing diversity in the workplace.
- Promoting, nurturing and developing talent.
- Promoting an understanding of how to manage work-related stress.
- Supporting and developing underachievers or poor performers.
- Observing work practices and providing impartial and high-quality feedback to enable development.
- Engaging employees in preparing to learn and reflect on learning.
- Supporting succession planning by developing the leaders of the future.
- Supporting shadowing and secondment.

This list is by no means complete. Coaching and mentoring that is provided either through a formal scheme or through coach mentoring behaviours as a part of effective leadership and management, for example in one-to-one sessions, will contribute to formal, informal and unconscious learning and development up and down the organization, and will, through practice and example, contribute to the development of a coaching and mentoring culture in the organization.

DEVELOPING A COACHING AND MENTORING SCHEME

There are a variety of workplace coaching and mentoring models and probably the most well known are the internal scheme using line managers and off-site managers or an external scheme using fee-paid coach mentors. Each of these models delivers clear advantages and disadvantages.

An internal scheme that trains, supports and uses only internal managers as coach mentors can be effective, especially as this gives a clear message about ownership of the scheme and coach mentoring practice in the organization's culture. By developing internal coach mentors, the organization gives a clear message about its investment in the scheme. The development of these skills in its workforce will directly contribute to the development of a 'coaching culture' in the workplace. However, the extent of creativity and innovation of learning could be diluted or stifled because learners may feel less comfortable or able to open up fully to internal colleagues and managers. Learners may also feel less able to challenge the coach mentor's practice and the quality of coaching and mentoring could be inhibited. Using only internal coach mentors also may minimize the impact on cultural change within the organization. Finally, personnel resources can become limited as, over time, it is often the same personnel who invariably come forward to take on coach mentoring roles.

External fee-paid coach mentors can provide benefits because they bring an external, impartial view to the organization. Rees and Porter (1996) suggest that external mentors may be able to develop a more confidential relationship with the person they are mentoring than would be possible with an internal mentor. The greater the trust, the more likely there is to be greater learning and development. It is also usually the case that external coaches or mentors are more professionally qualified. They can provide information about other organizations and can be dismissed more easily if a relationship does not work. However, they also have limitations. External coach mentors may not understand or appreciate the host organization's culture. They can be expensive and therefore are usually time-limited, and the cost also usually restricts coaching and mentoring to the fortunate few who are often at the top of the organization. External coach mentors can also result in leaders and managers off-loading problematic colleagues rather than dealing with poor performance and challenging behaviour. There may also be a loss of ownership of the skills of coaching and mentoring and this may negatively impact upon the development of an organizational coaching culture. The model that can provide all the same benefits as the schemes above and potentially minimize the weaknesses is an Inter-agency Coaching and Mentoring Scheme (ICMS).

DEVELOPING A MENTORING SCHEME
ACROSS DIFFERENT ORGANIZATIONS

A partnership of social care, health and housing providers in a London borough developed an ICMS. The project was launched as a pilot in 2002 in partnership with Social Services, Housing, an NHS Primary Care Trust and a local voluntary social care organization. The pilot was specifically developed to provide coaching and mentoring to a cohort of learners on a positive action, aspiring managers programme for black and other minority ethnic employees, women, gay men and disabled employees. The scheme ran originally for nine months, after which time it was evaluated. The feedback from those involved in the scheme was consistently positive, with each person involved reporting that the experience of either being coached mentored or being a coach mentor had been positive and developmental. Some talked about 'inspiration', 'extending skills', 'an enjoyable and positive experience' and 'finding own solutions', while others mentioned 'relieving pressure', 'management development' and 'learning about different organizations'. Following the evaluation, the scheme was re-launched in 2004 with a revised set of objectives:

- To support staff in professional development and welfare.
- To encourage inter-agency partnership and best practice.
- To enable learning and create a learning organization.
- To provide opportunities to develop a different perspective.

The scheme specifically aimed to:

- support employee professional development and career development;
- provide opportunities for individuals to reflect on their work issues in a safe environment;
- develop and build management capacity;
- support and celebrate diversity;
- enable the management of individual stress;
- demonstrate valuing and respect of staff;
- develop individual staff so that they input more effectively into plans that affect customers.

The project aimed to:

- develop greater shared understanding of each partner's work and perspectives;
- open boundaries and encourage inter-agency partnerships and work;
- encourage greater understanding of what other agencies do;
- build supportive networks;
- encourage and facilitate collaboration to improve service delivery;
- learn from experience;
- develop positive role models;
- encourage and develop the skills of self-reflection;
- support the development of informal learning.

The scheme was originally launched with a partnership of three organizations and, over time, grew and developed into a partnership of nine business partners, three local authorities, three National Health Service Trusts, one private and voluntary agency, a university and a consultancy group. The original group of only nine coach mentors and 19 learners grew to a group of over 40 coach mentors and a group of over 90 learners. At the centre of the ICMS is a steering group made up of members nominated by partner agencies. The steering group provides development and coordination of the scheme, and the recruitment, training and matching of coach mentors and learners. The scheme that was developed blended learning resources, including a facilitated coach mentoring skills learning course, an open learning pack, a coach mentors' network, an online discussion forum and a newsletter. The steering group members also supported and coach mentored the group's coach mentors. It also has quality assurance measures in place, such as the monitoring and evaluation of relationships and learning outcomes.

The steering group is supported by a volunteer coordinator who is also appointed through one of the partner agencies and who takes on the role in addition to their normal day job. The scheme members hope that in time it will be possible to raise funding to create a permanent, dedicated development and coordinator post, which can contribute to research and develop the scheme across other partner agencies. Some of the benefits of the inter-agency coach mentoring model is the sharing and cross-fertilization of learning beyond organizational and cultural borders. The actual coaching and mentoring sessions should ideally be free to the user at the point of delivery because of reciprocity and sharing time and human resources (Hafford-Letchfield and Chick, 2006a).

Figure 8.1 illustrates what the inter-agency model might look like and is based on the model described above.

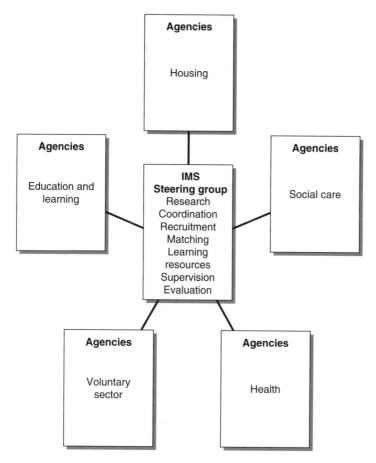

Figure 8.1   Model of an inter-agency mentoring scheme

Because coach mentors come from each partner and work across organizational boundaries, this results in the following:

- Widening participation – access to coaching and mentoring is available to a wider user-group up and down the organization because there is no funding issue, only time out.
- Learners have greater choice because they are able to request a match either in their own organization or from a partner agency. Experience shows that more people are likely to choose an external coach mentor.
- Learners report feeling freer to talk openly about their learning needs because of the trusting and confidential environment.
- Learners are less anxious about revealing their areas of weakness.

- There is increased networking across organizational and cultural boundaries.
- There is an opportunity to cross-fertilize learning.
- There is free access to knowledge and expertise that may not be so readily accessible through either an internal scheme or an external fee-paid scheme.

The actual overall cost of providing the scheme should be minimal because it relies mostly on personnel time rather than paying fees, and each organization contributes some time, some paper resources and a place to meet and learn. Finally, increasing access to coaching and mentoring, and the development of the skills of coaching and mentoring, should present a win–win situation. There are more opportunities for leaders and managers to learn the skills of coaching and mentoring if they have experienced being coach mentored. Ultimately, this should affect their own leadership and management style and affect the learning, development and performance of their colleagues. The practices, philosophies and values of coaching and mentoring will hopefully cascade through the organization and help embed a coaching and mentoring culture. If the development of a full inter-agency scheme seems too big or complex, why not simply start small and begin by developing your own relationship with one or two other agencies or providers in your area – perhaps an agency you work with and know well. Test out and invite the possibility of sharing coaching and mentoring resources across your agencies on a reciprocal basis and see how it works. Start small and who knows where it may lead.

CHAPTER SUMMARY

Social work and social care workers are concerned with defending, supporting and protecting the development, independence and potential of people in society who are often the most vulnerable and in need of support. Essentially, social work and social care is based on a philosophy that everyone has the right to learn, grow and develop, and maximize their own potential. Coaching and mentoring practices are based on the same beliefs. Managers who develop and use coach mentoring skills actively support their employees to learn, grow and develop and reach their potential at work. They actively demonstrate respect for their employees and promote diversity, creativity and talent. If you manage a social work or social care service, the skills of coach mentoring should be firmly rooted in your leadership and management practices and encouraged in your employees and in their work with service users. This chapter should help you get started and whet your appetite for more so that you can actively explore the benefits of coaching and mentoring in the workplace and beyond.

Recommended further reading

D. Clutterbuck (2001): *Everyone Needs a Mentor: Fostering Talent at Work* (3rd edition) (London: The Chartered Institute of Personnel and Development) explores many of the key issues to focus on when developing mentoring skills and a work-based mentoring scheme. David Clutterbuck is an acknowledged authority on mentoring. He gives practical advice on every stage of the process from matching mentors and learners through to identifying when the mentoring relationship should come to an end.

E. Parsloe and M. Wray (2000) *Coaching and Mentoring: Practical Methods to Improve Learning* (London: Kogan Page) is an accessible and easy-to-read book. It explores both the theory and practice of coaching and mentoring in the context of work, education and community action. It provides a very practical introduction to the subject and, like Clutterbuck above, is a good place to start exploring these important practices.

J. Starr (2003) *The Coaching Manual: The Definitive Guide to the Process, Principles and Skills of Personal Coaching* (Edinburgh: Pearson Education) provides guidance and advice for both new and experienced coaches. It looks at what to do and how to do it, encouraging the reader to engage in step-by-step exercises that aim to improve coaching skills.

Web-based resources

The Coaching and Mentoring Network (www.coaching network.org.uk) – provides information, resources and services for people providing coaching or mentoring services and for those seeking them. It aims to demystify coaching and mentoring and make them more accessible for people in business and in the community. It describes itself as a 'community portal and resource centre on the internet for information and services relating to coaching and mentoring'.

9 KNOWLEDGE MANAGEMENT IN SOCIAL CARE AND MANAGEMENT DEVELOPMENT

This chapter explores:

- The theories of knowledge management and their application to social care
- The role of practitioner evaluation and research in developing and improving services
- The importance of management development and strategies used to develop leadership and management in social care

---

INTRODUCTION

Throughout this book we have made constant reference to the concept of *knowledge* and the ways in which knowledge is acquired and transferred through the process of *learning*. Knowledge is an important strategic asset of many organizations (Clegg et al., 2005) and is closely interlinked with learning, both of which are two sides of the same coin. Increasing interest in the concept of *knowledge management* has been linked to the need for organizations to maintain a 'competitive' edge and to their survival in complex and ever-changing environments. One specific consequence of change for social care has been the need to have up-to-date and useful knowledge of the social, political, legislative, policy and economic environment, as well to be able to respond and reflect the diversity of service users' and carers' views. Therefore, our knowledge base has to be structured and organized in such a way that it can be easily accessed and utilized when required. Knowledge management describes this process, that is a process by which knowledge is created, stored, distributed and used for decision making. Knowledge management focuses on the actual creation, dissemination and transformation of knowledge, whereas learning involves change in the existing state of knowledge. Knowledge management also focuses on the existing resources within an organization, whereas learning focuses on the dynamic development of those resources.

At the beginning of this book we considered these processes in meeting the existing and future needs of the workforce, and those which enable an organization to develop and capitalize on opportunities to improve any services provided. In this last chapter we will look, first, at sources of knowledge that are specific to care and identify useful ways of classifying these. Understanding what constitutes the knowledge base of social care also requires examination of the contribution of different research and evaluative methodologies towards creating and providing evidence for practice. We will be looking at the contribution of the key methodologies commonly used in social care research before going on to look at how we might incorporate research and evaluation into practice and its development.

Attention to the active management of knowledge by organizational theorists first became prominent when change management became linked with management learning (Senge, 1996), so we will conclude this chapter, and indeed this book, by looking at approaches to leadership and management development. At the beginning of this book you were asked to think about your own leadership style in relation to the theories. Here you are asked to reconsider your own leadership style, learning and development needs. Leadership and management development in social care has, in reality, been a neglected area, lacking coherence and consistency and resulting in a fragmented *ad hoc* approach to developing its managers (McDonnell and Zutshi, 2006b). The Leadership and Management Standards for social care have set the direction for management development strategies by linking management and organizational development (Skills for Care, 2006a). It goes without saying, therefore, that to be effective in your role in developing others, attention to the nature, use and acquisition of your own managerial skills and other attributes is crucial.

TYPES OF KNOWLEDGE IN SOCIAL CARE

Experience from business and industry has identified the potential of knowledge management to increase the effectiveness of an organization and the preconditions required to ensure the success of a knowledge management strategy. In order to understand what approach is needed, it is important to first explore and review the types and quality of social care knowledge available. Work done by Pawson et al. (2003: 25) can help us here, as their comprehensive review has led to the development of a useful classification system. This is based on two aspects: first, by examining the process through which knowledge is created (e.g. through audit, review, survey, trial or evaluation); and, secondly, the vehicle through which knowledge is disseminated (e.g. through academic literature, education and training, policy and procedures, as well as less formal means). This approach dismisses any hierarchy in knowledge production while pointing to the potential for making quality judgements about a particular piece of evidence from each source. The five source domains offered by Pawson et al. (2003) are as follows.

ORGANIZATIONAL KNOWLEDGE

This represents the broad knowledge frameworks that shape social care and provide a comprehensive accountability framework mostly through governance and regulatory activities. Box 1.1 (see p. 19) identified the key bodies which promote and govern national standards. At the core of any organizational standards are regulatory requirements which lay down 'minimally acceptable' standards covering virtually every aspect of social care practice. While these are often thought of as 'given', it cannot be taken for granted that these standards are easily or actually implemented and evaluated, despite the complex national and local apparatus of training, inspection, audit and inquiry that appear to do this. High-performing organizations tend to consult a wider range of stakeholders and are more aspirational in setting standards which enable them to appraise and interact with their own local knowledge base (Clegg et al., 2005). Organizations grappling with more difficult issues, such as outcomes of certain interventions, or organizations that are more dynamic in developing risk management or risk aversion standards are more likely to learn and develop their knowledge base.

PRACTITIONER KNOWLEDGE

Social care is conducted through the medium of practitioners' knowledge. As we saw in Chapter 6, the idea of reflective practice lies at the heart of practitioners' knowledge and is acquired though the distillation of collective wisdom at many points, such as through education and training, supervision and consultation, team working as well as personal approaches where practitioners judge their efforts in terms of emotional rewards, peer approval, service user feedback and 'gut reactions'. Practitioner knowledge tends to be personal and context-specific, and therefore difficult to surface, articulate and aggregate. At the same time, practitioners' knowledge can operate through a highly systematic analytical and critical process on common issues pertinent to their direct work with service users.

USER AND CARER KNOWLEDGE

Increasing service user involvement, and the development of user-led and emancipatory research based on the social model, has aimed at creating a knowledge base which increases users' choice and control over their own lives and involving them in all decisions about the delivery of services. In Chapter 4, we explored the importance of harnessing the experiences of users and carers in a way that facilitates their leadership role and to develop outcome indicators and measures that give priority to user and carer perspectives on interventions.

RESEARCH KNOWLEDGE

This is among the most palpable sources of social care knowledge and is that derived from empirical inquiries based on predetermined research strategies. These provide the reports, evaluations, assessments, measurements and so forth, which are the most orthodox items in any evidence base. Debates about transparency, accuracy, purpose and propriety, as well as issues about ethics and quality, need to be further developed in social care research. Critical appraisal of research-based evidence has been incorporated as an essential skill and competency within continuing professional development in social care so that both practitioners and users are able to judge its quality and relevance.

POLICY COMMUNITY KNOWLEDGE

This category sets social care in its wider policy context by providing knowledge about what social care does and how it might fit into its complex political, social and economic environment. Structural models to understand social problems and issues, and vital knowledge about the organization and implementation of services, are derived from the broader policy community. The key contributors to policy community knowledge include central, regional and local government and its agencies and the members of think tanks, lobby groups, policy and research staff in political parties and scholars of public policy.

BOX 9.1　REFLECTION BREAK

Eraut (1994: 120) has stated that professional work of any complexity requires the concurrent use of several kinds of knowledge in an integrated and purposeful manner. The summary of the different domains of social care knowledge (outlined above) can be used as a foundation tool for organizing, understanding and accessing knowledge in

(Continued)

(Continued)

your specific area of practice. With this in mind, are you able to give any examples of the specific sources of knowledge that inform your area of practice? Are you aware of giving any priority to a particular domain and what might be the reasons for this? Can you identify any conflicts or tensions in accessing or promoting particular sources of knowledge? Finally, what opportunities are available in your service to acquire and share knowledge, and how is time allocated for potential users of knowledge to learn how to use it effectively?

In reflecting on the above, you may have recognized tensions in defining or giving particular emphasis to the different types of knowledge used in your organization. This raises issues about the problematic, uncertain and ambiguous nature of knowledge which reflects the character of social work and social care. Further, the subject matter, form and quality of responses are determined not just by the values, knowledge and skills of workers and managers, but also by the demands of government and the perceptions of other professionals, the media and the public (Lyons, 1999). In earlier chapters we acknowledged that our professional and personal experiences provide a framework through which new experiences are interpreted. The implications for professional education are that it needs to recognize that professionals already possess a great deal of relevant knowledge as a result of working in a particular organizational culture or environment. The continuous professional development (CPD) process provides the opportunity to develop a greater awareness of how knowledge is used and to re-examine taken-for-granted assumptions. The active use of critical reflection then helps to assimilate new learning into existing experiences. This process is based on a wider assent to the need for social work to be 'evidence-based' and become part of 'normal' practice (Shaw, 2005).

Running alongside, however, are tensions that arise with increasing moves to proceduralize social work practice by providing rapid assessment tools and procedures manuals which go hand in hand with management imperatives. According to Shaw (2004), this intertwining of evidence-based practice and managerialism in social care has given rise to the argument that good *management* practice and good *evaluation* practice are one and the same thing, and reflect a set of beliefs or doctrines, relationships and management techniques, aimed at enhancing the effectiveness, efficiency and productivity of social care services. However, reducing the evaluation of good practice merely to units that can be measured does not take account of other perspectives, such as service user involvement, the notion of reflective professional practitioner or the impact of its local context. While it has been argued that this approach offers some way towards standardizing practice, it may well restrict other benefits that can be achieved from evaluation.

DEVELOPING A KNOWLEDGE MANAGEMENT APPROACH

We have established that social care is an extremely knowledge-rich activity, and the potential to manage knowledge to improve the quality of care is important for all those interested in organizational and work-based learning. The relationship between knowledge and practice has been the subject of long, sometimes apparently interminable, debate (Sheppard et al., 2000). Knowledge is generally considered to be of two main types:

- *tacit* – the knowledge derived from practice and experience, which is context-specific and consists of personal beliefs and values and perspectives that individuals take for granted; and
- *explicit* – theoretically based knowledge which is more easily stored and accessible (Polanyi, 1983).

In the last decade, management theorists have noted that tacit knowledge contributes significantly to innovation processes and it is important for managers to know how to organize and manage tacit knowledge and how to transform elements of tacit knowledge into organizationally explicit knowledge. However, most knowledge management approaches consist only of storing explicit knowledge, albeit those from the social constructionist school (Lave and Wenger, 2002), who have highlighted the important interactive social process of creating and sharing knowledge.

Sandars (2004) describes a further four main elements of the knowledge management process which accounts for managing both tacit and explicit knowledge in an organization. First, Sandars talks about the generation of knowledge in which new explicit knowledge is created from research and involves the conversion of tacit into explicit knowledge which is subsequently stored and distributed as the 'evidence-base'. New tacit knowledge is developed by the daily experiences of individuals and by the internalization of explicit knowledge. Secondly, the storage of knowledge whereby explicit knowledge is stored in a variety of formats, particularly using IT and information libraries. Tacit knowledge is more difficult to articulate and store, and may be embodied within the notion of management, practitioner and service user 'expertise', which in turn can be accessed through direct observation of practice. Thirdly, the distribution or provision of the right knowledge at the right time is of major importance in enabling effective decision making and action. Information technology is now a dominant distributor of explicit knowledge. Tacit knowledge, however, can be distributed to people within an organization through work-based learning and the systems to support it, such as coach mentoring, supervision and team working, some of which we have already explored in much more detail in this book. Finally, Sandars (2004) reminds us that knowledge is useless unless it is utilized for problem solving and applied to inform decision making. Both explicit and tacit knowledge need to be acknowledged and translated into practice as an essential task of knowledge management and 'communities of practice' are an important vehicle here.

In the beginning of this book we referred to the influence of imaginative leadership and organizational culture in developing a learning organization. Learning is more powerful if there is a collective approach and trust is a critical factor in the sharing of tacit knowledge. Knowledge management can fail to understand the complexities of practice and the processes through which it is learned and then stored on the knowledge management system (Eraut, 2005). A robust physical structure, which provides the technical support and systems for staff to access and develop search strategies supported by time and relevant skill development (e.g. IT skills), provides the necessary conditions to realize the potential benefits of knowledge to improve services. Effective knowledge management in an organization enables it to identify which individuals and teams are performing in a way that provides examples of good practice. It also encourages ways of sharing aspects of practice that contribute to improved performance (Martin, 2003). On a strategic scale, the realization of the need for there to be an organization with lead responsibility for undertaking and/or commissioning systematic reviews of knowledge in social care led to the creation of the Social Care Institute of Excellence (SCIE). SCIE provides a specialist resource for knowledge management in social care by creating, reviewing and disseminating best practice in an accessible and systematic way, using an easily recognized format which carries credibility and authority (www.scie.org.uk). The Joint University Social Work Education Research Council (JUSWEC), in liaison with the Economic and Social Research Council (ESRC), also provide a UK-wide strategic framework for research, which includes applied and practice-based research and identifies appropriate priorities, training and governance. What is critical overall is that the social work academic and practice community maintains its drive and cohesiveness so that there is an authoritative voice for social work and social care knowledge.

In conclusion, all kinds of knowledge are necessary to improve professional performance and the systematic management of knowledge, and the transformation of this through learning is one of the features of a learning organization (Gould, 2000). What is also required, however, is the ability to make a realistic assessment of the relative strengths and weaknesses of the ideological and methodological position taken in appraising and selecting knowledge, combined with an awareness of the ethical issues when balancing what is known about individual rights and public welfare between individual responsibilities and structural inequality and oppression (Lishman, 2000). Whatever source of knowledge is preferred or utilized to promote or defend choices of intervention or practice, there will always be a balancing of rights, duties and responsibilities in social care, for which there may be no 'right answer'. As Lishman (1998: 90) reminds us: 'An ethical response may conflict with financial accountability and resource availability: it may inform or conflict with legal accountability.'

THE ROLE OF PRACTITIONER EVALUATION AND RESEARCH IN DEVELOPING AND IMPROVING SERVICES THROUGH THE USE OF KNOWLEDGE

Social care knowledge production needs research that begins with practice-relevant questions and ends with relevant material that can be usefully applied to practice (Marsh et al., 2005). Practitioners should be encouraged to engage in the evaluation of their own practice and possess the skills necessary to undertake the evaluative task (McIvor, 1995). Research and evaluation capability in social care depends on building its capacity and expertise. Social work research has already shown strengths in certain areas, as follows:

- qualitative and action research methods, data production and analysis;
- accessing hard-to-research groups;
- involving research users in research processes;
- incorporating a diversity of knowledge bases; and
- paying attention to impact: dissemination, application and implementation of findings.

However, weaknesses are also apparent, for example, in:

- basic and advanced quantitative research methods, data gathering and analysis, which do not always incorporate the perspectives of service users;
- advanced qualitative research methods;
- economic costing; and
- theory building. (www.ssrg.org.uk/consultations/juc/JUCSTRATE-GYMARCH20TH.doc)

Care councils that register social care staff and regulate training (e.g. General Social Care Council (GSCC)) and sector skills councils (e.g. Skills for Care and Children's Workforce Development Council (CWDC)) that promote workforce development both have a critical role in developing the research workforce. Re-registration and CPD also require staff to engage with knowledge evaluation and production as an integral part of professional responsibility, accountability and development. According to Pawson et al. (2003: xi), questions to be asked when appraising any piece of knowledge should include ones about its transparency, scrutiny, purpose, utility, propriety, accessibility and specificity. This implies the selection or integration of different methodological approaches to provide the infrastructure for social care knowledge production, which recognizes the multiple causes of social problems and issues and has a high commitment to interdisciplinary team perspectives and participatory and emancipatory approaches (Marsh et al., 2005). The complexity and contested nature of practice and knowledge further frustrates us in examining whether social care is effective, for whom and in what ways. Measuring outcomes has to include how practice is experienced and evaluated by both its users and practitioners, and whether these are attributable to our interventions or other factors and unrelated changes in the lives of service users, which may influence measured outcomes negatively or positively (Macdonald and Sheldon, 1998). As stated earlier, identifying appropriate measures highlights the tensions between these outcomes and the managerial or political agenda involving external audit and review, and there are many ethical issues at stake if we are to produce knowledge that is transformatory in delivering services.

PRACTITIONER RESEARCH AND CHOICE OF METHODS

The contributions of competing methodologies to the evaluation and evidence for social work practice often polarizes quantitative and qualitative methodologies, the former being associated with measurement, causality, experiment and fact and the latter with judgement, values, interpretation, meaning and experience. A pluralistic approach, utilizing both methods as appropriate, and outlined by Lishman (2000), may better encapsulate the complexity of social work practice and address the range of stakeholders and competing interests. We will not be exploring here how to develop different research and evaluation methods, and have recommended a suitable text if you want to read further at the end of this chapter. However, we want to focus on the potential of practitioners as a source of critical practice in social work and other professions, and their involvement in planned research, evaluation or inquiry as part of their primary practitioner role. Shaw (2005: 1235–6) suggests that practioners' research includes direct data collection and management, or reflection on existing data. Professionals should be involved in setting the aims and outcomes of any research so that it has immediate and instrumental practical benefits for professionals, service organizations and/or service users. Shaw further highlights the benefits of practitioners conducting a substantial proportion of the inquiry as 'insiders' and *about* practice, so that it focuses on their own practice and that of their immediate peers, is small-scale, short-term and self-contained.

Opportunities for practitioners to undertake research can be associated with career opportunities and pursuing a higher education degree (e.g. in the post-qualifying framework for social workers at higher specialist or advanced level), or can be agency-owned through promoting a new service development and delivery agenda. Practitioner researchers in these roles can assist in the building of theoretical knowledge directly from practice, so that the knowledge created is contextually relevant and flexible. Eraut (1994: 54) has argued that professional knowledge is usually defined by the research community rather than the professional community, which he describes as 'codified, published and public'. He argues that traditional researchers need to extend their roles from that of creator and transmitter of generalizable knowledge to that of enhancing the knowledge creation capacities of individuals from professional communities (Eraut, 1994: 57). This takes us back to the discussion at the beginning of this chapter, which questions fundamental assumptions about the types and hierarchies of knowledge that can often be devalued or discounted (Fook, 2001), and opens up possibilities for legitimating knowledge and perspectives which have previously been ignored, trivialized or disallowed. Fook (2001: 6) refers to the emancipatory possibilities for practitioners in making the links between theory, practice and research, by constructing these out of the everyday choices that practitioners make.

There are broadly three methodological approaches relevant to empirical evaluation or research in social care. The first is a positivist, *quantitative* approach which applies scientific perspectives and experimental design and methods in practice. The strengths of this approach include the direct linking of evaluation and individual cases and the way in which it emphasizes the practitioner's ownership of evaluation in practice. This helps to make it very specific, time-limited and based on evaluating predetermined aims and goals of actual interventions (Lishman, 2000). Critiques of scientific practice, however, highlight the failure of positivist approaches to recognize context, by supporting a view of knowledge that is rational and empirical and easily commodifiable from a managerial perspective. Glasby and Beresford (2006) go further to argue that objectivity is not a prerequisite for valid evidence, and can even be harmful in some circumstances, as it neglects the views and experiences of people who use and work in services.

The second is *qualitative* research, which has been said to have a natural synergy with the processes of professional practice in the way it starts with the service user or practice setting and fits with an emphasis on understanding the person within their environment. It uses case studies, ethnography, discourse analysis and narrative enquiry. Guilgun (1994), for example, has paralleled this approach with the individualized social work processes of assessment and intervention. The potential weaknesses of this approach include a lack of clarity about the specific purposes of intervention and related outcomes, and a focus on individual, specific experience rather than data which is generalizable (Lishman, 2000).

Finally, the most recent and relevant of research approaches are those developing within *emancipatory service user-controlled research*. These are led by movements of health and social care users and derived from the different user group's rights, perspectives and lifestyles. As we saw in Chapter 4, the strengths of participatory research paradigms lie in their inclusiveness and commitments to change, and in the more equal social relations of research production, which recognize accountability of practitioners to service users and not just to employing organizational hierarchies. Benefits in including the voices of people who may be excluded by race, gender, disability, mental health, age, learning disability or poverty, or a combination of these factors, can also be achieved (Lishman, 2000; Begum, 2006).

BOX 9.2 REFLECTION BREAK

What opportunities exist within your area of practice to promote practitioner research? What sorts of method would you advocate and what are the potential strengths and weaknesses of these approaches? How can knowledge generated by practioners be disseminated in your organizations and what support and resources are needed to develop practitioner research capacity and maximize its participatory elements?

Ultimately, the best method for researching any given topic is that which will answer the research or practice question most effectively and engages the 'practice wisdom' or 'tacit knowledge' of practitioners, which can be just as valid a way of understanding the world as any formal research study (Glasby and Beresford, 2006). According to Shaw (2005: 1245), the social work community should avoid being sanguine about the ability of practitioners' research, which can contribute to the knowledge agenda in 'direct proportion to the extent to which it yields diverse projects that take practicality and knowledge utilization seriously, that are supported by capacity and resources to deliver, and that include a central concern with providing a critique of practice and services, harnessed to a social justice agenda for and with service users'. This means that a strategic approach to research infrastructure development requires the recognition that practice itself is a key source of knowledge. With this in mind, you could generate debate in your service area about how practice identifies issues for the research agenda, and how research-based knowledge can be integrated with the knowledge that the practitioners you manage already use (Marsh et al., 2005).

BOX 9.3   DEVELOPING INFORMATION AND RESEARCH SKILLS TO SUPPORT EVIDENCE-BASED SOCIAL CARE

Booth et al. (2003) undertook a literature review and survey to determine attitudes to evidence-based practice, access to information and training requirements of 595 social care practioners in one region. Their literature review revealed a workforce that was poorly equipped with professional education and that relied heavily on personal communication and 'gut instinct' to deliver packages of care. They concluded that a culture of action, not reflection, and the absence of information resources and skills, make social care practioners less likely to consult research to improve their practice. Some of the barriers identified by staff were heavy workloads and a lack of accessibility to relevant information and time allocated to find and read research findings. The lack of a culture of questioning, where untrained managers expected staff to implement research findings without giving permission for debate or guidance, was influenced by budgets, and politics dictated services rather than research evidence itself.

They recommended that training in information and research skills should be available in both taught and self-directed formats, and that they should be pitched at a pragmatic level, to support existing work activities, rather than at an academic, detached, theoretical level. They also identified the need to recognize methods that were sensitive to differences between the

(Continued)

(Continued)

cultures of social care and health care in joint teams. They found that the implementation of evidence-based practice has generally led to a re-interpretation and distortion by different professional groups, with growing signs of a medically dominated model of evidence, with an emphasis on quantitative research and randomized controlled trials. While this has been modified through the influence of the caring professions, through greater joint working, moving to a more acceptable form which further aligns with the important influence of the service user within social services was recommended.

Source: Booth et al. (2003)

Given the interdisciplinary nature of evidence for practice, a major challenge is to provide arrangements that support integration of knowledge across the different communities and hierarchies involved in research production. To conclude this section, Fook's (2001: 6) recommendations are helpful in considering how new models for collaboration might be created in a number of spheres. These include inclusive research designs and methodologies that enable knowledge creation from practice (e.g. reflective approaches, case studies, practice-focused research). Conceptions of social work research should not be based on existing sciences but actively value-inclusive approaches that mirror the holistic and multidisciplinary nature of social work. Fook recommends the critical questioning of assumptions and practices which automatically silence or devalue the voices of practitioners. Self-reflexivity is one method that she promotes as proving useful for militating against cultures and environments which exclude the practitioner's perspective. The creation of infrastructures and processes which allow collaboration between researchers and practitioners, and their respective institutions, at both macro and micro levels are important, and Fook gives an example of setting up a student practice research unit in the practice organization itself. Any institutions which actively seek to transform the research and practice culture into an integrated one need not only policies and procedures to achieve this, but also CPD programmes which integrate relevant research approaches, especially into everyday practice, and encourage practitioners to *think* research. All of this should be enshrined within educational philosophies and practices which communicate and model an integration of practice, theory and research (Fook, 2001).

KNOWLEDGE IN SOCIAL CARE – A SUMMARY

In this section we have examined the unstated assumption about what is meant by 'knowledge' in social care (Sheppard, 1995) and considered the relationship between knowledge and practice, the notion of knowledge as a product which can be written down and formally used in practice as opposed to that knowledge which practitioners build up through their case experience and use to interpret meaning for action (Schön, 1991). We are unable to draw any conclusions from this ongoing debate, but nevertheless it is important to acknowledge that the process of knowledge application is problematic and such awareness is essential to those involved in both formal and work-based learning, where skilled and rigorous cognitive processes can help inform the conduct and recognition of good practice in social care (Sheppard et al., 2000). We will now conclude this chapter, and indeed this book, by giving attention to your own knowledge base and skill development as a leader, manager or facilitator of learning.

LEADERSHIP AND MANAGEMENT DEVELOPMENT

> None of us is perfect ... we inevitably have a profile of strengths and limits. (Goleman, 1998: 25)

Throughout this book we have been absolutely clear that if you are a manager in social care, you have a lead responsibility for promoting, developing and supporting learning in your everyday practice. What we have not discussed specifically, however, is the manager's own need for learning and professional development, and this provides us with the topic for the final and concluding section of this book.

Management is essentially a practical activity and all managers use a range of knowledge and skills that cannot easily be categorized yet needs to be integrated into their practice. This integrative task involves achieving synergy, balance and perspective (Harrison, 2005). Most management activity is undertaken through complex webs of social and political interaction involving a continuous process of adaptation to changing pressures and opportunities (Hafford-Letchfield, 2006). Particular aspects of social care make the role of management unique, setting it apart from other more traditional management roles. For example, the nature of public sector accountability, the contested power relations between professionals and managers, and the relatively recent emphasis on the role of managers in organizing effective service provision all point to the need for a multi-layered approach to any leadership and management development strategy. According to Kearney (2004: 103), managers are also the mediators and arbiters of standards and quality of practice in social care, and this has clearly been demonstrated throughout this book where we have closely examined aspects of what constitutes skilled and knowledgeable leadership in the learning and change process. Managing practice also involves combining available knowledge of external standards, statutory requirements and organizational procedures with internal knowledge and skills in how these operate. All of this knowledge and skill should provide integrated support to individuals and service users to bring about significant change.

First-line managers are particularly important as we depend on them to manage services, interpret thresholds, juggle resources and deliver policies.

> Managers are now having to commission and purchase services from the 'care market', devise contracts, integrate service provision through the development of new partnerships as well as manage multi-disciplinary teams. In addition to keeping down costs, they have to maintain standards of quality in accordance with government requirements. (Lawler and Harlow, 2005: 1167)

In addition, there is of course the vital 'people management' role that managers hold. During the past decade, management researchers have begun to pay particular attention to the concept of self-awareness and its effect on individual and organizational outcomes (Atwater and Yammarino, 1992). Self-awareness has been defined in the literature as one's ability to compare oneself and how others observe you against a certain standard. Individuals who self-observe are thought to have higher levels of organizational commitment and job satisfaction and to be more effective managers and leaders than those who are less self-aware (Atwater and Yammarino, 1992). The role of self-awareness has also received considerable attention in the emerging understanding of emotional intelligence and in the deployment of transformational leadership.

Emotional intelligence accompanies the technical know-how and intellectual abilities needed by managers, and focuses on demonstrating emotional competencies such as initiative, adaptability and persuasiveness. Emotional intelligence is thought to be learned from the experience of managing feelings so that they are expressed and controlled appropriately and effectively to enable those being managed to get along smoothly towards agreed common goals (Goleman, 1998). We established in Chapter 1 that emotional intelligence is central to leadership, a role whose essence is getting others to do their job more effectively. Personal ineptitude has the potential to influence an organization's culture negatively, by corroding motivation and building hostility and apathy in its members. Recognizing that sometimes control comes from giving up control is therefore a considerable role in self-management and is key to facilitating learning.

LEADERSHIP AND MANAGEMENT STANDARDS FOR SOCIAL CARE

This complex role of management is recognized in the development of leadership and management standards in social care. These cover six functional areas: managing self and personal skills; providing direction; facilitating change; working with people; using resources; and achieving results (Skills for Care, 2004). Leaders and managers are more likely to stay in the sector if leadership qualities and management skills are recognized, nurtured and developed at all levels in your organization. Continual management learning or CPD for managers also describes the ongoing, planned, learning process that contributes to personal and professional development. The CPD framework for social care aims to provide a flexible system that can meet the needs of the range of individual leaders and managers within any organization and ensure that particular requirements for this group of professionals are met. This includes the achievement of formal accreditation, for example through the National Vocational Qualification (NVQ) and post-qualifying awards framework for social work, as well as key areas of development of knowledge, skills, behaviours and reflective practice in each service area and specialist practice.

Skills for Care (2006b) have identified a number of key principles for its leadership and management strategy. This gives pointers as to how active your own organization is in meeting the learning needs of its managers and aspiring managers. What is required is:

- a systematic and consistent approach, integrating individual, team and organizational development;
- that leadership and management are part of the same continuum rather than being separate activities;
- national occupational standards which offer a flexible route to describing leadership and management roles, enabling learning needs to be identified and competence to be developed;
- continuing professional development as a core part of every leader's and manager's responsibility in the future. (Skills for Care, 2006b: 1)

This strategy is aimed at developing a 'whole systems' model which is consistent but can still be individualized and tailored to the specific needs of managers in a particular organization. The process begins with a matching exercise between the requirements of the job you do,

Table 9.1   The CPD Framework for Leadership and Management in Social Care

CPD process	CPD methods	CPD tools/activities
Stage 1 Assessment of individual and organizational need	Develop person management specification	Audit learning needs against competences to develop a personal CPD profile
Stage 2 Identify development needs	Assessment of development needs	Diagnostics, e.g. 360° feedback or benchmarking of skills within the PQ framework for leadership and management standards, supervision and the performance appraisal process
Stage 3 Identify learning opportunities	Identify learning objectives	Identify types of learning to meet objectives: work-based learning, action learning, networking, mentoring, and secondment, project work, e-learning, external events and activities, formal study leading to accreditation
Stage 4 Plan development opportunities	Identify goals	Identify strengths, weaknesses, opportunities and threats that might help or hinder these goals
Stage 5 Implement learning opportunities	Experience different types of learning – both planned and *ad hoc*	Keep a learning log or reflective diary, which can be an on-line recording system
Stage 6 Record outcomes	Reflect upon and record development	Record of achievement or record of learning into practice, for example, for the GSCC re-registration requirements or a locally developed tool
Stage 7 Review and accredit learning	Review person management specification and include any additional responsibilities or roles	Audit learning against updated skills, competences and knowledge and update CPD profile. Accredit CPD through regulatory and professional bodies

Source: Adapted and reprinted with kind permission from Skills for Care (2006b: 8, products)

the areas in which you are competent or in which you need to be competent, and your individual development needs. Tables 9.1 and 9.2 provide the framework in which a unique mix of learning opportunities, qualifications and organizational training can be put together for the individual or the agency. This should be an ongoing process. You may find it useful as a model to plan your own learning and development needs.

Table 9.2   **Person management specification for developing managers**

Person management specification	Personal development plan (PDP)	Continuing professional development
Profile based on a selection of current competences drawn from: • generic leadership and management standards • specialist competences, specific to social care • partnership competences	Discrete learning and other development opportunities: • organization-specific for updating and further development • external non-qualifying programme	This could include a range of activities: • record of achievement • record of learning • reflective learning diary • demonstration of how professional leadership and management institute requirements are being met
The overall competence profile resulting would be: • related to job role of that level and type of manager • related to individual leadership and management role in the organization	Required qualifications essential to the management role and matching the competence profile or other awards. An initial award for new managers could relate to foundation learning Organizational basics for new managers: • induction and foundation learning	The CPD process should be closely linked to the person management specification and the PDP

Reproduced by kind permission of Skills for Care.

EMERGING MANAGERS AND SUCCESSION PLANNING IN MANAGEMENT DEVELOPMENT

In order to understand the management learning process we need to recognize that people in managerial roles do not suddenly 'become' managers and once established do not cease to learn and develop either as individuals or managers (Watson, 2001; Hafford-Letchfield and Chick, 2006b). Theoretical trends in the study of management learning utilize thinking in both organizational theory and psychology to develop an understanding of the process by which individuals emerge through learning. This is a continuous process and looks at how individuals make the transition into management and how they learn and develop once they are in managerial posts. Induction, foundation, achievement of the relevant academic awards, updating of knowledge to meet organizational requirements, regular appraisal leading to personal development planning and CPD activities are all important building blocks to management learning (Skills for Care, 2006a). Watson's research (2001), however, refers specifically to the life experiences, identity and biographies of managers as a whole, much of which influences people prior to formally taking up a managerial post. She goes as far as to interpret management as 'a social and moral activity' (Watson, 2001: 222). Such a view of management emphasizes social and moral practice over the technical specialized activities of managers. The skills we might expect to see people developing in social care are more likely to be social, political, cultural and rhetorical skills. For example, to be effective, the use of 'political skills' gives managers the ability to effectively understand others at work, and to use such knowledge to influence others to act in ways that enhance one's personal and/or organizational objectives (Mintzberg, 1985). By working with and through others, managers can become more effective at networking, coalition building, and creating social capital. According to House (1995), leaders who network are in a better position to secure more resources for their units and are valued more by their teams. The accumulation of friendships, connections and alliances allows them to then leverage this social capital to facilitate change. These are not skills that are necessarily or specifically taught on a management development programme but emerge through the development of tacit knowledge and its application to practice.

Within the concept of the emergent or aspiring manager, you will no doubt realize from your own experiences that there is no obvious point at which one suddenly 'becomes' a manager. Even when individuals accept the status or role of manager, they will inevitably continue to learn about managing and will go on through their career to modify or develop their understandings and practices. For managers who are moving up within their organization, there is often emphasis on how important their previous jobs in the organization were in helping them to know about and understand the details of the organization or the 'business' of social care. Burgoyne and Reynolds (1997) refer to management learning as understanding the whole person as mediated through experience. They pay more attention to the manager's connectedness to daily personal and professional life and in avoiding the passivity thought to be associated with more conventional educational methods, as offering managers more opportunity for development than seemed possible in focusing exclusively on the acquisition of knowledge and skills. This fits very well with writing on experiential learning and reflective practice in social care (Schön, 1983; Kolb, 1984) discussed throughout this book. Recognizing that preparation for management begins much earlier in an individual's life than the point at which they formally enter or prepare for management work also links to the philosophies on continuous or life-long learning.

> **BOX 9.4   REFLECTION BREAK**
>
> How have you learned to become a leader or manager? What particular influences have been significant and how have these affected your own leadership style, either negatively or positively? Do you have a clear plan for your own learning and development, and who can help you with this?

The influence of previous managers, both good and bad, has been seen as helpful in learning to become a manager (Bryans and Mavin, 2003). The emphasis is not always on subject and task expertise but on complex interactions with others. Bryans and Mavin's (2003: 123) research demonstrated that 'feeling like a manager is a complex balance between an individual's self-perception and the perception of others towards them, a fragile, dynamic and continual process easily threatened by one's own lack of confidence and the response of others'.

Earlier, we referred to the concept of social capital which harnesses levels of trust between people. This refers to the extent to which they work collaboratively, are mutually supportive and tied by strong networks. Intellectual capital grows through the creation and transfer of knowledge between situations and people and is therefore strengthened by high levels of social capital. Good quality management learning can ensure that managers provide support for their colleagues and find new ways of working and learning together. This provides fertile ground for the development of intellectual capital going beyond the general provision of CPD or a spirit of enquiry. As managers develop specific strategies and responses through their leadership within their own service or community of practice, and share this knowledge and process across their network, this is a powerful means of building organizational knowledge and capital.

CHAPTER SUMMARY

This chapter has looked specifically at the concept of knowledge and the ways in which knowledge can be generated, stored and disseminated in order for it to be utilized for informed decision making and the improvement of services. We established that knowledge can be transformed through the learning process in a number of different ways. Despite the abundance of knowledge in social care, there is no guarantee that this will lead to evidence-based practice or even quality services, and the role of the research-minded practitioner has a key role to play in this process. Taking an interest in knowledge management can enable your staff and teams to make best use of the knowledge available, by recognizing the interplay between knowledge, experiential practice, and critical reflection embedded in everyday practice and supported by the organizational culture and infrastructure.

As organizations continue to evolve, facilitative management capabilities are required, reinforcing the importance of continuous management development and learning. We hope that this book has extended your understanding about the role of learning in social care and the underpinning values, beliefs and principles as well as theoretical aspects, to help you become an exemplary facilitator of learning. This is the key to developing the responsibility needed to create a culture where practitioners are able to develop mutually supportive relationships in order to learn in and from their practice.

Recommended further reading

I. Shaw, J. Greene and M. Mark (2006) *Handbook of Evaluation: Policy, Programme and Practice* (London: Sage) provides a useful reference for any practitioner or student interested in examining the complexities of contemporary evaluation and the ongoing dialogue that arises in professional efforts to evaluate people, services, policies and practices.

Web-based resources

SWAP (www.swap.ac.uk) – is the Social Policy and Social Work subject centre and is one of 24 discipline-based centres, which form the UK-wide Higher Education academy. Its main aim is promoting high-quality learning, teaching and assessment in all subject areas. It was formerly part of the Learning and Teaching Support Network (LTSN).

ESRC Evidence Network (www.evidencenetwork.org) – provides a focal point for those interested in evidence-based policy and practice in social science.

Department of Health (www.dh.gov.uk/policyandguidance/ researchanddevelopment) – provides a research governance framework for health and social care which defines the broad principles of good research governance and is key to ensuring that health and social care research are conducted to high standards and ethics.

REFERENCES

Adair, J. (1983) *Effective leadership*. London: Pan Books.

Ahearn, K.K., Ferris, G.R., Hochwater, W.A., Douglas, C. and Ammeter, A. (2004) Leader political skill and team performance. *Journal of Management*, 30(3): 309–27.

Annelies, E.M., Van Vianen, A. and Fischer, H. (2002) Illuminating the glass ceiling: the role of organisational culture. *Journal of Occupational and Organisational Psychology*, 75(3): 315–38.

Argyris, C. and Schön, D. (1990) *Overcoming organizational defenses*. Needham Heights, MA: Allyn & Bacon.

Arnstein, S.R. (1969) A ladder of citizen participation in the USA. *Journal of the American Institute of Planners*, 35(4): 216–24.

Association of Directors of Social Services (nd) *Round pegs – round holes? Recognising the future of human resource management: a discussion paper on how organisations learn*. Report by Linda Tapey. London: ADSS. Available from www.adss.org.uk/publications, pp. 1–24.

Association of Directors of Social Services (2004) *Race Equality Through Leadership*. London: ADSS with Social Care Institute for Excellence, Commission for Social Care Inspection and Race Equality Unit.

Association of Directors of Social Services (2005) *Independence, Well-being and Choice: The ADSS Response to the Green Paper on Adult Social Care*. July 2005, available on www.adss.org.uk (accessed on 21/8/2005).

Atwater, L.E. and Yammarino, F.J. (1992) Does self-other agreement on leadership perceptions moderate the validity of leadership and performance predictors? *Personnel Psychology*, 45: 141–64.

Audit Commission (2002a) *Recruitment and Retention: A Public Service Workforce for the Twenty-First Century*. London: Audit Commission.

Audit Commission (2002b) *Directions in Diversity*. London: Audit Commission.

Aynsley-Green, A. (2004) Introduction. In Department of Health, *The National Framework for Children, Young People and Maternity Services*. London: The Stationery Office.

Balloch, S., Andrew, T., Ginn, T., McLean, J. and Williams, J. (1995) *Working in the Social Services*. London: National Institute Social Work Research Unit.

Bandura, A. (1977) *Social Learning Theory*. Englewood Cliffs, NJ: Prentice-Hall.

Barker, R.A. (1997) How can we train leaders if we do not know what leadership is? *Human Relations*, 50(4): 343–62.

Barnes, C. and Mercer, G. (2006) *Independent Futures: Creating User-led Disability Services in a Disabling Society*. Bristol: British Association of Social Workers and Policy Press.

Barnett, R. (1994) *The Limits of Competence: Knowledge, Higher Education and Society*. Buckingham: Open University.

Barr, H. (1998) Competent to collaborate: towards a competency-based model for interprofessional education. *Journal of Interprofessional Care*, 12(2): 181–88.

Barr, H. (2002) *Interprofessional Education Today, Yesterday and Tomorrow*. York: Learning and Teaching Support Network.

Barr, H., Freeth, D., Hammick, M., Reeves, S. and Koppel, I. (1999) *Evaluating Interprofessional Education.* Macclesfield: British Education Research Association and Centre for Advancement of Professional Education.

Barr, H., Freeth, D., Hammick, M., Koppel, I. and Reeves, S. (2006) The evidence base and recommendations for interprofessional education in health and social care. *Journal of Interprofessional Care,* 20(1): 75–8.

Barr, H., Koppel, I., Reeves, S., Hammick, M. and Reeth, D. (2005) *Effective Interprofessional Education: Argument, Assumption and Evidence.* Oxford: Blackwell and CAIPE.

Barrett, S. and Rogers, A. (2003) *Leadership, Power and Authority.* Unit 15 K205. London: Open University Press.

Bashford, L. (1999) Shared learning: a phenomena for celebration and a challenge to health educators. *Nurse Education Today,* 19: 345–6.

Bass, B.M. (1990) *Handbook of Leadership: A Survey of Theory and Research.* New York: Free Press.

Begum, N. (2006) Doing it for themselves: participation and black and minority ethnic service users. *Report 14.* London: Social Care Institute of Excellence. Available from www.scie.org.uk/publications.

Begum, N., Hill, M. and Stevens, A. (1994) *Reflections: Views of Black Disabled People on their Lives and Community Care.* Cambridge: Black Bear Press and Central Council for Education and Training in Social Work (CCETSW).

Bell, M. (1994) Towards self-managed appraisal. *Management Development Review,* 7(4): 3–8.

Benner, P. (2001) *From Novice to Expert.* Englewood Cliffs, NJ: Prentice-Hall.

Beresford, P. and Croft, S. (1993) *Citizen Involvement: A Practical Guide for Change.* London: Macmillan and British Association of Social Workers.

Beresford, P. and Croft, S. (2003) Involving service users in management: citizenship, access and support. In J. Sedan and J. Reynolds (eds), *Managing Care in Practice.* London: Routledge in association with the Open University Press, pp. 21–8.

Beresford, P., Croft, S., Evans, C. and Harding, T. (1997) Quality in personal social services: the developing role of user involvement in the UK. In A. Evers, R. Haverinin, K. Leichsenting and G. Wistow (eds), *Developing Quality in Personal Social Services.* Aldershot: Ashgate, pp. 63–81.

Blake, R.R. and Mouton, J.S. (1985) *The Managerial Grid III.* Houston, TX: Gulf.

Bloom, B.S. (ed.) (1956) *Taxonomy of Educational Objectives: Cognitive Domain.* New York: McKay.

Boje, D.M. and Dennehey, R. (1999) *Managing in the Postmodern World.* Dubuque, IA: Kendall Hunt.

Booth, S.H., Booth, A. and Falzon, L.J. (2003) The need for information and research skills training to support evidence-based social care: a literature review and survey. *Learning in Health and Social Care,* 2/4(9): 191–201.

Boud, D., Keogh, R. and Walker, D. (1985) *Reflection: Turning Experience into Learning.* London: Kogan Page.

Boud, D. and Walker, D. (2002) Promoting reflection in professional courses. In R. Harrison, F. Reeve, A. Hanson and J. Clarke (eds), *Supporting Lifelong Learning, Volume 1: Perspectives on Learning.* London and New York: Routledge and The Open University Press, pp. 111–26.

Boyd, E. and Fales, A. (1983) Reflective learning: key to learning through experience. *Journal of Humanistic Psychology,* 23(2): 99–117.

Boydell, T. and Leary, M. (1994) From management development to managing development: the changing role of the manager in the learning organisation. *Transitions,* 94(9): 8–9.

Braye, S. (ed.) (2000) *Participation and Involvement in Social Care*. London: Jessica Kingsley Publishers.

Britnore Guest, A. (1999) A *Coach, a Mentor... a What? Success Now*, 13. Available at: http://www.coachingnetwork.org.uk/ResourceCentre/Articles/ViewArticle.asp?artId=72.

Brown, J.S. and Duisguid, P. (1991) Organizational learning and communities of practice: towards a unified way of working, learning and innovation. *Organizational Science*, 2(1): 40–57.

Brown, S. (1999) Assessing practice. In S. Brown and A. Glasner (eds), *Assessment Matters in Higher Education*. Milton Keynes. The Society for Research into Higher Education and The Open University Press, pp. 95–205.

Bryans, P. and Mavin, S. (2003) Women learning to become managers: learning to fit in or to play a different game? *Management Learning*, 34(1): 111–34.

Burgess, R.C. (2005) A model for enhancing individual and organisational learning of 'emotional intelligence': the drama and winner's triangles, *Social Work Education*, 24(1): 97–112.

Burgoyne, J. and Reynolds, M. (1997) *Management Learning: Integrating Perspectives in Theory and Practice*. London: Sage.

Butt, J. (2006) 'Are we there yet?' Identifying the characteristics of social care organisations that successfully promote diversity. In J. Butt, B. Patel and O. Stuart (eds), *Race Equality Discussion Papers*. London: Social Care Institute for Excellence. Available in print and online from www.scie.org.uk.

Butt, J. and Davey, B. (1997) The experience of black workers in the social care workforce. In M. May, E. Brundsdon and G. Craig (eds), *Social Policy Review* 9. London: Social Policy Association, pp. 141–61.

Butt, J., Gorback, P. and Ahmed, B. (1991) *Equally Fair: A Report on Social Services Departments' Development, Implementation and Monitoring of Services for the Black and Minority Ethnic Community*. London: National Institute for Social Work Research Unit, Race Equality Unit and the Social Services Research Group.

Butt, J., Patel, B. and Stuart, O. (eds) (2006) *Race Equality Discussion Papers*. London: Social Care Institute for Excellence. Available in print and online from www.scie.org.uk.

Buxton, V., James, T. and Harding, W. (1998) Using research in community nursing. *Nursing Times*, 94(35): 57–60.

Calder, J. (ed.) (1993) *Disaffection and Diversity: Overcoming Barriers for Adult Learners*. London: The Falmer Press.

Carpenter, J. (2005) Evaluating outcomes in social work education, evaluation and evidence, Discussion Paper 1. Dundee: Scottish Institute for Excellence in Social Work Education (SIESWE) and London: The Social Care Institute for Excellence (SCIE).

Carr, S. (2004) *Has Service User Prticipation Made a Difference to Social Care Services*? Bristol: Social Care Institute for Excellence and Policy Press.

Carter, J. (2003) *Ethnicity, Exclusion and the Workplace*. Oxford: Oxford Brookes University and Palgrave Macmillan.

Choy, A. (1990) The winner's triangle. *Transactional Analysis Journal*, 20(1): 40–66.

Clarke, N. (2001) The impact of in-service training within social services. *British Journal of Social Work*, 31: 757–74.

Claxton, G. (1999) *Wise Up: The Challenge of Lifelong Learning*. London: Bloomsbury.

Clegg, S., Kornberger, M. and Pitsis, T. (2005) *Managing and Organisations: An Introduction to Theory and Practice*. London: Sage.

Clutterbuck, D. (2001) *Everyone Needs a Mentor: Fostering Talent at Work* (3rd edition). London: Chartered Institute of Personnel and Development.

Coffield, F. (2000) *Differing Visions of a Learning Society* (Vols 1 & 2). Bristol: Policy Press.

Cole, M. (2004) The practice of developing practice: facilitating the capture and use of informal learning in the workplace. *Work Based Learning in Primary Care*, 2: 1–5.

Colyer, H., Helme, M. and Jones, I. (2005) *The Theory–Practice Relationship in Interprofessional Education.* London: Higher Education Academy Health and Sciences and Practice. Available from www.heacademy.ac.uk.

Comerford, S. (2005) Engaging through learning – learning through engaging: an alternative approach to professional learning about diversity. *Social Work Education*, 4(1): 113–35.

Cropper, A. (2000) Mentoring as an inclusive device for the excluded: black students' experience of a mentoring scheme. *Social Work Education*, 19(10): 597–607.

Dass, P. and Parker, B. (1999) Strategies for managing human resource diversity: from resistance to learning. *The Academy of Management Executive*, 13(2): 68–80.

Davidson, M.J. (1997) *The Black and Ethnic Minority Women Manager: Cracking the Concrete Ceiling.* London: Sage.

Davis, J., Rendell, P. and Sims, D. (1999) The joint practitioner: a new concept in professional training. *Journal of Interprofessional Care*, 3: 17–30.

Department for Education and Employment (1998) *The Learning Age.* London: The Stationery Office. Available at: www.lifelonglearning.co.uk/greenpaper/index.htm (accessed on 30/12/2003).

Department for Education and Skills (2003) *Twenty-first Century Skills: Realising Our Potential: Individuals, Employers, Nation.* White Paper. London: The Stationery Office. Available at: www.dfes.gov.uk/skillsstrategy (accessed on 12/05/2007).

Department for Education and Skills (2005a) *Multi-agency Working: Toolkit for Managers of Multi-agency Teams.* London: The Stationery Office.

Department of Education and Skills (2005b) *The Common Core of Skills and Knowledge for the Children's Workforce.* London: The Stationery Office.

Department of Health (1995) *Challenge of Partnership in Child Protection: A Practice Guide.* London: The Stationery Office.

Department of Health (1998) *Modernising Social Services, Promoting Independence, Improving Protection, Raising Standards.* Cm 4169. London: The Stationery Office.

Department of Health (1999) *Modernising Health and Social Services: Developing the Workforce.* London: The Stationery Office.

Department of Health (2000) *A Quality Strategy for Social Care.* London: The Stationery Office.

Department of Health (2001a) *Positively Diverse – The Field Book: A Practical Guide to Managing Diversity in the NHS.* London: The Stationery Office.

Department of Health (2001b) *The Expert Patient: A New Approach to Chronic Disease Management for the Twenty-First Century.* London: The Stationery Office.

Department of Health (2002a) *Requirements for Social Work Training.* London: The Stationery Office.

Department of Health (2002b) *Employment Improves Your Health, Volume 2: Learning from Other People's Experiences.* London: The Stationery Office.

Department of Health (2002c) *Working Together – Learning Together: A Framework for Lifelong Learning for the NHS.* London: The Stationery Office.

Department of Health (2003) *Every Child Matters: Summary.* London: The Stationery Office.

Department of Health (2004a) *Every Child Matters: Change for Children.* London: The Stationery Office.

Department of Health (2004b) *The Children Act 2004.* London: The Stationery Office.

Department of Health (2004c) *The National Service Framework for Children, Young People and Maternity Services*. London: The Stationery Office.

Department of Health (2004d) *The NHS Knowledge and Skills Framework and the Development Review Process*. London: The Stationery Office.

Department of Health (2005a) *Independence, Well-being and Choice: The Vision for the Future of Social Care in England*. A Green Paper. London: The Stationery Office.

Department of Health (2005b) *Delivering Race Equality in Mental Health Care and the Government's Response to the Independent Inquiry into the Death of David Bennett*. London: The Stationery Office.

Department of Health (2006a) *Our Health, Our Care, Our Say*. London: The Stationery Office.

Department of Health (2006b) *Reward and Recognition: The Principles and Practice of Service User Payments in Health and Social Care*. London: The Stationery Office. Available at: www.dh.gov.uk/publications (accessed on 8/8/2006).

Department of Health and Department for Education and Skills (October 2006) *Options for Excellence: Building the Social Care Workforce of the Future*. London: The Stationery Office.

Disability Rights Commission (2006) Making the Duty Work. Stratford-upon-Avon: Disability Rights Commission. Available at: www.drc-gb.org and www.dotheduty.org (accessed on 21/10/2006).

Doel, M., Shardlow, S. and Sawdon, D. (1996) *Teaching Social Work Practice*. Aldershot: Arena.

Dominelli, L. (2002) *Anti-oppressive Social Work Theory and Practice*. Basingstoke: Palgrave Macmillan.

Dovey, K. (1997) The learning organization and the organization of learning: power, transformation and the search for form in learning organizations. *Management Learning*, 28(3): 331–49.

Downie, C.M. and Basford, P. (1998) *Teaching and Assessing in Clinical Practice: A Reader* (2nd edition). London: Greenwich University Press.

Dreyfus, H.L. and Dreyfus, S.E. (1986) *Mind over Machine: The Power of Human Intuition and Expertise in the Era of the Computer*. Oxford: Basil Blackwell.

Driver, M. (2002) Learning and leadership in organizations: towards complementary communities of practice. *Management Learning*, 33(1): 99–126.

Elkajaer, B. (2003) Organizational learning with a pragmatic slant. *International Journal of Lifelong Education*, 22(4): 481–94.

Ellinger, A.D. and Bostrom, R.P. (2002) An examination of managers' beliefs about their role as facilitators of learning. *Management Learning*, 33(2): 147–79.

Equal Opportunities Commission (2003) Facts about Women and Men in Great Britain: Annual Compilation of Gender Statistics. London: EOC. Available at: www.eoc.org.uk (accessed on 8/8/2006).

Eraut, M. (1994) *Developing Professional Knowledge and Confidence*. London and New York: Routledge Falmer.

Eraut, M. (1998) *Development of Knowledge and Skills in Employment*. Brighton: University of Sussex, Institute of Education.

Eraut, M., Alderton, J., Cole, G. and Senker, P. (2002) Learning from other people at work. In R. Harrison, F. Reeve, A. Hanson and J. Clarke (eds), *Supporting Lifelong Learning: Volume 1: Perspectives on Learning*. London: Routledge Falmer, pp. 127–45.

Eraut, M. (2004) Editorial: Learning to change and/or changing to learn. *Learning in Health and Social Care*, 3(3): 111–17.

Eraut, M. (2005) Editorial: Uncertainty in research. *Learning in Health and Social Care*, 4(2): 47–52.

Eraut, M. (2006) Editorial: Learning contexts. *Learning in Health and Social Care*, 5(1): 1–8.

Erikson, E.H. (1959) *Identity and the Life Cycle: Selected Papers*. Madison, WI: International Universities Press.

Evans, D. (1999) *Practice Learning in the Caring Professions*. Aldershot: Ashgate.

Field, J. (2001) Lifelong education. *International Journal of Lifelong Education*, 29(1/2): 5–15.

Fish, J. (2006) *Heterosexism in Health and Social Care*. Basingstoke: Palgrave Macmillan.

Flood, R.L. and Romm, N.R.A. (1996) *Diversity Management: Triple Loop Learning*. Chichester: John Wiley.

Fook, J. (2001) Linking theory, practice and research. *Critical Social Work*, 2(1).

Fook. J. (2004) Critical reflection and organizational learning and change: a case study. In N. Gould and M. Baldwin (eds), *Social Work, Critical Reflection and the Learning Organization*. Ashgate: Aldershot, pp. 57–73.

Fook, J. Ryan, M. and Hawkings, L. (2000) *Professional Expertise: Practice Theory and Education for Working in Uncertainty*. London and Concord, MA: Whiting and Birch.

Freeth, D., Hammick, M., Barr, H., Koppel, I. and Reeves, S. (2002) *A Critical Review of Evaluations of Interprofessional Education*. London: Learning and Teaching Support Network Health Sciences and Practice.

Freeth, D., Hammick, M., Reeves, S., Koppel, I. and Barr, H. (2005) *Effective Interprofessional Education: Development, Delivery and Evaluation*. Oxford: Blackwell and CAIPE.

Freire, P. (1986) *Pedagogy of the Oppressed*. New York: Continuum.

Friday, E. and Friday, S.S. (2003) Managing diversity using a strategic planned change approach. *Journal of Management Development,* 22: 863–80.

Frost, N. (2005) *Professionalism, Partnership and Joined-up Thinking*: *A Research Review of Front-line Working with Children and Families*. Dartington: Research in Practice (www.rip.org.uk).

Fryer, R. (1997) *Learning for the Twenty-first Century*. First report of the National Advisory Group for Continuing Education and Lifelong Learning. London: NAGCELL.

Garvin, D. (1993) Building a learning organization. *Harvard Business Review*, 71(4): 78–91.

Geddes, J. (2004) Evidence-based practice in mental health. In L. Trinder and S. Reynolds (eds), *Evidence-based Practice: A Critical Appraisal*. Oxford: Blackwell, pp. 66–88.

Glasby, J. and Beresford, P. (2006) Who knows best? Evidence-based practice and the service user contribution. *Critical Social Policy*, 26(1): 268–84.

Glen, S. and Leiba, T. (eds) (2004) *Interprofessional Post-Qualifying Education for Nurses: Working Together in Health and Social Care*. Basingstoke: Palgrave Macmillan.

Goleman, D. (1996) *Emotional Intelligence*. London: Bloomsbury.

Goleman, D. (1998) *Working with Emotional Intelligence*. London: Bloomsbury.

Gorard, S. and Rees, G. (2002) *Creating a Learning Society*. Bristol: Policy Press.

Gould, N. (2000) Becoming a learning organisation: a social work example. *Social Work Education*, 19(6): 585–96.

Grint, K. (ed.) (1997) *Leadership: Classical, Contemporary and Critical Approaches*. Oxford: Oxford University Press.

GSCC (2002) *Codes of Practice for Social Care Workers and Employers*. London: General Social Care Council. Available at: www.gscc.org.uk/codes/.

GSCC/TOPSS (2002) *Guidance on the Assessment of Practice in the Workplace.* London: General Social Care Council.

GSCC (2005a) *Post-qualifying Framework in Social Work Education and Training.* London: General Social Care Council.

GSCC [2005b] *Specialist Standards and Requirements for Post-qualifying Social Work Education and Training: Children and Young People, Their Families and Carers.* London: General Social Care Council.

GSCC (2006) GSCC works with Disability Rights Commission to end discrimination. *Media releases*, 22/05/2006. Available at: www.gscc.org.uk/mediareleases/ (accessed on 8/11/2006).

Guilgun, J. (1994) Hand in glove: the grounded theory approach and social work practice research. In E. Sherman and W.J. Reid (eds), *Qualitative Research in Social Work*. New York: Columbia University Press, pp. 115–25.

Hafford-Letchfield, T. (2006) *Management and Organizations in Social Work*. Exeter: Learning Matters.

Hafford-Letchfield, T. and Chick, N.F. (2006a) Talking across purposes: the benefits of an interagency mentoring scheme for managers working in health and social care settings in the UK. *Work Based Learning in Primary Care*, 4(1): 13–25.

Hafford-Letchfield, T. and Chick, N.F. (2006b) Succession planning: developing management potential in a social service department. *Diversity in Health and Social Care*, 3(2): 191–202.

Haines, B. and Haines, A. (1998) Getting research findings into practice: Barriers and bridges to evidence-based clinical practice. *British Medical Journal*, 317: 273–6.

Harlow, E. (2004) Why don't women want to be social workers anymore? New managerialism, post-feminism and the shortage of social workers in social services departments in England and Wales. *European Journal of Social Work*, 7(2): 167–79.

Harris, (2003) *The Social Work Business*. London: Routledge.

Harrison, J. (1994) A counselling approach to staff development. *Employee Counselling Today*, 6(3): 11–4.

Harrison, R. (2005) *Learning and Development* (4th edition). London: Chartered Institute of Personnel and Development.

Hawkins, P. and Shohet, R. (2006) *Supervision in the Helping Professions*. Maidenhead: The Open University Press with McGraw-Hill.

Hawkins, P. and Smith, N. (2006) *Coaching, Mentoring and Organizational Consultancy: Supervision and Development*. Maidenhead: Open University Press.

Hay, J. (1999) *Transformational Mentoring, Creating Developmental Alliances for Changing Organisational Cultures*. Watford: Sherwood.

Hewison, J., Dowswell, T. and Millar, B. (2000) Changing patterns of training provision in the National Health Service: an overview. In F. Coffield (ed.), *Differing Visions of a Learning Society: Research Findings* (Vol. 1). Bristol: Policy Press, pp. 167–98.

Higginson, J. (1990) Partners not problems: developing new roles for staff and consumers. In G. Darvill and G. Smale (eds), *Partners in Empowerment: Networks of Innovation in Social Work*. London: National Institute for Social Work.

Higham, P., Sharp, M. and Booth, C. (2001) Changes in the quality and regulation of social work education: confronting the dilemmas of workforce planning and competing qualifications frameworks. *Social Work Education*, 20(2): 187–98.

Holmes, L. and Robinson, G. (1999) *The making of black managers: unspoken issues of identity formation*. Paper presented at first International Conference on Critical Management Studies, UMIST, Manchester. Available at: www.re-skill.org.uk (accessed 8/8/2006).

hooks, b. (1994) *Teaching to Transgress: Education as the Practice of Freedom*. New York: Routledge.

House, R.J. (1995) Leadership in the twenty-first century. In A. Howard (ed.), *The Changing Nature of Work*. San Francisco: Jossey-Bass, pp. 411–50.

Howell, J.M. and Frost, P.J. (1989) A laboratory study of charismatic leadership. *Organizational Behaviour and Human Decisions Process,* 43: 243–69.

IDeA with Leadership Research and Development Ltd (2004) *Perceptions and Prospects: Diversity Issues in Local Government Management*. London: The Improvement and Development Agency.

Improvement and Development Agency (2004) *Prospects*. A study co-funded by Leadership Research and Development Ltd. London: Improvement and Development Agency.

Issitt, M. and Woodward, M. (1992) Competence and contradiction. In P. Carter, T. Jeffs and M.K. Smith (eds), *Changing Social Work and Welfare*. Buckingham: Open University Press, pp. 40–54.

Jarvis, P. (1987) *Adult Learning in the Social context*. London: Croom Helm.

Jarvis, P. (1999) *The Practitioner Researcher: Developing Theory from Practice*. San Francisco: Jossey-Bass.

Jarvis, P. and Gibson, S. (1997) *The Teacher Practitioner and Mentor in Nursing, Midwifery, Health Visiting and the Social Services* (2nd edition). Cheltenham: Stanley Thornes.

Johnson-Bailey, J. (2004) Hitting and climbing the proverbial wall: participation and retention issues for black graduate women. *Race, Ethnicity and Education,* 7(4): 331–49.

Joint University Council Social Work Education Council Social Work Education Committee, Research Sub-Committee (JUC SWEC) 2006 *A Social Work Research Strategy in Higher Education 2006–2020*. London: The Social Care Workforce Research Unit.

Jones, K. (2006) Valuing diversity and widening participation: the experiences of access to social work students in further and higher education. *Social Work Education,* 25(5): 485–500.

Jones, S. and Joss, R. (eds) (1995) *Models of Professionalism in Learning and Teaching in Social Work: Towards Reflective Practice*. London: Jessica Kingsley.

Jordan, B. and Jordan, C. (2002) *Social Work and the Third Way: Tough Love as Social Policy*. London: Sage.

Kadushin, A. and Harkness, D. (2002) *Supervision in Social Work* (4th edition). New York: Columbia University Press.

Karpman, S. (1968) Fairytales and script drama analysis. *Transactional Analysis Bulletin,* 7(26): 39–43.

Kearney, P. (2004) First-line managers, the mediators of standards and the quality of practice. In D. Statham (ed.), *Managing Frontline Practice in Social Care*. Research Highlights in Social Work 40. London: Jessica Kingsley.

Kemshall, H. (1993) Assessing competence: scientific process of subjective interference? Do we really see it? *Social Work Education,* 12: 36–45.

Kenny, D. and Field, S. (2003) *Black people: pushing back the boundaries II. Key facts on public services and black and minority ethnic people in London*. London: Greater London Authority. Available at: www.london.gov.uk.

King's Fund (1990) *The Work of the Equal Opportunities Task Force 1986–1990: A Final Report*. London: King Edward's Hospital Fund for London.

Kirkpatrick, D.L. (1967) Evaluation of training. In R.L. Craig and L.R. Bittel (eds), *Training and Development Handbook*. New York: McGraw-Hill, pp. 87–112.

Kitson, A., Harvey G. and McCormack B. (1988) Enabling the implementation of evidence-based practice: a conceptual framework. *Quality in Health Care*, 7: 149–58.

Knight, P. (2001) *A Briefing on Key Concepts: Formative and Summative Criteria and Norm-referenced Assessment*. LTSN Generic Assessment Series No 7. York: Learning and Teaching Support Network.

Knowles, M.S. (1984) *Androgogy in Action: Applying Modern Principles of Adult Learning*. San Francisco: Jossey-Bass.

Kolb, D. (1984) *Experiential Learning: Experience as the Source of Learning and Development*. Englewood Cliffs, NJ: Prentice-Hall.

Kotter, J.P. (1988) *The Leadership Factor*. New York: Free Press.

Kotter, J.P. (1992) *A Force for Change*. London: Free Press.

Laming, H. (2003) *The Victoria Climbie Enquiry: Report of an enquiry by Lord Laming*. Cm 5730. London: The Stationery Office.

Lave, J. and Wenger, E. (1991) *Situated Learning: Legitimate Peripheral Participation*. Cambridge: Cambridge University Press.

Lave, J. and Wenger, E. (2002) Legitimate peripheral participation in communities of practice. In R. Harrison, F. Reeve, A. Hanson and J. Clarke (eds), *Supporting LIfelong Learning, Volume 1: Perspectives on Learning*. London: Routledge, pp. 111–26.

Lawler, J. and Harlow, E. (2005) Postmodernization: A phase we're going through? Management in social care. *British Journal of Social Work*, 35: 1163–74.

Leat, M.J., Lovel, M.J. and Murray, J. (1997) Training needs analysis: weaknesses in the conventional approach. *Journal of European Industrial Training*, 21(4): 143–53.

Leathard, A. (ed.) (1994) *Going Interprofessional: Working Together in Health and Social Care*. London: Routledge.

Lefevre, M. (2005) Facilitating practice learning and assessment: the influence of relationship. *Social Work Education*, 24(5): 565–83.

Leiba, T. and Leonard, K. (2003) Interprofessional education: the reality of an inter-professional practice teacher course. *Journal of Practice Teaching*, 4: 14–28.

Levin, E. (2004) *Involving Users and Carers in Social Work Education: Resource Guide No. 2*. London: Social Care Institute for Excellence.

Lewis, J. (2001) What works in community care? *Managing Community Care*, 9(1): 3–6.

Liff, S. and Dale, K. (1994) Formal opportunity, informal barriers: black women managers within a local authority, *Work, Employment and Society*, 8(2): 177–95.

Lishman, J. (1998) A comment on theory and practice in social work. *British Journal of Social Work*, 8(11): 23–5.

Lishman, J. (2000) Evidence for practice: the contribution of competing research methodologies. Paper presented in ESRC seminar series *Theorising Social Work Research*. Cardiff, 27 April 2000, ISpp. only. Available at: www.scie.org.uk/publications/misc/tswr/seminar5/lishman.asp (accessed 29/3/2006).

Lorbiecki, A. (2001) Changing views on diversity management: the rise of the learning perspective and the need to recognize social and political contradictions. *Management Learning*, 32(3): 345–61.

Low, H. and Weinstein, J. (2000) Interprofessional education in innovative education and training for health care professionals. In R. Pierce and J. Weinstein (eds), *Innovative Education and Training for Care Professionals: A Providers' Guide*. London: Jessica Kingsley, pp. 205–20.

Lumby, J., Harris, A., Morrison, M., Muijs, D., Sood, K., Glover, D. and Wilson, M. with Briggs, A.R.J. and Middlewood, D. (2005) *Leadership, Development and Diversity in* the *Learning and Skills Sector.* London: Learning and Skills Research Centre and Learning and Skills Development Agency.

Lymbery, M. (2004) Responding to crisis: the changing nature of welfare organisations. In M. Lymbery and S. Butler (eds), *Social Work Ideals and Practical Realities.* Basingstoke: Palgrave Macmillan.

Lyons, K. (1999) *Social Work in Higher Education: Demise or Development.* Aldershot: Ashgate.

Macaulay, C. (2000) Transfer of learning. In V. Cree and C. Macaulay (eds), *Transfer of Learning in Professional and Vocational Education.* London and New York: Routledge, pp. 1–26.

Macdonald, G. (2000) Social care: rhetoric and reality. In H.T.O. Davies, S. Nutley and P. Smith (eds), *What Works? Evidence-based Policy and Practice in Public Services.* Bristol: Policy Press, pp. 117–40.

Macdonald, G. and Sheldon, B. (1998) Changing one's mind: the final frontier? *Issues in Social Work Education,* 18(1): 3–25.

Marini, A. and Genereau, R. (1995) The challenge of teaching for transfer. In A. McKeough, J. Lupart and A. Marini (eds), *Teaching for Transfer: Fostering Generalizations in Learning.* Mahwah, NJ: Lawrence Erlbaum Associates, pp. 1–21.

Marsh, P. and Fisher, M. (1992) *Good Intentions: Developing Partnership in Social Services.* York: Joseph Rowntree Trust.

Marsh, P. and Fisher, M., in collaboration with Mathers, N. and Fish, S. (2005) *Developing the Evidence Base for Social Work and Social Care Practice: Using Knowledge in Social Care.* Report 10. Bristol: Policy Press and Social Care Institute for Excellence (www.scie.org.uk).

Marsick, V.J. and Watkins, K.E. (1999) *Facilitating Learning Organizations: Making Learning Count.* Aldershot: Gower.

Martin, V. (2003) *Leading Change in Health and Social Care.* London: Routledge.

Mastrangelo, A. (2004) The importance of personal and professional leadership. *The Leadership and Organizational Development Journal,* 25(5): 435–51.

McDonnell, F. and Zutshi, H. (2006a) *Managing Effective Supervision: A Unit of Competence for Managers in Social Care.* Leadership and Management Product No. 6. Leeds: Skills for Care. Available at: www.skillsforcare.org.uk. (accessed on 07/11/2006).

McDonnell, F. and Zutshi, H. (2006b) *Leadership and Management: A Strategy for the Social Care Workforce.* Main Report. Leeds: Skills for Care. Available at: www. skillsforcare.org.uk. (accessed on 07/11/2006).

McDougall, M. (1996) Equal opportunities versus managing diversity: another challenge for public sector management? *The International Journal of Public Sector Management,* 9(5/6): 62–73.

McGill, I. and Beaty, L. (2001) *Action Learning: A Guide for Professional, Management and Educational Development.* London: Kogan Page.

McGregor, D. (1960) *The Human Side of Enterprise.* New York: McGraw-Hill.

McIvor, G. (1995) Practitioner research in probation. In J. McGuire (ed.), *What Works: Reducing Offending.* New York: Wiley.

McLean, J. (1998) Anti-discriminatory practice: gender, sexuality and disclosure by social services staff. *Issues in Social Work Education,* 18(2): 75–81.

McLenachan, J. (2006) Facing up to a recruitment crisis. *Society Guardian,* 27 November. Available at: www.societyguardian.co.uk.

Mead, G., Ashcroft, J., with Barr, H., Scott, R. and Wild, A. (2005) *The Case for Interprofessional Collaboration.* Oxford: Blackwell and CAIPE.

Mezirow, J. (1991) *Transformative Dimensions of Adult Learning.* San Francisco: Jossey-Bass.

Miller, C., Woolf, C. and Mackintosh, N. (2006) *Evaluation of common learning pilots and allied health professions first wave sites.* Research commissioned by DoH. Prof C Miller, University of Brighton, Centre for nursing & Midwifery Research, Mayfield house, Village Way Brighton, E. Sx BN1 9PH.

Mintzberg, H. (1985) The organization as political arena. *Journal of Management Studies,* 22: 133–54.

Moriarty, J. (2004) *Main Messages and Bibliography from the NISW [National Institute for social work] Workforce Studies.* London: Social Care Workforce Research Unit.

Morris, J. (1994) *The Shape of Things to Come? User-led Social Services.* Social Services Policy Forum Paper No. 3. London: National Institute for Social Work.

Morrison, T. (2002) *Staff Supervision in Social Care: Making a Real Difference for Staff and Service Users.* Brighton: Pavilion.

Myers, P., Barnes, J. and Brodie, I. (2004) *Partnership Working in Sure Start Local Programmes: Early Findings from Local Programme Evaluations. NESS Synthesis Report No. 1.* National Evaluation of Sure Start. London: Institute of the Study of Children, Families and Social Issues, Birkbeck, University of London. Available at www.ness.bbk.ac.uk.

OECD (1996) *Lifelong Learning for All.* Paris: Organization for Economic Cooperation and Development.

OECD (2003) *The Role of National Qualifications Systems in Promoting Lifelong Learning.* Paris: Organization for Economic Cooperation and Development.

Ovretveit, J. (1993) *Co-ordinating Community Care: Multi-Disciplinary Teams and Care Management.* Buckingham: Open University Press.

Ovretveit, J., Mathias, P. and Thompson, T. (1997) *Interprofessional Working for Health and Social Care.* Basingstoke: Macmillan.

Owen, D. (2003) The demographic characteristics of people from minority ethnic groups in Britain. In: D. Mason (ed.), *Explaining Ethnic Differences.* Bristol: The Policy Press.

Parker. J. [2004] *Effective Practice Learning in Social Work.* Exeter: Learning Matters

Parsloe, E. and Wray, M. (2000), *Coaching and Mentoring. Practical Methods to Improve Learning.* London: Kogan Page.

Pattison, S. (2003) Virtues and values. in J. Reynolds, J. Henderson, J. Sedan, J. Charlesworth and A. Bullman (eds), *The Managing Care Reader.* London: Routledge and Open University Press.

Pawson, R., Boaz, A., Grayson, L., Long., A and Barnes, C. (2003) Types and quality of knowledge in social care: *Knowledge Review No 3.* Bristol: Policy Press and Social Care Institute for Excellence.

Payne, M. (2000) *Teamwork in Multiprofessional Care,* Basingstoke: Macmillan.

Payne, M. (2005) *Modern Social Work Theory.* Basingstoke: (3rd edition) Palgrave Macmillan.

Peel, M. (2003) Managing professional development in Sedan, J., Reynolds, J. (eds), *Managing care in practice.* London: Routledge, The Open University Press.

Pepper, S. (1942) *World Hypothesis: A Study in Evidence.* London: University of California Press Ltd.

Polanyi, M. (1983) *The Tacit Dimension,* Gloucester, MA: Peter Smith

Popper, M. (2003) Main principles and practices in leader development. *Leadership and Organization Development Journal,* 26(1): 62–75.

Postle, K., Edwards, C., Moon, R., Rumsey, H. and Thomas, T. (2002) Continuing professional development after qualification: partnerships, pitfalls and potential. *Social Work Education,* 21(2): 157–69.

QCA (2006) *The Story of NVQs.* London: Qualifications and Curriculum Authority. Available at: www.qca.org.uk (accessed on 21/9/06).

Race, P. (2001) *A Briefing on Self, Peer and Group Assessment.* LTSN Generic Assessment Series No. 9. York: Learning and Teaching Support Network.

Rawson, D. (1994) Models of interprofessional work: likely theories and possibilities. In A. Leathard (ed.), *Going InterProfessional: Working Together in Health and Social Care.* London: Routledge, pp. 38–63.

Reder, P. and Duncan, S. (2004) From Colwell to Climbie: Inquiring into fatal child abuse. In N. Stanley and J. Manthorpe (eds), *The Age of the Inquiry: Learning and Blame in Health and Social Care.* London: Routledge, pp. 92–115.

Rees, W.D. and Porter, C. (1996) *Skills of Management* (5th edition). London: Thomson Learning.

Revans, R. (1980) *Action Learning.* London: Blond and Biggs.

Ribbins, P. (2004) Knowing and knowing more on education and its administration: two cheers for reviews and reviewers of research? Paper in support of the closing keynote lecture given at the 7th International BELMAS Research Conference in partnership with SCRELM, New Understandings in Educational Leadership and Management, 8–10 July 2004, St Catherine's College, Oxford.

Research in Practice (2003) *A Review of Literature on Leading Evidence-Informed Practice* (EIP). Research in Practice. Available at: www.rip.org.uk (accessed on 14/5/2007).

Robson, P., Begum , N. and Locke, M. (2003) *Developing User Involvement: Working Towards User-Centred Practice in Voluntary Organisations.* Bristol: Policy Press.

Rogers, C. (2002) The interpersonal relationship in the facilitation of learning. In R. Harrison, F. Reeve, A. Hanson and J. Clarke (eds), *Supporting Lifelong Learning, Volume 1: Perspectives on Learning.* London: Routledge and Open University Press, pp. 25–39.

Rorty, R. (1989) *Contingency, Irony and Solidarity.* Cambridge: Cambridge University Press.

Rowntree, D. (1987) *Assessing Students: How Shall We Know Them?* London: Kogan Page.

Sackett, D., Strauss, S., Richardons, W., Rosenberg, W. and Haynes, R. (2000) *Evidence-Based Medicine: How to Practice and Teach EBM.* London: Churchill Livingstone.

Salaman, G. (1995) *Managing.* Buckingham: Open University Press.

Sandars, J. (2004) Knowledge management: something old, something new! *Work Based Learning in Primary Care*, 2: 9–17. pp. 202–7.

Sandars, J. (2006) Transformative learning: the challenge for reflective practice. *Work Based Learning in Primary Care*, 4(1): 6–10.

Sang, B. (2005) Whose outcome is it anyway: leadership development – a consumer perspective. *British Journal of Leadership in Public Services*, 1(7): 9–16.

Schein, E. (1993) How can organisations learn faster? The challenge of entering the green room. *Sloan Management Review*, 34(2): 85–92.

Schein, E. (1997) *Organisational Culture and Leadership.* San Francisco: Jossey-Bass.

Schön, D. (1983) *The Reflective Practitioner.* New York: Basic Books.

Schön, D. (1991) *The Reflective Practitioner* (2nd edition). Aldershot: Arena.

SCIE (2003) *Types and Quality of Knowledge in Social Care.* Knowledge Review No. 3. Bristol: Policy Press and Social Care Institute for Excellence.

SCIE (2004) *Learning Organisations: A Self-assessment Resource Pack.* Bristol: Social Care Institute for Excellence. Available at www.scie.org.uk.

SCIE (2005) *SCIE consultation Response to Independence, Well-being and Choice.* Bristol: Social Care Institute for Excellence. Available at: www.scie.org.uk.

SCIE (2006) *The Learning, Teaching and Assessment of Partnership in Social Work Education.* Bristol: Policy Press, and Social Care Institute for Excellence.

Senge, P. (1996) *The Fifth Discipline: The Art and Practice of the Learning Organization.* New York: Doubleday.

Senge, P.M. (1996) *The Fifth Discipline.* London: Random House

Shardlow, S. and Doel, M. (1996) *Practice Learning and Teaching.* Basingstoke: Macmillan.

Sharp, M. and Danbury, H. (1999) *The Management of Failing DipSW Students: Activities and Exercises to Prepare Practice Teachers for Work with Failing Students.* Aldershot: Arena.

Shaw, I. (2004) Evidence-based social work practice: a review of developments. Paper given to the Inter-Centre Network for the Evaluation of Social Work Practice (Intsoceval) at the 7th Annual Workshop, 30 September–2 October. Available at: www.intsoceval.org/files/switzerland/IAN%20SHAW_2004.doc (accessed on 12/05/2007).

Shaw, I. (2005) Practitioner research: evidence or critique? *British Journal of Social Work*, 35: 1231–48.

Sheppard, M. (1995) Social work, social science and practice wisdom. *British Journal of Social Work*, 25: 265–93.

Sheppard, M., Newstead, S., Di Caccavo, A. and Ryan, K. (2000) Reflexivity and process knowledge in social work. *British Journal of Social Work*,30(4): 465–88.

Sims, D. and Leonard, K. (2004) Interprofessional practice teacher education. In S. Glen and T. Leiba (eds), *Interprofessional Post-Qualifying Education for Nurses: Working Together in Health and Social Care.* Basingstoke: Palgrave Macmillan, pp. 61–78.

Singh, B. (2005) *Improving Support for Black Disabled People: Lessons from Community Organisations on Making Change Happen.* York: York Publishing Services Ltd.

Singh, V. (2002) *Managing Diversity for Strategic Advantage: Management and Leadership Council Reports.* London: Council for Excellence in Management and Leadership. www.managementandleadershipcouncil.org.uk/reports (accessed on 7/6/2005).

Skills for Care (2004) *What Leaders and Managers in Social Care Do: A Statement for a Leadership and Management Development Strategy for Social Care.* No. 1. Leeds: Skills for Care. Available at: www.skillsforcare.org.uk. (accessed on 11/05/2007).

Skills for Care (2005a) *The State of the Social Care Workforce 2004: The Second Skills Research and Intelligence Annual Report, April 2005.* Leeds: Skills for Care. Available at: www.topssengland.org.uk (accessed on 1/6/2005).

Skills for Care (2005b) *New Types of Worker Project.* Leeds: Skills for Care. Available at: www.skillsforcare.org.uk (accessed on 12/05/07).

Skills for Care (2006a) Leadership and Management 2006: Update Pack. Leeds: Skills for Care. Available at: www.skillsforcare.org.uk (accessed on 21/05/2006).

Skills for Care (2006b) *What Leaders and Managers in Social Care Do: A Statement for a Leadership and Management Development Strategy for Social Care.* No.1. Leeds: Skills for Care.

Skinner, B.F. (1989) *The Origins of Cognitive Thought.* American Psychologist. 44: 13–8.

Skinner, K.and Whyte, B. (2004) Going beyond training: theory and practice in managing learning. *Social Work Education*, 23(4): 265–381.

Smith, K. and Tillema, H. (2001) Long-term influences of portfolios on professional development. *Scandanavian Journal of Educational Research*, 2: 183–203.

Smyth, M. (1996) *Qualified Social Workers and Probation Officers.* London: Office for National Statistics Social Survey Division.

Stanley, N. (2004) Women and mental health inquiries. In N. Stanley and J. Manthorpe (eds), *The Age of Inquiry: Learning and Blaming in Health and Social Care.* London: Routledge, pp. 151–64.

Stanley, N. and Manthorpe, J. (eds) (2004) *The Age of Inquiry: Learning and Blaming in Health and Social Care.* London:, Routledge.

Starratt, R. (1993) *The Drama of Leadership.* London: The Falmer Press.

Stephens, F. (2001) Positive moves to end inequality, *NHS Magazine,* 22(July/August): 3.

Stevenson, K.M., Leung, P. and Cheung, K.M. (1992) Competency-based evaluation of interviewing skills in child sexual abuse cases. *Social Work Research and Abstracts,* 28(3): 11–16.

Thompson, N. (2003) *Communication and Language.* Basingstoke: Palgrave Macmillan.

Thomsen, H.K. and Hoest, V. (2001) Employees' perception of the learning organization. *Management Learning,* 32(4): 469–91.

TOPSS (National Training Organization for Social Care) (2000) *Modernizing the Social Care Workforce: The First National Training Strategy for England. Leeds:* TOPSS.

TOPSS (2002) *Occupational Standards for Social Work.* Leeds: TOPSS.

Townend, M. (2005) Interprofessional supervision from the perspectives of both mental health nurses and other professionals in the field of cognitive behavioural psychotherapy. *Journal of Psychiatric and Mental Health Nursing,* 12: 582–8.

Trinder, L. and Reynolds, S. (eds) (2004) *Evidence-Based Practice: A Critical Appraisal.* Oxford: Blackwell.

Tsui, Ming-sum (2005) *Social Work Supervision: Contexts and Concepts.* London: Sage.

Turner, M. (2003) *Shaping Our Lives – From Outset to Outcome: What people Think of the Social Care Services They Use.* York: Joseph Rowntree Foundation.

Turner, M. (2005) Service user participation: implications for the leadership in social care programmes. Unpublished discussion paper. London: Social Care Institute for Excellence (SCIE).

Turner, M. and Beresford, P. (2005) *Contributing on Equal Terms: Service User Involvement and the Benefits System.* Adult Services Report 08. London: Social Care Institute for Excellence.

UCAS (2003) Educational Background and Qualifications Data (online). Available at: ftp://ftp.ucas.ac.uk/pub/web/equalsol.exe.

Uttley, S. (1994) Professionals moving down: rationalisation, routinisation and displacement. *Advances in Social Work and Welfare Education,* 2(1): 46–58.

Walton, R. (2005) Social work as a social institution. *British Journal of Social Work,* 35: 587–607.

Ward, F. (2004) *Caring for Your Workforce,* Regional Conference Materials, TOPPS, England Workforce Intelligence Unit. Leeds: TOPPS. Available at: www.topps.org.uk (accessed on 9/8/2006).

Watson, T.J. (2001) The emergent manager and processes of management pre-learning. *Management Learning,* 32(2): 221–35.

Weinstein, J. (1998) The professions and their interrelationships. In P. Mathias and T. Thompson (eds), *Standards and Learning Disability.* London: Ballière Tindall, Chapter 20.

Weinstein J. and Leonard K. (forthcoming 2007). In S. Shardlow and M. Doel (eds), *Practice Education in Health and Social Care.* Aldershot: Arena.

Wenger, E. (1998) *Communities of Practice Learning, Meaning and Identity.* Cambridge: Cambridge University Press.

Whittington, C. (2003) A model of collaboaration. In C. Weinstein, C. Whittington and T. Leiba (eds), *Collaboration in Social Work Practice*. London: Jessica Kingsley Chapter 2.

Whittington, C. (2005) Interprofessional education and identity. In H. Colyer, M. Helme and I. Jones (eds), *The Theory – Practice Relationship in Interprofessional Education*. Occasional Paper No. 7. Available at www.heacademy.ac.uk (accessed on 04/05/2006).

Wolf, A. (1995) *Competence-Based Assessment*. Buckingham: Open University Press.

Wright, P. Turner, C., Clay, D. and Mills, H. (2006) Participation of children and young people in developing social care. *Practice Guide 2006*. London: Social Care Institute for Excellence.

Yelloloy, M. and Henkel, M. (eds) (1995) *Professional Competence in Higher Education in Learning and Teaching in Social Work: towards reflective practice*. London: JKP.

Zeus, P. and Skiffington, S. (2002) *The Coaching at Work Toolkit: A Complete Guide to Techniques and Practices*. Roseville, *Victoria,* Australia: McGraw-Hill.

Zwarenstein, M., Atkins, J., Barr, H., Hammick, M., Koppel, I. and Reeves, S. (1999) A systematic review of interprofessional education. *Journal of Interprofessional Care*, 13: 417–24.

INDEX